Cathy Williams

FROM SLAVE TO
FEMALE BUFFALO SOLDIER

PHILLIP THOMAS TUCKER

STACKPOLE
BOOKS

Library of Congress Cataloging-in-Publication Data

Tucker, Phillip Thomas, 1953–
    Cathy Williams: from slave to Buffalo Soldier / Phillip Thomas Tucker.— 1st ed.
      p. cm.
    Includes bibliographical references and index.
    ISBN 0-8117-0340-1
    1. Williams, Cathy, b. 1844. 2. African American women—Biography. 3. African
Americans—Biography. 4. Women slaves—Missouri—Independence—Biography. 5.
Women soldiers—West (U.S.)—Biography. 6. African American soldiers—West
(U.S.)—Biography. 7. United States. Army. Infantry Regiment, 38th—Biography. 8.
United States. Army—African American troops—History—19th century. 9. Frontier and
pioneer life—West (U.S.) 10. Indians of North America—Wars—1866–1895. I. Title.

E185.97.W694 T83 2002
973.8'1'092—dc21
[B]
                                                                        2001049746

TABLE OF CONTENTS

For Betty,
Who Has Always Been There

ACKNOWLEDGMENTS

I WOULD LIKE TO THANK A GOOD MANY PEOPLE WHO HELPED TO MAKE THIS work possible. One of the foremost of these was Dr. Frank N. Schubert, one of the nation's leading authorities on the Buffalo Soldiers and a veteran historian at the Office of the Chairman, Joint Chiefs of Staff, at the Pentagon, Washington, D.C. Dr. Schubert selflessly provided encouragement, insight, and expertise on all occasions. Equally important, he shared information and research on the Buffalo Soldiers that proved most helpful.

Mr. Carlton G. Philpot, of Weatherby Lake, Missouri, an authority on the Buffalo Soldiers and the life of Cathy Williams, gave encouragement and assistance. He has played a leading role in the Buffalo Soldier Project at Fort Leavenworth, Kansas.

Also, I wish to thank Ms. Cynthia Savage, Midland, Texas, for sharing her research and information on the life of Cathy Williams.

I would like to thank Mr. Marty Brazil, of Keesler AFB, Mississippi, who provided insight on the Buffalo Soldiers, as well as his usual masterful artwork that has graced this book. Also, the gifted artist Mr. William Jennings allowed the use of the first portrait of Pvt. William Cathay ever painted. I extend my thanks to Mr. Jennings as well.

Finally, I would like to thank the good people—including Mr. Philpot—of the Buffalo Soldier Educational and Historical Committee who have embarked upon the effort to create a reference and research library dedicated to the Buffalo Soldiers at Fort Leavenworth, Kansas.

INTRODUCTION

IN DEDICATING THE BUFFALO SOLDIER MONUMENT AT FORT LEAVENWORTH, Kansas, on July 25, 1992, Pres. George Bush bestowed a measure of long-overdue recognition due to African Americans in uniform. He emphasized how it was finally time for Americans to recognize that "the many invaluable contributions that the Buffalo Soldiers made to the preservation and development of our great Nation [while serving in some of] the most decorated of all United States military regiments."

Then general Colin Powell, fresh from his own brilliant performance in the War in the Persian Gulf, reinforced his commander in chief's comments, remarking that "through this monument, such due recognition and reward have finally begun" to be bestowed upon the Buffalo Soldiers. Powell himself had initiated the Buffalo Soldier Project to honor the little-known but important contributions of these African Americans during the early 1980s when he was Fort Leavenworth's commander.

Then secretary of state Dick Cheney placed the distinguished role of the Buffalo Soldiers in proper historical perspective, declaring "the Buffalo Soldiers were the first African Americans allowed to enlist in the Army during peacetime, but it was their valor, bravery, and dedication to duty that earned these soldiers a special place in our history. By their efforts, they also brought closer the day when African American men and women would serve not in separate units, but on the basis of full equality."

Another project intended to recognize the contributions of African Americans in uniform is the "Walkway of Patriots," proposed by the Buffalo Soldier

Educational and Historical Committee. The committee is presently soliciting funding to include the busts of Colin Powell, the first African American chairman of the Joint Chiefs of Staff; Lt. Henry O. Flipper, the first black graduate of the U.S. Military Academy; and Pvt. William Cathay, one of the long-forgotten Buffalo Soldiers of the 38th United States Infantry.

Not surprisingly, few people have heard of Pvt. William Cathay. Who was this mysterious soldier and why is he deserving of such a distinguished place in the proposed memorial?

Private Cathay was in fact a woman named Cathy Williams. She disguised herself as a man for nearly two years to serve in the ranks of the Buffalo Soldiers: the first and only African American woman to accomplish this feat.

How did this enterprising young woman become Private Cathay and why did she decide to wear a blue uniform? How did she successfully serve so long as a Buffalo Soldier when service by a female in the U.S. Regular Army was illegal? What did she accomplish while in the ranks? What became of Cathy Williams after her life as a soldier of the West? What did she have to endure and overcome as a single black woman first in a life of slavery, then as a Buffalo Soldier, and finally as a woman on her own in the Western frontier? These are intriguing questions about the remarkable life of Cathy Williams that have never been answered—until now.

Few Americans today, black or white, have ever heard about the remarkable life of Cathy Williams or her personal saga as she rose up from a lowly slave to a proud Buffalo Soldier in the service of her country. By disguising her gender in order to fulfill her dreams of embarking upon a new life in the American West and believing that she could accomplish what no other woman had previously achieved, Cathy Williams remains the only documented black female to serve for nearly two years, from 1866 to 1868, as a Buffalo Soldier in the U.S. Regular Army.

Despite the fact that it was illegal for women to enlist in the U.S. Army, Cathy Williams was in many ways merely exercising her right as a former slave by serving as Private Cathay in the Buffalo Soldiers' ranks. As Cathy saw it, her gender was no greater a reason to deny her equality than was her race.

Duty as a Buffalo Soldier under the name of Pvt. William Cathay led Cathy Williams on a personal odyssey of adventure from her home state of Missouri to the Mexican border. Wearing a blue uniform and serving beside her male comrades, Cathy Williams experienced hard duty during a winter campaign against the Apache of southwest New Mexico.

By accepting this host of challenges, Cathy Williams went where no other African American woman—or any woman, for that matter—had previously gone. During nearly two years of service, she successfully challenged and eventually overcame a host of demeaning stereotypes about both her race and gender. All the while, she maintained her dignity, pride, and self-respect in a world that sought to deprive her of these virtues simply because she was an African American woman. Continuing a tradition of personal independence and self-sufficiency, Cathy Williams continued to reach high to fulfill her own dream of creating a life for herself on the Western frontier after her military service.

The story of Cathy Williams is significant for a number of reasons. First, the important roles of former slaves have been overlooked in the telling of our greatest national epic, the winning of the West. The Western saga today defines much of the American nation's character, self-identity, and democratic spirit. Generations of historians, however, have long overlooked the key roles played by African Americans, as if blacks played no significant part in the dramatic story of the Western saga. Nothing could be further from the truth. From beginning to end, African Americans—both men and women—contributed a great deal to the winning of the West.

For too long these courageous men and women of African heritage have been the forgotten players, largely nameless and faceless individuals leaving few written traces, lost to the historical record. The relatively few blacks in the West made significant contributions that went far beyond their numbers. Included among these forgotten African Americans who found personal fulfillment and an independent life on the frontier was the young ex-slave Cathy Williams.

The winning of the West epitomized the triumph of the American spirit. Cathy Williams orchestrated her own personal triumph by fulfilling her dreams of an independent life. The experience of slavery was not sufficient to shatter her sense of self or personal dignity. Cathy was a survivor who successfully adapted to the many changes in her life. Resilient to the last, she not only survived, but succeeded in accomplishing what most other women could only dream of achieving, by relying on her intelligence, determination, and the strength of her unbreakable will to succeed in life.

Cathy Williams's odyssey offers an inspiring example of a courageous African American woman who made her hopes and dreams come true in the West by her own initiative and desire to succeed. In fact, both Cathy's struggle and longing for equality were greater for her than for white Americans because of her race, gender, and tragic past rooted in slavery.

In the same way, the fulfillment of Cathy's dream of achieving a life for herself in the West was much more difficult to obtain than for whites. By enduring adversity, surviving against the odds, and never giving up hope for a brighter future despite a host of setbacks and disadvantages that would have discouraged others less determined to succeed, Cathy Williams finally achieved equality—first as a soldier and later as a businesswoman on the frontier.

In the West, Cathy Williams made her American dream come true in a land of immense potential and promise. Here, she discovered a place that was more egalitarian and more tolerant than any other she had previously known. In this encouraging environment, Cathy blossomed. On the Western frontier, she was able to rise more rapidly on her own ability, initiative, and hard work: the great dream of African Americans throughout our nation's history.

As a private in the famed regiment of Buffalo Soldiers, Cathy Williams was part of a distinguished historical legacy. These regulars of African descent were not only the guardians of the Western frontier but they also served as the vanguard of civilization and national progress. In the blue uniform, the Buffalo Soldiers, hardened by lives of slavery and service in the Civil War, led the way for the young nation's expansion and development, battling Native Americans, and opening up the West for settlement.

After her faithful military service at frontier outposts, Cathy made the West her home. Never sacrificing her dream to win independence, she created a life for herself in southeast Colorado, where more equality for African Americans—both men and women—existed than perhaps any other region of the country in the years immediately following the Civil War. As she did throughout her life, Cathy Williams shattered the stereotype that blacks, and especially African American women, made few, if any, significant contributions to the West's settlement.

Symbolically, Cathy's life revolved around the historic Santa Fe Trail: one of the main routes leading the way west for thousands of Americans, black and white, to start a new life on the frontier. As a strange fate would have it, the Santa Fe Trail, a 900-mile link across the frontier that connected Hispanic and Anglo cultures and the ancient lands of Native Americans, remained a central theme in Cathy Williams's life before, during, and after her service as a Buffalo Soldier.

After growing up as a slave in Independence, Missouri—the Santa Fe Trail's starting point—and then near the Missouri state capital of Jefferson City, Cathy joined the men of Company A, 38th U.S. Infantry, on November 15, 1866. During her period of service, Cathy Williams and her regiment marched hundreds of miles down the Santa Fe Trail, protecting this vital gateway to frontier development and expansion.

Filling a void in the historical record, the story of Cathy Williams's life fits well into the overall context of the West's settlement. The frontier West was multicultural to an extent unimaginable by popular Hollywood scriptwriters, filmmakers, and producers. Her life story provides a more balanced and accurate view of Western history, while offering a rare glimpse into the struggle of one forgotten, but remarkable, African American woman.

Western historian Frederick Jackson Turner became famous in 1893—the same year that Cathy Williams struggled in vain to gain her well-deserved army service pension—by proposing his famous frontier thesis. Turner analyzed the almost Darwinian process by which an emigrant people in a new land—in the absence of conventional cultural and social norms and restrictions—were transformed into self-reliant and self-sufficient Americans, while at the same time creating the egalitarian spirit that served as the central foundation for American democracy.

Turner, however, excluded both minorities and women from his thesis. What has been forgotten is the fact that the women of the West, including Cathy Williams, as a result of the Western frontier experience, underwent this same process of development and Americanization as their male counterparts.

In a comparable personal evolution, the combined effect of the cultural legacies of West Africa, the positive lessons of perseverance and survival drawn from her slave past, service with Civil War armies on both sides of the Mississippi from 1861 to 1865, and nearly two years of service with the Buffalo Soldiers successfully transformed Cathy Williams into a stronger, more independent, and self-reliant woman of the West: in short, she was an American success story.

In many ways, therefore, this is a feminine Horatio Alger story. Against the odds, Cathy Williams rose up to turn personal misfortune and tragedy into success by living her life as she desired. In the process, she achieved beyond all expectations. In fact, Private Cathay's military service was only one chapter of a most remarkable life. Thanks to her service in the 38th U.S. Infantry, Cathy Williams has emerged from the shadows of the prejudice that has long ensured obscurity for African American women in American history.

As one of the "Guardians of the Plains" from 1866 to 1868, Cathy Williams and other blacks in blue uniform earned the name of "Buffalo Soldiers" and the rare respect of the Indians. She marched in the ranks as Pvt. William Cathay while serving her country in the most arduous duty in the U.S. Army during the post–Civil War period. As in her service across the South during the Civil War, she risked her life both on the Great Plains and in the Indian Wars.

Cathy Williams's story also brings to light the most forgotten of the Buffalo Soldiers: the black infantrymen of the post–Civil War period. Throughout the past, historians have focused primarily on the heroics of the hard-riding horse soldiers, while ignoring the many equally impressive contributions and sacrifices of the African American infantrymen.

In fact, thousands of Buffalo Soldiers served on foot and not on horseback: half of all the Buffalo Soldiers on the Western frontier served as infantry. The Cathy Williams story illuminates the role of these forgotten Buffalo Soldiers who fought as infantry across the West.

The story of Cathy Williams also serves as an inspirational example to other women, both black and white. Quite unknowingly and unintentionally, Pvt. William Cathay charted a new course by leading the way for today's important role of women in all branches of the American military. This resourceful former slave can be viewed today as a pioneer for the thousands of American women, both black and white, serving in today's U.S. armed forces.

Cathy Williams's story makes a meaningful contribution to the annals of women's, American, African American, military, and Western history. But her remarkable life is especially valuable as an inspiring example for all Americans—black and white, man or woman—emphasizing the importance of the power of the will to survive against the odds, and as an enduring testament to the strength and resiliency of the human spirit.

CHAPTER ONE

A Young Slave
Named Cathy Williams

THE FORGOTTEN STORY OF CATHY WILLIAMS'S LIFE FIRST BEGAN IN AN AN-
cient land across the wide breadth of the Atlantic Ocean, West Africa. Before
enslavement, Cathy's ancestors probably hailed from the culturally rich, luxu-
rious tropical lands of the Gold Coast, the Niger Delta, and Dahomey. Unlike
the hunting and fishing tribes that were more nomadic and warlike, America's
slaves came primarily from agricultural tribes of West Africa. The highly developed agrarian skills of these West Africans were needed to develop and exploit the plantations of the New World.[1]

Consequently, on the northern coast of the Gulf of Guinea, the Gold
Coast, Niger Delta, and Dahomey region along the Atlantic Coast—today's
countries of Sierra Leone, Senegal, Guinea, Liberia—and the Ivory, Gold, and
Slave Coasts from west to east—respectively, Ghana and Nigeria—was most
probably the native homeland of Cathy Williams's ancestors. Among the most
dominant tribes of this coastal region were the Asante, Ibo, Kru, Ewe, Awikam,
and Fanti.

From the lush area where the Niger, Sassandra, Nzi, Volta, and Komoe
Rivers flowed through the rich, fertile lands to enter the blue waters of the
Gulf of Guinea, Cathy Williams's ancestors were brought in chains to the
shores of the New World at some unknown date. For huge profits unattainable in any other business venture, ruthless slave traders, both black and white,
severed their unfortunate captives' bonds with the African homeland to feed
the hungry labor markets of America. The institution of slavery became essential for America's economic development from an early date. The invaluable

labor supplied by slaves played a key role in conquering the untamed wilderness of the New World, resulting in civilization in America.

Without exaggeration, one concerned New Englander in 1645 spoke to the importance of the role of African Americans in the nation's early settlement along the Atlantic coast: "I doe not see how wee can thrive untill we gett into a stock of slaves sufficient to doe all our business, for our children's children will hardly see this great Continent filled with people."[2]

Engaging in such a lucrative trade only fueled the sinister greed of slave traders both black and white, Christian and Islamic, to new heights. These flesh merchants were guilty of the atrocity known as the slave trade, selling thousands of human beings, who were viewed as nothing but "black gold," from West Africa to America.

The horrors of slavery had existed since Biblical times. But the curse had not originally been inflicted upon Africa by ruthless Europeans: not the Portuguese, Dutch, Spanish, or English. Instead, long before the Europeans' arrival, the warring tribes of West Africa had first turned captives into slaves, making it an established tradition. In this way, the powerful Asante tribe, wrote one African, gained prestige and influence from "the slave market, where the great wealth of the Asante was created."

Cathy Williams's ancestors left behind them in Africa a vibrant culture, far beyond the stereotypical view of a primitive tribe of debased heathens. These enslaved West Africans were fortunate if they survived the infamous Middle Passage across the Atlantic, a six-week journey in fair weather or up to a three-month trip in bad weather.

Thanks to strong-willed slaves bent on preserving what they cherished, this distinctive West African culture was destined to survive for generations within the institution of slavery. West African culture was destined to thrive in the New World, much like the slaves' hopes of returning one day to their faraway African homeland.

One surviving element of this resilient culture and agrarian tribal society was that women held not inferior but complementary, or equal, positions to men. This heritage of equality would be perpetuated by Cathy Williams as a Buffalo Soldier from 1866 to 1868. In this sense, she was destined to continue the noble tradition of her ancestors.

The various West African tribal cultures from which thousands of slaves were stolen were energetic and thriving. These complex maternal and agrarian societies were deeply rooted in the traditional values of the importance of the family, worship of the homeland, and ancestral ways of life.

Many West African peoples enjoyed a life "at least as sophisticated as that of Anglo-Saxon England." Once these unlucky people were transplanted across the Atlantic to American soil, the brutality of slavery caused them to more closely embrace the last remaining vestiges of their distant homeland, the rich cultural life of West Africa. In this way, the faraway cultural traditions of their lost homelands forged a sense of "togetherness" among the slave communities in America.

Trapped and isolated in a foreign land across the Atlantic and surrounded by unfamiliar white faces who spoke an unintelligible tongue, the most resilient of these enslaved blacks were determined that their cherished traditions would not die. If they allowed their culture to perish, then they themselves were finished. It was a survival mechanism that ensured that the cultural legacies of West Africa would survive for generations even amid the hell of slavery. Although the memory of the African homeland would be lost to the children of the first Africans on American soil, the enduring legacy of West Africa would continue to live on in the hearts and minds of the transplanted Africans in America.

How might the ancestors of Cathy Williams have looked? Then, as today, a wide variety in stature, color hues, and other physical characteristics marked the people of Africa. According to one writer, the men and women of West Africa were noted for distinctive physical features that distinguished people from this region: "The West African Negroes (sometimes called Guinea Coast or 'true' Negroes) are generally about five feet eight inches tall, with skin that ranges from dark brown to blue-black. They have very little body hair, and their head hair is dark and kinky [and] their noses are broad and more or less flattened." By all accounts, these people were robust, strong, and hardy.[3]

Cathy Williams was destined to inherit the physical characteristics of her ancestors. As a mature adult, she would be described by a white journalist in 1875 as "tall and powerfully built, black as night, muscular looking."[4]

Born of a slave mother who took her last name from her master, Williams, and a free black father whose name is unknown, a slave named Cathy Williams began her life in a slave cabin just outside the small western Missouri town of Independence, in September 1844.[5]

In her own words: "[M]y father was a free man but my mother a slave [and] I was born near Independence, Jackson County, Missouri." Her start in life drew no special notice, other than the fact that her mother and friends might have celebrated her birth with a traditional West African ritual.[6]

This infant slave girl would never see her ancestral homeland but its legacy would be passed down to her. Cathy would embrace this cultural legacy as she grew and matured into a young woman. Here, in a cabin just south of the Missouri River was anything but a promising beginning for the young slave girl. As powerless in the antebellum world as it was possible to be, she was born into the lowest social and economic level of American society. As fate would have it she would have to make the best of what little life would offer her.[7]

Ironically, Cathy was born with no rights in a democratic nation that had been founded on equal rights. This infant girl who was born on the eastern edge of the Great Plains came into a world where she would have little, if any, hope of ever gaining her own personal freedom from bondage. Considered little more than chattel, she was a slave for life from the very moment she was born.

However, the odds for Cathy Williams's future survival in life were enhanced because she inherited qualities of strength of character, resiliency, and determination from her parents. Like her father's birthplace, the place of birth of Cathy's mother is unknown, but she was probably born in the 1820s. Her mother is likely to have come originally from an Upper South state, such as Tennessee or Kentucky, like most of Missouri's early settlers, before migrating west of the Mississippi River with a white family in a covered wagon to the promised land of Missouri.

As a free black, Cathy's father from an early date must have provided her with a symbolic example that nourished a deep longing for personal freedom. It is not known if she knew him personally as a young girl, but for the rest of her days the inspiration of her father's life would not be lost to the daughter. Cathy's father symbolized the freedom that an African American could enjoy outside of slavery.

The haunting irony of a black slave named Cathy Williams born near a western Missouri community called Independence in the world's largest democracy, was merely a hypocritical fact of life in America for tens of thousands of blacks for more than half a century.

This central tragedy of American history caused the black nationalist David Walker, in his famous 1829 *Appeal to the Coloured Citizens of the World,* to lament of "our miseries and wretchedness in this Republican Land of Liberty!" This fertile land of the free along the Mississippi and Missouri Rivers was blighted by the curse of slavery. That awful legacy had been successfully transplanted from the Old World to the New World to now become Cathy Williams's world.[8]

The fact that Cathy Williams's father was a free black was an exception to the rule for African Americans on the Western frontier, especially in Missouri and the Upper South.[9] In the largest city, prosperous St. Louis, within the most noted slave state west of the Mississippi River, Missouri, more than 500 free blacks worked in both skilled and unskilled positions in 1860. Meanwhile, more than 1,500 African Americans toiled as slaves in that bustling port city during the same year.

However, in general, the institution of slavery was less harsh in the western cities of the Mississippi Valley than in the South. Here, greater economic and social opportunities beckoned African Americans from the rural areas. In the more cosmopolitan and urban environment of the western cities, especially in the ports along the Mississippi, the line between slave and free was much more blurred than in the countryside. In overall terms, the free black community had the effect of gradually diminishing and then eventually undermining the overall strength of the institution of slavery during the antebellum period, especially in the West.

In the western Missouri town of Independence, Cathy Williams's father enjoyed life as a free black man, while her mother endured the brutal oppression of slavery. This difference of status meant that marriage between Cathy's parents was forbidden by law. Therefore, a long-term relationship between this free black man and slave woman was doomed from the start unless the master freed Cathy's mother, which he did not do. Most likely, Cathy's father lived in Independence while her mother lived on a nearby Jackson County farm outside the town, a situation that ensured a permanent separation.

Most of all, the last thing that a white master wanted was to have his slaves in close association with free blacks. Free African Americans were viewed by slave owners with suspicion and as potential threats undermining the stability of the institution of slavery. For slave owners, historical lessons supported the validity of this ever-present fear among whites, especially in the Deep South.

Slave revolts and less overt forms of resistance were common among slave communities, both in the cities and the rural areas across the South. Inspired by the successful slave revolt of Toussaint L'Ouverture on the French West Indies island of St. Domingue, or Haiti, during the early 1790s, Denmark Vesey, a free black from Charleston, South Carolina, organized the largest slave insurrection in American history in 1822. To liberate his long-suffering people in bondage, Vesey not only depended upon aid from Haiti but also from Africa.

For slaves in America, the shining example of the revolt on St. Domingue was an inspiration. However, Vesey's revolt was discovered, and white retaliation was swift. With fellow black revolutionaries who planned to strike back against the hated institution of slavery, Vesey was hanged on a hot July day in Charleston.[10]

By 1840 Missouri was the most prosperous state west of the Mississippi. Less than two decades old, this frontier state benefitted from the soil's richness and the hard work of her people, both black and white. In 1840 and four years before Cathy's birth, 57,891 African Americans toiled in Missouri's fields, woodland, river bottoms, and prairies.

The total number of African Americans in bondage across Missouri was more than double the number of blacks found only ten years before, indicating the success of slavery in the Mississippi Valley. Most Missouri slaves, including Cathy Williams, were clustered not on vast plantations as in the Deep South, but on the small farmsteads in the fertile valleys of the state's two major river systems, the Missouri and the Mississippi.

In this land of plenty, the institution of slavery was destined to thrive for generations. The Missouri slave population doubled each decade from 1820 to 1840 until nearly 115,000 slaves were living and working in the state by 1860. The fertile agricultural lands of Missouri were the enduring dream of thousands of land-hungry white settlers on the Western frontier. Here, the small Western farmers could own their own land and reap the benefits of their hard work from tilling the soil.

Ironically, however, these early settlers also benefitted a great deal from the toil of a good many others who were legally denied the fruits of their labors: the African American people in bondage, including Cathy's mother. So great was the contribution of black slaves in helping to turn the wilderness of America into a nation that David Walker without exaggeration declared in his 1829 appeal that "America is more our country than it is the whites."[11]

Throughout the antebellum period, most of Missouri's slave population lived in the counties bordering the Missouri River, which cut across Missouri's center, and along the Mississippi River that ran along the state's eastern boundary.

Cathy's native county of Jackson bordered the free state of Kansas to the west. In the early years of Cathy's life, therefore, Kansas was the closest land of freedom for her and her fellow slaves. Her Jackson homeland was the easternmost Missouri county south of the Missouri River, and by 1860 contained the fourth highest percentage of slaves—21 percent—of any of the state's 110 counties.

Cathy's birthplace near Independence served as the county seat for the agrarian society of yeoman farmers who dominated Jackson County. Busy Independence was the scene of bustling steamboat commerce from the Missouri River and wagon traffic from the Santa Fe Trail.[12]

Jackson County was part of the culturally, economically, and socially distinctive region of Missouri known as "Little Dixie." The sobriquet was appropriate because this region's cultural influences were predominately Southern in nature. "Little Dixie" had been settled primarily by migrants from the Upper South, after they pushed west across the Mississippi River.

The fertile lands of "Little Dixie" consisted of the dissected till plains, lying mostly north of the Missouri, and the Osage Plains primarily located south of the Missouri. The southern part of Jackson County was covered in broad expanses of rolling prairie once traversed by buffalo herds. The northern section of the county, which bordered the Missouri River, was dominated by thick forests of bottomland hardwoods.

Both the Missouri and the Blue Rivers flowed through the rich farmlands of Cathy Williams's Jackson County, promising agricultural abundance and prosperity for the region. Here, in the promised land of the Western frontier, thousands of white settlers found their dreams in the fulfillment of the Jeffersonian vision of a free democracy of yeomen farmers. However, this idealistic and romantic dream of Mr. Jefferson that was fulfilled west of the Mississippi was in reality a nightmare for the slaves that made it possible.

While African Americans of western Missouri languished in bondage and reaped little, if anything, from their efforts in working this land, white settlers grew increasingly prosperous. So much prosperity came that "Little Dixie" became known as the "Canaan of America."

These anonymous black slaves, both men and women, who helped to carve a civilization out of a wilderness with sweat, blood, and toil have been all but forgotten by generations of American historians, especially in regard to the West's settlement. Along with her family members, one such "invisible" African American of "Little Dixie" was Cathy Williams. Only because her life was destined to take an unusual twist due to her own perseverance and determination to succeed would her story be preserved for all time.[13]

Creating a civilization from an untamed wilderness imbued the American people with a sense of destiny, and a hunger for even more lands that would bring additional agricultural wealth and riches. Before Cathy Williams was two years old, Jackson County and all of the Missouri River country were intoxicated by the spirit of Manifest Destiny—an imperialistic nationalism—that swept the West like a wildfire. The people of "Little Dixie" were consumed by a desire to spread what they saw as the benefits of democratic government southward by expanding the young republic's boundaries to lands owned by their neighbors to the south, the Mexican people.

Southerners and Westerners, especially, embraced this aggressive and imperialistic doctrine of expansionism with an unbridled enthusiasm. At this time, the American republic was seen as "the nation of progress," which was charged with a special mission. In the showdown with the Republic of Mexico in 1846–48, Americans felt that a divine sanction had presented them with an opportunity to spread republican ideals and the blessings of democracy to less fortunate peoples—in this case the Mexicans—by expanding the nation's borders by any means possible, including military conquest.

Hence, Americans believed that they could uplift the Mexican people from centuries of autocratic government, corruption, anarchy, civil war, and economic underdevelopment. At this time, Americans felt that they were specially ordained to bring the vast lands of Mexico to the level of the booming American republic, ironically made prosperous by slave labor.

Consequently, for those Westerners infected by the intoxicating dream of Manifest Destiny, a blatant imperialism was seen as a beneficial gift to its victims in much the same way as slave owners rationalized slavery as a means of Christianizing "pagan" Africans and saving their souls while owning their bodies. In this sense, the American people felt more paternalism toward the Mexican people than their own African American slaves who were culturally more similar to them by the time of Cathy's birth than Hispanics south of the border.

Like Missouri and most of the West and the South, the populace of Jackson County was inspired by the spirit of Manifest Destiny. Fighting finally erupted in the spring of 1846 over the disputed border between Mexico and the United States. Consequently, hundreds of young Missourians from across "Little Dixie" rallied to Col. Alexander Doniphan's regiment of 1st Mounted Missouri Volunteers. These zealous men, primarily the officers, brought their own African American body servants into service to accompany them on their campaigns into northern Mexico, the nation's first foreign war.

During the hot summer of 1846, the Missouri Volunteers joined Gen. Stephen Watts Kearny's army as it pushed west along the dusty Santa Fe Trail with the goal of capturing the old Spanish city and commercial center of Santa Fe, New Mexico.

The city was occupied without a fight in August, and in the autumn, leading his Missouri soldiers southward, Colonel Doniphan set out on the longest military expedition in American history. From Santa Fe the Missourians marched southward down the Rio Grande River and into the depths of northern Mexico. The soldiers, including men from Jackson County, pushed along the all-important commerce trail that led south to Chihuahua City, Mexico.

However, the farther that Colonel Doniphan's Missouri soldiers pushed southward from Santa Fe, the greater the distance they moved away from American forces, logistical support, and safety. When caught unprepared by the advance of a strong Mexican army defending El Paso del Norte or today's El Paso, Texas, Colonel Doniphan's lengthy column was vulnerable. The Missouri troops were strung out for miles along the line of march. Meanwhile, the regiment's lead elements were setting up the night's encampment in leisurely fashion along a wide bend of the Rio Grande called El Brazito. With the Mexicans' unexpected appearance, the "gringos" from Missouri, rallied in haste, falling into line as best they could amidst a growing crisis.

The African Americans with the regiment also came forward to stand in the front lines and assist the manpower-short Missouri soldiers. By this time eager for the chance to prove themselves as equal to the white soldiers on the battlefield, African Americans from "Little Dixie" were "fired with military ardor," wrote one veteran.

North of El Paso, the attacking Mexican army struck Colonel Doniphan's men on Christmas Day 1846. Both black and white Missourians rallied in time, and during the Mexican attack, the blacks stood side-by-side with the white soldiers to meet the challenge.

Missouri soldiers of both colors fought with their backs to the Rio Grande, standing firm before the Mexican onslaught. Despite having been caught by surprise deep in hostile territory, the black and white Missouri soldiers from "Little Dixie" and Jackson County repulsed the attackers with an accurate musketry. Shortly afterwards, the surprising victory at El Brazito cleared the way for Colonel Doniphan's triumphant march into El Paso del Norte.

Helping to hurl back the Mexican tide when every man was needed in the ranks, the African Americans exhibited what the whites called "Negro Valor" on the battlefield, when at last given the chance to fight for themselves and their country.[14]

After Colonel Doniphan's improbable victory at the battle of El Brazito, the African Americans of Doniphan's Expedition were allowed to organize into a regular company because of their steadfast performance on Christmas Day. Inspired by Doniphan's order, those blacks without weapons armed themselves from rifles and pistols picked up from the bodies of dead Mexicans on the battlefield.

Inflamed by a fighting spirit demonstrated at El Brazito, the African Americans in Colonel Doniphan's command banded together. They were "determined to form a company of their own," and no one now could deny them that right. The commander of their company was a slave from "Little Dixie" named Captain Joe. One Missouri soldier described that he was "the blackest of the crowd, and sported a . . . small [Mexican] sabre, with an intensely bright brass hilt."

After marching farther south with Colonel Doniphan's regiment and deeper into northern Mexico, the company of Missouri slaves from "Little

Dixie" also joined in the assault during the Missourians' next battle at Sacramento. The victory there resulted in Doniphan's capture of Chihuahua City. Chihuahua, like El Paso del Norte, was another vital Mexican commercial city with a link to Santa Fe and the Santa Fe Trail. With the bold Missouri soldiers motivated by a sense of invincibility, another surprising victory was won by Colonel Doniphan and his men when few, if any, on either side expected them to succeed.[15]

It is not known but perhaps some of these Missouri River country slaves who fought with Colonel Doniphan's regiment might have been either friends or acquaintances of Cathy Williams's family in Jackson County. Or perhaps one of them was even a brother, cousin, or another relative of the Williams family. If so, then such an influence might have helped to explain Cathy's later interest in military life. The people of Jackson County of her generation were more influenced by the heroics of Colonel Doniphan's Expedition than any other single military event.

Perhaps Cathy's own father served with Colonel Doniphan, since some troops, including their slaves, were from Independence. If so, then such service as he had demonstrated might explain why he had been freed, and was a free slave at the time of Cathy's birth.[16]

About to complete an amazing 5,000-mile saga, the members of Colonel Doniphan's Expedition—including the African Americans—embarked upon their return to "Little Dixie" as conquering heroes. After traveling up the Mississippi from New Orleans the soldiers from Missouri received a grand reception at St. Louis. Here, the entire city turned out to greet their bearded, long-haired men now in buckskins, and Mexican and Indian clothes. But, despite the cheers, those Missouri blacks who had fought with such distinction at El Brazito and Sacramento were also returning to a state of slavery.

Ironically, the same tragic fate also befell many African Americans who had fought on the patriots' side during the American Revolution. It was a pattern sadly prevalent throughout American history. Military assistance from African Americans was eagerly sought by America and appreciated by whites only during the crisis of war but seldom afterward when the threat to national security was over.[17]

Colonel Doniphan's Expedition, in the words of a New York newspaperman, was "the most wonderful march in the annals of warfare." In awe of what they had accomplished against the odds, historian Bernard DeVoto in his classic work, *The Year of Decision: 1846*, wrote of the homespun Missouri soldiers, both white and black, of Colonel Doniphan's Expedition, which had accomplished so much on its own: "[T]hey had made their march, thirty-five hundred miles of it, from Fort Leavenworth to the Rio Grande by way of

Santa Fe and the Navajo country, El Paso, Chihuahua, and Buena Vista. As long as they lived, the twelve-months march would splash their past with carmine—prairie grass in the wind, night guard at the wagons, the high breasts of the Spanish Peaks and all New Mexico spread out before them from the Raton, fandangos at Santa Fe, glare ice above the Canyon de Chelly, the hot gladness of the charge at Sacramento [that was part of] the March of the One Thousand [Missourians of Colonel Doniphan's command]—thirty-five hundred miles of prairie, desert, and mountain . . . they too had found the West and left their mark on it, an honorable signature"—a long list of accomplishments not unlike the imprint left by the Buffalo Soldiers on the Western frontier two decades later. Indeed, the soldiers, both black and white, of Colonel Doniphan's Missouri regiment played a key role in the conquering of Western lands and setting the stage for future settlement of an immense expanse of American southwest, including the communities that Cathy Williams would one day call home.[18]

In fact, much of Cathy Williams's life and military service would parallel the trek of Colonel Doniphan's regiment, the Santa Fe Trail, and the course of the Rio Grande River during both her time in uniform and in the decades after.[19]

Following in the tracks of Colonel Doniphan's Missourians, she would be destined to march as a Buffalo Soldier from Kansas to the blazing deserts of New Mexico, while serving in defense of the Santa Fe Trail. Then, after her military service, she would finally settle in Trinidad, Colorado, and later briefly in Raton, New Mexico, both also located on the Trail.[20]

Cathy would spend the longest period of her life in the small community of Trinidad. Here, in the untamed West, Cathy Williams would become a businesswoman, making a living with her own enterprising ways and business sense.[21]

Significantly, the Santa Fe Trail was as interwoven into the fabric of Cathy Williams's life and army service as her rich West African heritage that survived the oppression of slavery.[22]

Long fueling the dreams of expansionism and mercantilism under Manifest Destiny's banner was the goal of opening the doors of trade with Santa Fe, which possessed established links into northern Mexico, including the centers of El Paso del Norte and Chihuahua, and Mexico's interior. An international trade route for decades, commercially exploited by Missouri traders from Independence, other western Missouri towns, and St. Louis, the lucrative Santa Fe trade first began in the early 1820s. This early commercial traffic helped to lay a foundation for the westward migration of Americans along the Santa Fe Trail.

Symbolically, the small Jackson County community of Independence was a principal starting point and supply base for this vital route of commerce and expansionism. In the year of Cathy's birth, Josiah Gregg, of the Blue River country of Jackson County, published his successful work entitled *Commerce of the Prairies,* on the commercial opportunities of the Santa Fe Trail.[23]

After the close of the Mexican War and as peace came once more, Cathy grew from an infant to a young girl in Jackson County. Here, she blossomed amid the Missouri River country and the sprawling prairie lands of western Missouri at the eastern edge of the Great Plains.[24]

This early and formative period of life was a blissful haven for this young woman. Like another young African American raised in the Upper South, on the eastern shore of Maryland in this case, Frederick Douglass grew up in harmony with the world around him for "it was a long time before I knew myself to be a slave." Interestingly, Douglass was raised by his maternal grandparents, and his grandfather was a free black like Cathy's own father.[25]

However, this comforting existence of Cathy's early innocence would not linger long. Indeed, the full realization of her slave status would shortly become a painful reality to Cathy. A slave woman named Linda Brent, who was a mulatto and the great granddaughter of a South Carolina planter, described her own anguish upon the initial realization of her dismal fate, explaining in her 1861 book, *Incidents in the Life of a Slave Girl:* "I was born a slave; but I never knew it till six years of happy childhood had passed away [for] I was so fondly shielded [by my parents] that I never dreamed I was a piece of merchandise [but] when I was six years old, my mother died; and then, for the first time, I learned, by the talk around me, that I was a slave."

No doubt for Cathy Williams, the brutal realization that what lay in store for her was a lifetime of servitude and oppression came as a stunning blow. Such a realization that her world would be dominated by horror could easily shatter the self-image of a young fatherless slave girl. Whatever her early aspirations for a bright future, they were probably now no more. And like a fellow slave, Harriet Brent Jacobs, Cathy probably felt a deep anguish with the discovery that she was a slave until death, her "soul revolt[ing] against the mean tyranny" of her fate.[26]

However, within the narrow context of the slave community that was matriarchal in nature like the tribal societies of West Africa, Cathy Williams soon gained a measure of equality absent from the sheltered upbringing of the average white female of the antebellum period, especially those from among the privileged planter class. At this time, white women were placed on a pedestal in Southern and Missouri society. In general, such a pampered existence was the exact opposite of the experience of black women and girls under slavery, who developed more self-sufficiency and strength of character out of the need for self-preservation. These black females became heads of the household out of necessity. The emasculating effect of slavery on the African American male left many females serving as figures of authority.

Quite unlike anything experienced in white society and based upon the West African cultural heritage, the lowly status of slaves resulted in a measure of greater equality between the young black man and woman that continued well into adulthood. This unique condition under slavery was part of the early upbringing of Cathy Williams. Because of their status as property and because both male and female slaves worked together under similar circumstances in the fields and endured the same hardships, African American men and women were generally treated as equals on the plantation or farm by their white owners.

In the slave community, female slaves never gained the level of privileged status normally enjoyed by the "fair sex," because they were forced to shoulder more responsibility than black males, who were deprived of their traditional role of authority by the institution of slavery. For the most part, consequently, African American women were not imbued with a pronounced femininity or social dependence like white women. In a process of equality that was at least one indirect benefit of slavery, if one was at all possible under the circumstances, black women were forced to work as hard as men and labor as long from dawn to dusk and gained a measure of equal status in doing so.

For instance, one observant Swedish woman, Frederika Bremer, who visited the South during the antebellum period emphasized the egalitarian tendencies of slave life for black females, in contrast to the less "liberated" lives of white women, writing with some surprise: "[B]lack [female slaves] are not considered to belong to the weaker sex." In this narrow sense and despite its brutal repression, one positive outcome of slavery was its liberating experience for the black female, where she took the principal role in family and community life.

From early in her life, a female slave was forced by harsh circumstances to remain stronger than a white woman to ensure the survival of herself and her children. In this repressive environment, maternal instincts rose to the fore, creating a woman who shouldered more responsibility because the male was made powerless by slavery. This liberating experience helped to strengthen the character, will, and determination of black women not only despite of but also because of slavery.[27]

Based upon the future course of her life, Cathy Williams probably embraced this spirit of equality and sense of self-reliance that was part of her heritage. Indeed, such qualities would later develop to best define her character, enabling Cathy to endure the worst that the world had to offer a young African American woman.

In this sense, certain elements of Frederick Jackson Turner's frontier thesis of the 1890s can be applied to the evolution of the character of slave women, who out of necessity were transformed by the slavery experience into self-reliant and resilient individuals during their struggle to survive. For black women, the toughening process that was the life of the average female slave forged strong, resilient, and survival-oriented personalities. Such strengths of character would help to set the stage for Cathy Williams's future role as a Buffalo Soldier and for her later success on the Western frontier.[28]

At some point before reaching adulthood, Cathy was forced to leave Jackson County. She explained the sudden move from western Missouri to the heartland of Missouri: "While I was a small girl my master and family moved to Jefferson City." Because of the move and the fact that he was a free man, Cathy was now forced to permanently break with her father.[29]

Unfortunately, little is known about the details of Cathy Williams's early slave life before 1850 and her move eastward around 150 miles from Jackson County to Cole County, Missouri. In departing her birthplace, she was now transported, probably by steamboat, down the Missouri River. During this journey, she traveled from western Missouri to the rich agricultural belt of central Missouri. Cathy remained the property of a farmer William Johnson who was now a resident of Cole County.[30]

Having made money in Jackson County, Johnson became a wealthy planter who lived near the state capital, Jefferson City. Fortunately for her, the master could afford to relocate to midstate without having to sell Cathy to raise cash to finance the move or to purchase property.[31]

Cathy's new home, the small town of Jefferson City stood on the bluffs overlooking the wide, brown Missouri River. In 1850, the Kentucky-born William Johnson was forty-four years old and his wife, the Virginia-born Elizabeth Russell Johnson, was thirty-seven. They had been married on June 27, 1830. The Johnson family also looked with pride on their only son, Joseph, who was fifteen years of age. He had been born in Missouri in 1835, nine years before Cathy.

The place that Cathy Williams now called home was still "Little Dixie," where slavery and crops thrived. It was in the old Boonslick country of mid-Missouri where William Johnson had his plantation, or farm.[32]

Exactly when Cathy was sent to Cole County from western Missouri is not known. She recorded neither the time of year nor the date of the move to Jefferson City. All that Cathy mentioned was the fact that the move was made when she was "a small girl."[33]

By moving to Jefferson City, perhaps she was uprooted from her family in Jackson County, if they were owned by someone other than William Johnson at that time. If so, then such a tragic event, which was an ever-present possibility in a slave's life, would have been especially stressful and painful, if not traumatic for Cathy. She would not only have lost her father, but she may have also left her mother, who was apparently a field hand, behind. It is not known for certain, but Cathy quite likely never saw either of her parents again after relocating to Cole County.

Such sudden shattering of bonds with her family and local slave community was probably devastating to the young girl. Like her mother, Cathy retained the surname of her former Jackson County owner, Williams, before William Johnson purchased them both at some unknown date. She kept the name of Williams in her new location near Jefferson City, where, as she later explained, "she grew up" and matured into a young woman.

Even though able to bear children, Cathy Williams apparently never conceived. For whatever reason, she would never have children in her long life, even after she married, not long after her military service.[34]

The tortured realization that any child of her own would instantly become a slave might explain why Cathy Williams never bore a child. Some evidence exists that slave women went so far as to kill their own children so that they would not suffer slavery's oppression, sparing them from a fate that they considered worse than death. Such a tragic end for the child not only reveals the extent of slavery's horrors but also perhaps demonstrates the ultimate act of love by a slave mother. In this way, at least the mother possessed some vital personal choices in her life that not even the master himself or the white world could control. This was both a defiant and independent act of resistance, denying the master the means of generating additional wealth. But most of all, she would sacrifice what she loved the most because she did not want the child to suffer in slavery like herself. Such a desperate act indicated the strength of will and unbeatable spirit of the slave woman, who would make the ultimate sacrifice as an indirect means of striking back against the master and slavery.

In regard to her infant son, Linda Brent explained the most heart-wrenching dilemma for many slave women: "I could never forget that he was a slave [and] sometimes I wished that he might die in infancy [and when sick] I prayed for his death. . . . Death is better than slavery."[365]

What did slave life mean for the young Cathy Williams in mid-Missouri during the antebellum period? Trapped within the grip of slavery, what kind of hell did Cathy have to endure to survive? As a powerless slave, how was she able to cope with adversity, hardship, and disappointment? How strong did she have to become in order to endure the worst aspects of slavery without losing hope or faith in the future? The words of slave Linda Brent emphasized what life meant for black women, especially during "the trials of girlhood" across the South: "Slavery is terrible for men but it is far more terrible for women."

At an early age, Cathy Williams came to the painful realization that she, in the eyes of the law, was nothing more than mere chattel owned by another human being. Despite being based upon the premise that "all men are created equal," the greatest democracy on earth denied Cathy her basic humanity from the moment of her birth. Such powerlessness nurtured in slavery meant that she was without personal choice in regard to her own future destiny and even personal happiness. Like other slaves, Cathy Williams was little different in legal terms from the plantation owner's horses, which were fed, sheltered, and forced to work for the owner's economic benefit, discretion, or amusement.

At this time, her white owners, the Johnson family, most likely viewed this young slave girl as an investment; barely human because of little more than her skin color, the irreversible physical characteristic that determined inferiority and, hence, justified slave status in the eyes of white America. Because of property rights guaranteed in the U.S. Constitution by the Founding Fathers, including slave owners such as Thomas Jefferson and George Washington in Virginia, Cathy Williams was merely personal property that could be sold on a master's whim at the auction block.

But like most African American slaves, Cathy Williams also probably knew that the fundamental premise of slavery was a lie. The master's view that slave status was based solely on God's will was unthinkable to any slave who understood Biblical teachings that proclaimed God's love for all people. In time, Cathy probably came to realize that she was every bit as human and deserving of fair treatment—as proclaimed in the Bible—as her white owners.

Cathy also realized that she possessed the same feelings, hopes, and fears as her white owners and their children. She cried, hurt, dreamed, and prayed, and no doubt hated slavery that stripped her and other African Americans of their personal dignity. Perhaps such a hatred of slavery even resulted in a hatred of the whites who owned her.

Consequently, it was not unusual for slaves, including women, to rise up and kill their masters in anger and righteous indignation. For example, Celia, a teenage female slave of "Little Dixie," killed her sexually abusive owner in the early summer of 1855 in Callaway County. On the north side of the Missouri River, Callaway County bordered Cole County, located on the south side of the Missouri River, to the northeast.[36]

Or perhaps Cathy Williams may have felt some affection for the whites of the William Johnson family, if they demonstrated kindness toward her, accepting her as part of an extended family as was sometimes the case. For the most part, Cathy's exact feelings toward her masters and mistress, Mrs. Johnson, partly depended upon the kind of treatment she received from them.

More than anything else, color was the major distinction between slave and free across antebellum society. In the colonial period, white America had seized upon this biological difference as an indication of racial inferiority to justify the moral righteousness of slavery, the denial of the Africans' basic humanity and human rights, and their systematic brutalization.

Here, in the Western frontier lands of Missouri, slaves like Cathy Williams were forced to survive in a harsh world without legal protection more than five thousand miles from their West Africa homeland. Cathy Williams, however, was more fortunate than most slaves by the time she reached adolescence. She worked as a servant in the "big house" on the Cole County plantation of William Johnson. During this period near the Missouri River port of Jefferson City, she described herself merely as "a house girl."[37]

However, Cathy would probably occasionally toil in the fields for owner William Johnson, whenever necessary. Such field work by domestic servants most often occurred during planting or harvesting periods when almost everyone, including black children and even whites if on a small farm, were required to labor.

Cathy's role as a house servant was easier than the much harder life of a field hand, which was the lowest standing in the slave social order. Most likely Cathy's job at the "big house" included a wide variety of menial tasks. These responsibilities probably included serving food and attending to the dinner table, drawing bath water, setting the table, acting as a chamber maid or a hostess for visitors, food preparations in the kitchens, cleaning-up, sewing and making clothes, running personal errands, maintaining the house, and serving as a domestic body servant to Mrs. Johnson.[38]

Because Mrs. Johnson had no daughter, Cathy did not have to attend to the petty whims of a young white mistress. Nevertheless, she probably attended to both Mr. and Mrs. Johnson, who were both old enough to have been Cathy's parents. In addition, Cathy might have learned to do a variety of household and farm chores on the Johnson plantation, such as milking cows, churning butter, hauling water and firewood, and building fires. As she grew older and stronger in body, mind, and spirit, no doubt Cathy began to resent these menial chores as much as she did the white owners who assigned them.

Cathy Williams's role as a house servant gave her a privileged status. And such a position was unique for Cathy, who possessed none of the white blood often passed down by house servants' ancestors. The most famous mulatto slave families were the Hemings, including Sally Heming, most of whom served as house slaves at Jefferson's Monticello estate. The household slaves of George Washington's beloved Mount Vernon were also mulattoes. Because of the racism which had determined that light skin indicated higher intelligence, lighter-skinned African Americans most frequently served as household servants. Retaining her black West African physical characteristics, however, Cathy was quite dark, and in this sense unlike the typical house servant.

In contrast to the hard-working field slaves, a number of benefits were derived from Cathy Williams's service as a household servant, the highest status in slave society. Some advantages included better clothes, which often were second-hand garments from the white owners or children, and overall better working conditions. Most likely, Cathy Williams's position as a servant with its elevated status, and the accompanying benefits helped to boost her self-image and self-esteem.

If accepted as an extended family member like the Hemings of Monticello, perhaps Cathy Williams learned some basic reading skills because of her status in the household. If so, then she more than likely would have read the Bible.

A stereotype exists that all slaves were illiterate but such was not the case. For instance, one female slave, who traveled west by wagon train and later settled in New Mexico like Cathy Williams, was self-taught and learned the basics of education on her own. "Aunt Addie" learned "other methods [than from teachers, by] playing with rocks and beans in the field[, where] she learned to add and subtract. Her masters were good to her and after serving a delicious meal, she was given 3 or 4 dollars."

Cathy might have learned to read from other slaves or white children but almost certainly not from her masters, as such an act was unlawful. Because she worked at the "big house," however, Cathy might have been fortunate enough to have gained special privileges outside the law, which might have included reading and writing. But she never learned to write as a young girl, as the different spellings of her name—Cathay or Cathey—in her military papers indicate that she did not sign them herself.

Fortunately for Cathy Williams, the institution of slavery in the Upper South, including Missouri—the region's westernmost state—was more benign than slavery in the Deep South. Below the Mason-Dixon line, the large, sprawling plantations of staple crops flourished, especially cotton. On these extensive plantations of the Deep South, hundreds of African Americans worked in large slave gangs.

For Missouri slaves including Cathy Williams, the ever-present threat of eventually being sold "down river" to a harsh owner of a cotton plantation and heartless slave overseer, who controlled the slave gangs in the rich deltas and river bottoms of Mississippi or Louisiana, was the greatest fear of all.

Clearly, the daily life for a young slave girl in mid-Missouri was precarious at best. A great deal of uncertainty, especially if fate or the master were unkind, surrounded the life of Cathy Williams on the Johnson plantation.

But existence for the average slave was generally better on the western Missouri frontier, where Cathy spent her early days, than in the Deep South. For example, in the Missouri river county of Lafayette, which bordered Jackson County to the east, an astounded visitor to Lexington, Missouri, wrote an interesting entry in his diary in the summer of 1846, when Cathy was age two. At that time, he reflected with some bewilderment upon the relatively easy association and interaction between black and white, because the slaves of this section of "Little Dixie," "all have their own way and do very much as they please. So it is with all the families I saw—a slave calls his master's horse, his horse [and] his master's wagon, his wagon—and whatever he has charge of he denominates in intercourse with other[s] as mine. If you ask a slave when you meet, whose is that fine horse he is riding, he will say 'Mine, Sir.' I saw nothing while at L[exington and Lafayette County] but comfort and happiness and perfect contentment among [the slaves]."

The relative mildness of slavery in Missouri was noted by other whites as well. In 1854 when Cathy Williams was ten years of age, a Missouri farmer described in a letter that the trusted slaves who harvested corn in the broad fields of his Howard County farm in "Little Dixie" "require[d] no overseeing" by their white owners. And, in a January 1858 letter, a slave owner of Polk County wrote with some pride how he personally treated his slaves when they were ill because "both duty and interest required me to stay at home and give them medicine and attend to them and it is probable [that this] was the means of saving some of them."[39]

This greater benevolence and paternalism of slavery in Missouri and the Upper South resulted in more miscegenation and a sizable mulatto population. By this time, the Upper South was "the heartland of mulattoness," where these "new people" emerged by the thousands. By 1850, one in every seven slaves in Missouri was a mulatto. Along with nonmulatto blacks like Cathy Williams, these "new people" also played significant roles in the West's settlement and development.

The majority of the unions that created these "new people" of the West came from the master's sexual exploitation. However, not all of these relationships between slaves and master were exploitative or abusive in nature. Virginia Meacham Gould, in writing about the relationships of slave and free black women with white men in New Orleans, Louisiana, Pensacola, Florida, and Mobile, Alabama, explained that "to focus only on the exploitative nature of the relations between white men and slave women and free women of color would be to ignore the reality of the world in which they lived." And one of the most famous residents of another Upper South state, Virginia, had a long-term relationship with Sally Heming that was almost certainly more loving than exploitative because it apparently continued for decades. This, of course, was Thomas Jefferson.

During the antebellum period, the vast majority of Missouri slave owners possessed fewer than five slaves. For the most part, these owners were small, middle-class farmers, working the land to raise enough to support their families. In general, therefore, white Missourians and other Upper South slave owners were more paternalistic because they often treated slaves in relative terms, almost like family, compared with the harsher relationship between owner and slave on the big plantations of the Deep South.

This closer association between slave and master contributed to the high level of miscegenation in the Upper South, including Missouri. In the early frontier days before Missouri statehood in 1821, both black and white needed each other to survive, often forming bonds that went deeper than simply that of master and slave. Such close association partly resulted in white masters and black slaves fighting side by side in the ranks of Colonel Doniphan's regiment during the Mexican War.[40]

Regardless of these mitigating factors, slavery remained a barbaric legalized institution that caused America to betray its own heritage and the values founded upon Jefferson's principles that all men were created equal. Most of all, the institution of slavery was a hell on earth, both in Missouri and the Deep South. With a sense of disgust, light-skinned Linda Brent, who was a house servant like Cathy Williams and endured similar indignities, described life as an adolescent female slave on a plantation, where sexual exploitation and other humiliations were ever-present to serve as constant reminders of the female slave's lowly status: "No pen can give an adequate description of the all-pervading corruption produced by slavery. The slave girl is reared in an atmosphere of licentiousness and fear [and] the lash and the foul talk of her master and his sons are her teachers. When she is fourteen or fifteen, her owner, or his sons, or the overseer, or perhaps all of them, begin to bribe her with presents. If these fail to accomplish their purpose, she is whipped or starved into submission to their will. She may have had religious principles inculcated by some pious mother or grandmother, or some good mistress; she may have a lover, whose good opinion and peace of mind are dear to her heart; or the profligate men who have power over her may be exceedingly odious to her. But resistance is hopeless."

Especially when compared with the pampered existence of white women in antebellum Southern society, Cathy Williams's lot in life was difficult under the twin oppression of racism and sexism. Color relegated her to life as a slave without rights or much future hope. And this permanent mark of repression could never be erased. Nevertheless, to combat the constant threat of brutalization, a measure of carefully nurtured personal dignity, self-respect, and pride could be maintained in secret from whites by a young female slave, though this was not achieved without difficulty.

Linda Brent described the lingering resentment from slavery's brutalities, not to mention the damage inflicted upon the psychological makeup of the average female slave: "Notwithstanding my grandmother's long and faithful service to her owners, not one of her children escaped the auction block[, for] these God-breathing machines are no more, in the sight of their masters, than the cotton they plant, or the horses they tend." By any measure, the auction block was one of the most searing experiences that a slave could endure, especially if the slave was a young woman. The pain inflicted by sale on the auction block was more damaging and often caused longer-lasting suffering than physical punishments from masters.

Despite Cathy Williams's elevated status as a household slave, sale at an auction block in Jefferson City or on the Johnson plantation could come at any time for her. If she caused any type of displeasure for her master, then she could be sold without hesitation. It is not known for certain, but she might have endured the horror of the auction block experience in Jackson County or at Independence—perhaps witnessing the sale of either her mother or other siblings before she moved to Cole County.[41]

Cathy Williams's health was a problem to her for much of her life, and the reason, perhaps, was that she had not always been a house servant. Most likely she had worked in the fields and labored as a field hand at some point in her life as a slave. By any measure, work in the fields was rough and demanding with no reward except food, shelter, and a meager existence.

In the words of Mary Raines, who was born a slave only a few years before Cathy Williams: "I was a strong gal, went to de fields when I's twelve years old, hoe my acre of cotton, 'long wid de grown ones, and pick my 150 pounds of cotton. As I wasn't scared of de cows, they set me to milkin' and churnin'. Bless God! Dat took me out of de field. House servants 'bove de field servants [in slave society]."[42]

The average slave's life in Missouri consisted of tedious labor, poor sanitation, inferior living conditions in drafty log cabins, and a scanty diet of the basic Upper South staples of corn bread and pork. These staples were both protein and vitamin deficient. One Missouri slave, Eliza Overton, recalled that "many times we ran short of food." Slave life in antebellum Missouri resulted in the spread of many diseases that could strike down the enslaved

African Americans suddenly and without mercy. Throughout the antebellum period, thousands of slaves became the victims of illness such as dysentery, cholera, smallpox, and pneumonia. At least Cathy Williams was not taken with smallpox, for she would later acquire the disease as a Buffalo Soldier in her mid-twenties.[43]

If a master was cruel, frugal, or forgetful, even the necessary clothes to ward off the sharp cold of winter in mid-Missouri could be denied a slave. Even George Washington forgot to adequately care for his slaves of Mount Vernon. The father of our country had to be reminded by a concerned overseer to provide adequate clothing for slave children and blankets for the adults on his lavish estate.[44]

Even with a privileged status, a slave could suffer severely from a master's neglect, either intentional or accidental. Frederick Douglass, despite being the son of the master and a slave woman, suffered greatly in the winter along the windswept eastern shore of Maryland along the Chesapeake Bay. His yearly allotment of clothing consisted only of two linen shirts, and Douglass went without either shoes or socks in winter.[45]

However, Cathy Williams's life as a slave was not one entirely of hardship, pain, and drudgery. The average slave in antebellum Missouri enjoyed a lively and vibrant social life from sundown to sunup. This period of the night was the slaves' own time and not their masters, who were fast asleep in the "big house." For instance, one white described how the slaves' "nocturnal revels [consisted] of music and dancing."

Although Cathy occupied the lowest level in society, such was not the case within the slave community because she was a house servant. Here, in this secondary environment of the slave community, described as "a nation within a nation," and beyond the prying eyes of the white world, a strong sense of black identity and solidarity were forged.

The evolution of slave personality within the context of the black community led to the development of a positive self-image and a measure of self-respect for the average female slave. In addition, some of the most cherished cultural traditions such as art, music, and folklore of the tribes of West Africa were perpetuated by African Americans. This preservation of West African cultural life served as a strong foundation for the vibrancy of the slave community and rich slave life after sundown. For the slaves, the development of a lively social life was a means of survival under harsh repression.

By retaining the respected traditions of their long-lost West African past, instead of allowing these precious cultural legacies to slip away forever, and then merging them into newly developed American slave traditions, black slaves created a vibrant way of life and resilient slave community. Even under the oppression of slavery, African American cultural life was distinctive and culturally rich. Most important, the diversity of slave culture followed westward expansion as migrating African Americans were brought by their masters to the new Western lands.

Although victimized by slavery daily, the slaves compensated by combining a variety of West African tribal beliefs, traditions, and music with local influences to develop a rich and varied community life. In this way within the slave community, African Americans were able to control their own personal destiny in a cultural sense instead of becoming completely manipulated victims of events beyond their control.

Therefore, important elements of black pride, a distinctive sense of community, and personal identity and cultural distinctiveness not only survived but thrived. Within this dynamic local African American community, Cathy Williams's strong and independent personality was first forged. This young African American woman began to develop a character distinguished by strength, endurance, and persistence. However, these traits, essential for survival in slavery, were exhibited only within the security of a black cultural world that was completely unknown to the white master, mistress, and overseer.[46]

While on the Johnson plantation, Cathy Williams probably lived in a slave cabin not far from the "big house" of her master's family.[47] As elsewhere among these isolated slave communities in the Missouri River country, the slave quarters served as a safe refuge from the psychological torment of slavery. Nevertheless, a Spartan existence defined the life of the average Missouri slave in "Little Dixie."

Solomon Northrop described the conditions of his slave life with some bitterness, and for good reason: "[T]he softest couches in the world are not to be found in the log mansion of the slaves [as] my pillow was a stick of wood [and] the bedding was a coarse blanket and not a rag or shred beside . . . the cabin was constructed of logs, without floor or window."

Another slave named Mattie Logan possessed only slightly less painful memories of her living quarters. She recalled that "each slave cabin had a stone fireplace in the end, just like ours, and over the flames at daybreak was prepared the morning meal . . . the peas, the beans, the turnips, the potatoes, all seasoned up with fat meats and sometimes a ham bone, was cooked in a big iron kettle and when meal time come they all gathered around the pot for a-plenty of helpings! Corn bread and buttermilk made up the rest of the meal . . . once in a while we had rabbits and fish, but the best dish of all was the 'possum and sweet potatoes—baked together over red-hot coals in the fireplace. Now, that was something to eat." However, in reality, the majority of slave quarters were squalid. For instance, the wife of a South Carolina aristocrat, Fanny Kemble-Butler, wrote with horror that "such of these [slave] dwellings as I visited today were filthy and wretched in the extreme."[48]

But in the absence of physical comforts and equal treatment, the strength of character of the slaves was forged by hardships, denial, and suffering. In addition, other support systems aided the average slave's chances for survival. Based upon a central pillar of West African communities, the kinship system was transferred by the enslaved Africans to America. Here, in a new land the system survived and endured and helped to serve as a comforting and secure buffer for slave women against the most searing aspects of slavery.

Most important, the kinship system provided a sturdy foundation and stabilizing force that strengthened community bonds. Adapted to function as smoothly as possible outside the harsh restrictions that slavery imposed, the slaves' extended and protective kinship system was maternal, like the West African culture from which it originated. Here, in the Missouri River country of "Little Dixie," kinship provided both an extended family environment and a strong community pillar to support a rich slave society and culture.

Ironically, the enduring strength of this resilient kinship system was both dominated and nurtured by the most powerless individuals of antebellum society, African American women. Because the white master stripped away the power of the black male as a family provider, the African American female became the sturdy foundation for the survival of the black family and community.

African American women were the unbreakable force that fed vitality into the kinship system, strengthening and ensuring the survival of the black family and the black community. One of the means by which African American women maintained the kinship system's vibrancy was by creating a maternal support system within the immediate slave community. In this way, African American women created a maternal network that supported the extended family community and gave it renewed strength.

For instance, in the Missouri River town of St. Joseph, Missouri, located immediately north of Cathy Williams's hometown of Independence, black women, both slave and free, often gathered in designated slave cabins to socialize at regular periods. Here, slave women strengthened the all-important maternal bonds with each other to forge more durable ties of an extended slave family and community network. One such respected matriarch of a regular gathering of slave women in Platte County, Missouri, just north of Cathy's native Jackson County, was an elder woman by the name of Mymee. Highly respected within her community, Mymee was "the child of a Guinea sorceress [and] a great conjurer."[49]

In Sedalia, Missouri, the county seat of Pettis County located just southeast of Jackson County and south of the Missouri River, African American women of this "Little Dixie" plantation socialized together while cleaning laundry every Saturday afternoon. During these lengthy gatherings, the slave women "would get to talk and spend the day together."

The Missouri slave Alice Sewell recorded how black women in antebellum Missouri often gathered to conduct their own prayer meetings. Powerless in white society and without the support or protection from equally powerless black males, African American women found strength not only in themselves but also in the power of God, an irrepressible religious faith, and worship.

Such religious worship services also strengthened the deep cultural bonds of a maternal society and kinship system. Another Missouri slave woman, Minksie Walker, recalled that after Sunday church services her mother and other slave women on a Missouri plantation, "would be jumpin' up and dancin' around . . . pattin' their hands until all [the] grass [beneath their feet] was wore slick."

Despite slavery's horrors, the resiliency of slave women resulted in a positive response that not only forged a vibrant community, but also laid the foundation for a strong matriarchal society. Black women in slavery strengthened maternal bonds with each other and their families to ensure a secure social haven for the development of the black family and community.

By these means, female slaves also enhanced the chances for their own mutual survival in an oppressive world from which there was little hope for escape. Consequently, these African American women triumphed by retaining their West African culture and by nurturing the development of the slave community. They also laid a foundation for their children's ability to cope with the repression of slavery as best they could.[50]

Certainly a critical feature of life that assisted Cathy Williams and other Missouri slaves of "Little Dixie" to survive the harshness of slavery was religion. Religion became a spiritual refuge that served as a buffer for the average slave against the brutal reality of life. What was most important was that this protective shield of slave religion, in contrast to the masters' paternalistic brand that emphasized obedience, "most preserved the West African impulse and identity [as well as providing] the basis for an independent struggle against slavery and racism."

The slaves' passionate embrace of a highly musical, emotional, and mystical brand of religion became an enthusiastic form of expression not only of worship but also of recreation, socialization, and most important, both psychological and spiritual revitalization. All in all, this vibrant spiritualism and strong religious faith provided the African American with a beacon of hope amid the dark world of slavery. For a young slave like Cathy Williams, the brutality of her world could be momentarily forgotten and endured thanks to the passionate embrace of religious rituals, including praying, fasting, and singing.[51]

After the day's monotonous labors were completed and especially on Sunday, the nocturnal hours provided that precious time for the slaves to "Steal Away to Jesus." African Americans would flock to rustic houses of worship—out-of-sight from the "big house"—to find God and spiritual healing.

A primary outlet for the development of slave spiritualism was black church meetings, which were held in the woods or log churches by often fiery black preachers. Here, in the secluded forests near a peaceful flowing river or creek, the slaves worshipped with an almost mystical passion that brought much-needed psychological, emotional, and spiritual release and redemption. In addition, they sang a wide variety of songs of complex rhythms that evolved from the rich musical traditions of West Africa. These were combined with American influences to produce a distinctive musical heritage.

Most of all, these African Americans prayed for a new day in the future without the curse of slavery. Slave worship also unleashed pent-up frustrations outside the stifling bonds of slavery and beyond the sight of whites, providing a means of survival in a regime that could not be overthrown by revolt. All the while, a burning religious faith emphasizing hope for a brighter future strengthened the bonds of the black community, enriching African American culture and social life in the process.[52]

Most of all, the slaves' passionate embracing of a personal and emotional religious spirit laid an invaluable psychological and spiritual foundation for their belief that they were equal to whites before the eyes of God. This intoxicating religious faith proved the spiritual equality of blacks and whites.

While religion strengthened the bonds of the overall slave community, the egalitarian spirit of religion also enhanced a more positive self-image of slaves, especially young female slaves like Cathy Williams. Strong religious faith also served as the breeding ground for resistance. Slave religion fueled the fiery resolve of the most successful black revolutionary of the antebellum period, Nat Turner. Turner, like Denmark Vesey before him was executed in November 1831 after a failed bid to spark a slave uprising.[53]

From the depths of slavery's degradation rose the uplifting words and music of the inspirational slave spirituals. Religious songs sung by African Americans at the slave prayer meetings contained inspiring words of faith that reminded them that it was important to maintain hope for their eventual deliverance. Their prayers, in consequence, focused on the long-awaited day of release and redemption, when freedom would not be a dream but a sweet reality.

Slave music was spiritually and psychologically uplifting, beckoning the day of liberation and final release from slavery. Rooted in the complex rhythms and cadences of West African music, which was more sophisticated than American styles of the time, slave spiritual songs revealed the depth of the slaves' personal reflection, expression, and creativity, while providing solace and relief from the pain of life. Most important, these songs proclaimed the slaves' longing for freedom in both this world and the next:

> When we get to heaven
> There'll be no slaves no more.[54]

From beginning to end, religion and the African American churches served as a foundation that supported both the individual slave and the black community. As in the case of Cathy Williams, the vibrancy of slave religion kept hope alive for better days ahead, enhancing chances for both personal survival and spiritual salvation. The important legacy of slave religion was destined to be continued on the Western frontier when Cathy Williams served as a Buffalo Soldier after the Civil War.[55]

All of these diverse influences endured for each generation of slaves, helping to forge a strong personality and sense of independence in young and impressionable slaves like Cathy Williams. The roots of Cathy's self-reliance were first developed beyond the white world and deep within the bosom of the nurturing slave community. Here, in the community of rustic log cabins and black churches, Cathy's self-identity and positive self-image found fertile ground in the positive aspects of her black culture, African heritage, and slave life.

What is more, a subtle form of resistance to slavery developed when the slave retained the spirit and distinctiveness of West African culture. Such reliance on cultural antecedents assisted in making slaves stronger in mind and spirit. Like other slaves, Cathy Williams was able to cope with slavery's horrors by stubbornly clinging onto the remnant of the West African past, culture, and heritage. This survival mechanism helped to mold a positive self-image when combined with the positive influence of a religious faith, a vibrant slave community, a kinship network, and a matriarchal society.

At a relatively early date, like so many other slaves, Cathy Williams became toughened both spiritually and psychologically by drawing positive strength from the negative aspects of the slave experience. In this way, she was able to better deal with adversity, while learning to become a survivor rather than a victim. Most important, Cathy was able to cope with a harsh environment beyond her control without losing either her dignity, positive self-image, or self-respect.

The irrepressible Linda Brent underwent a comparable type of personal development by successfully utilizing positive lessons from the inhumanity of slavery. She described with typical defiance that after "fourteen years in slavery . . . I resolved never to be conquered." Despite slavery's indignities and humiliations, slave women like Cathy Williams and Linda Brent remained strong in mind and spirit, allowing them to survive slavery's horrors and to remain free-thinking individuals in the process.[56]

However, successfully combating the affects of slavery was no small challenge because the human spirit could be crushed by the worst aspects of the institution. The horror of the sale of family members on the auction block could destroy a psyche, especially that of a young person like Cathy. The instability and uncertainty of slave life were ever-present because the life of a slave was entirely in the hands of the owner.

Linda Brent described the sudden uncertainty resulting from the death of her mistress, when she was only twelve years old: "[A]fter a brief period of suspense, the will of my mistress was read, and we learned that she had bequeathed me to her sister's daughter, a child of five years old. So vanished our hopes [for freedom, even though] my mistress had taught me the precepts of God's Word: 'Thou shalt love thy neighbor as thyself' [and] 'Whatsoever ye would that men should do unto you, do ye even so unto them.' But I was her slave, and I suppose she did not recognize me as her neighbor." Like Cathy Williams was forced to do upon relocating from Jackson County to Cole County with the William Johnson family, Linda Brent was also forced to move to a new area to start a new life because of circumstances beyond her control.[57]

In overall terms, the toughening process of slavery played a role in Cathy Williams's subsequent service as a Buffalo Soldier, because slavery proved in some ways to be a liberating influence to the African American women who successfully coped. As in the West African homelands, black women enjoyed an unmatched measure of equality to black males under the institution of slavery. In general, African American males were unable to place African American women in a permanent subordinate role because the white master played the dominant male role. In this way, the most powerless people in American society, black women, possessed the authority to compile their own distinguished legacy of survival and endurance during slavery and long afterward. Such characteristics of strength and survival would play a role in explaining why Cathy Williams would serve for nearly two years on the Western frontier as a Buffalo Soldier.

What the brutality of slavery was unable to take away from her was the power of her own will, determination, and resilience of personality. Despite the experience of slavery, Cathy would continue to possess her own free and irrepressible spirit, hopes for the future, pride in self, and strength of will that could not be taken away from her.[58]

CHAPTER TWO

The Civil War
Descends upon the Land

BY THE SPRING OF 1861 AND THE START OF THE CIVIL WAR, CATHY WILLIAMS could not possibly have imagined how much her life was about to change. Her master, William Johnson, died at Jefferson City at some point before the war. In Cathy's words, "my master died there," though she remained with the Johnson family. Fortunately, for her, she avoided being sold to pay any debts that Johnson might have owed.[1]

At the outbreak of war leaders in both South and North, especially Pres. Abraham Lincoln, recognized the strategic importance of the West and the vital Mississippi Valley. As the conflict intensified, the military and political maneuvers for possession of the most vital state west of the Mississippi River, Missouri, would soon play a role in determining the unusual course of Cathy's life.

After May 10, 1861, and the capture of the pro-Southern Missouri Volunteer Militia encampment at Camp Jackson, outside St. Louis, by the Union forces of Gen. Nathaniel Lyon, the state capital of Jefferson City—Cathy's hometown—became the most important center supporting the growing rebellion in Missouri. Here, at Jefferson City, Cathy Williams was about to be caught in the eye of the sectional storm that was soon to sweep over the state with a vengeance.

Because Jefferson City was located in the pro-Southern area of "Little Dixie," the Rebel cause was warmly embraced by the local populace. One appalled pro-Union German citizen of Jefferson City wrote on May 25, 1861, that "yesterday a large flag of the Confederate States was raised once more in front of the governor's house . . . this flag had been raised earlier by members of the [Missouri state] legislature, and it is waving right now as I write this."[2]

Since mid-April 1861 and the outbreak of war between North and South, Jefferson City had been a thoroughly Rebel city. The state capital had enthusiastically celebrated the fall of Fort Sumter. Cathy Williams no doubt heard or watched the celebrations of the excited people of Cole County and mid-Missouri. In their naïveté and innocence these Missourians had yet to learn the meaning and harsh realities of war.

Meanwhile, throughout the spring of 1861, hundreds of Rebel volunteers from the rural Missouri counties of "Little Dixie" poured into Jefferson City like a flood. The town was soon turned into an armed encampment of Abe Lincoln haters. These rustic Missouri volunteers, heavily armed and full of bravado, appeared almost as threatening to the locals as the Yankees—especially to slaves, who had never seen so many armed white men before.

One incredulous soldier described how the gathering Missouri volunteers consisted of "a queer, promiscuous, undisciplined sort of a rabble which assembled at Jefferson City in obedience to the governor's call. Every man regarded himself as a host, capable of whipping any quantity of 'Dutch' [Germans], and especially qualified to command and govern men[, while their] uniforms were as unique and various as the costumes in Barnum's brazen 'cavalcade of nations' . . . and were typical of just about as much lying and humbug."[3]

Here, in Jefferson City, the fertile Missouri River country, Gov. Claiborne Fox Jackson and his military commander, Gen. Sterling Price, busily prepared the state and its revolutionary army, the budding Missouri State Guard, for war. From the hills, valleys, and grasslands, Rebel volunteers continued to pour into the capital to defend it against the expected advance of the Germans and Unionists of St. Louis.

An alarmed resident of the state capital watched the arrival of additional Rebel volunteers from the prairies of western Missouri as they proudly "marched through Jefferson City with continuous hurrahs for Jefferson Davis, flying the flag of secession."

Jefferson City appeared more warlike when cannon, captured in the first weeks of war from the Liberty arsenal in Ray County, were unloaded from a steamboat on City's docks. On the north side of the Missouri River, Ray County bordered Cathy Williams's native county of Jackson and her former home of Independence to the northeast. These captured artillery pieces added muscle to the growing Rebel force now preparing to defend the state capital against the St. Louis Unionists.

By the end of May 1861, explained one German citizen of Jefferson City, General Price promised his gathering force of Missouri Rebels that "the taking of Camp Jackson and the murder of innocent women and children had not yet been avenged, but the time shall come when they shall rise up in full force and smite their enemies to the ground."

Just outside Jefferson City, Cathy Williams continued to work as a house servant on the Johnson plantation. She and other African American slaves, awaited developments as events continued to swirl around them. Perhaps the slaves of the area realized that if Union forces captured Jefferson City, then this meant freedom for them. If Cathy knew as much, then she probably prayed for a speedy day of liberation. The Civil War was about to descend upon Jefferson City and nothing, including the life of Cathy Williams, would ever be the same.[4]

Union authorities in St. Louis and Washington, D.C., realized that the growing Rebel threat at Jefferson City had to be eliminated as soon as possible. Pressing military and political needs required the capture of the state capital and the heart of rebellion in Missouri. Therefore, Jefferson City was targeted for capture by the most aggressive Union commander in Missouri at this time, General Lyon of Connecticut.

With the capture of prosecessionist Camp Jackson just outside St. Louis in May 1861, General Lyon had already become a Northern hero. By this time, the New England Yankee was the conqueror of both Camp Jackson and St. Louis, winning this vital port city on the Mississippi for the Union. Never would St. Louis slip out of Union control after General Lyon's timely efforts during the decisive spring of 1861.

However, no great clash for possession of the Missouri state capital was forthcoming during the late spring of 1861. General Lyon, meanwhile, continued to make plans to eliminate the Rebel threat there. Fortunately for the Union, the disorganized and ill-prepared Missouri Rebels in Jefferson City could do little more than talk and brag about how many St. Louis Germans and Yankees they could whip in battle.

A bold commander, General Lyon prepared to launch an amphibious operation to capture the state capital in June. In the early summer heat and against the river current, Lyon's expedition pushed north up the Missouri from St. Louis, then turned westward at the confluence of the Missouri and Mississippi. Then, the Union task force headed up the wide Missouri toward Jefferson City. Steaming upriver and with no Rebel steamboats or gunboats to bar the way, the Union flotilla eased westward up the swirling river and ever-closer toward Jefferson City.

Learning of General Lyon's rapid approach on the lightly defended state capital, the pro-Southern governor and his state government immediately fled. The hasty Rebel exit left the capital of the most vital Trans-Mississippi state for General Lyon's taking. After their recent victory at Camp Jackson, the ruthless reputation of the German troops from St. Louis among the pro-Southerners produced widespread panic in Jefferson City.

One St. Louis Rebel, H. E. Clark, on May 12, 1861, had warned in a letter to Jefferson City authorities that "the parties or troops going there [Jefferson City], on the part of Abe [Lincoln], are nearly all Dutch merciless savages [so] lookout for Jefferson City . . . they are certainly going [and] they will get there before you know it." Such a fear helped to quell the budding rebellion of volunteers in Missouri.[5]

After the panicked Rebel evacuation of Jefferson City, General Lyon and his Federal troops disembarked from their steamboats, landing on the Missouri's south bank. The Federals marched proudly into Jefferson City with spirits high and flags flying. Without firing a shot, the North now gained possession of Missouri's capital. Cathy Williams, in her own words, never forgot when "the United States soldiers came to Jefferson City."[6]

General Lyon eliminated much of the legitimacy of the existing state government and defused the Rebel bid to take Missouri out of the Union by force. The sixteen-year-old Cathy Williams must have viewed these startling new developments with interest. Her hometown of Jefferson City was now an occupied city and armed camp filled with thousands of Federal soldiers.

During the Union occupation Cathy Williams no doubt felt admiration for the "liberators" in blue uniforms. These Union men were different from the local people, sounding and talking strangely to the young slave girl who had spent her entire life in the Missouri River country. Many of the Yankees spoke German or English in thick accents. These "Hessians" talked of places in their distant homeland like Berlin and the Rhine River. In contrast, the local people that Cathy had known her entire life were mostly people with antecedents going back to the Upper South, primarily Tennessee, Kentucky, North Carolina, and Virginia.

More importantly, these soldiers of General Lyon's army thought differently in regard to African Americans and the issue of slavery. Probably an astounding realization to this young African American woman, the German soldiers from St. Louis and nearby western Illinois, having migrated to escape autocratic rule in Europe, were mostly antislavery abolitionists.

Many men in Yankee blue, especially the Germans, believed in equality for African Americans, unlike the people of Jefferson City. For Cathy Williams, the world that she had long known was rapidly changing around her, and changing for the better. Slavery was dying a quick death in Cole County, Missouri. At long last, a new day of "jubilee" had come for African Americans of the area, answering the prayers of the slaves of this agricultural region.[7]

After withdrawing from mid-Missouri and despite the lack of assistance from Confederate authorities elsewhere, Gen. Sterling Price was still attempting to form an army of Missouri Rebels at Cowskin Prairie. Here, in the far southwest corner of the state and immediately north of the Arkansas line, the Missourians gathered strength in preparation for meeting the conquerer of Jefferson City, General Lyon. In the words of Bruce Catton: "[N]ot even in the American Revolution was there ever a more completely backwoods army . . . these men were not so much soldiers as rangy characters who had come down from the north fork of the creek to get into a fight." One of General Price's frustrated officers simply described that "our army was such a free democracy that my feeble efforts to check that petty rapine, and enforce discipline, were but partially successful."

In a letter, another Missouri Rebel described this most unorthodox of frontier armies as a "ragged, half-fed, and ill-armed band of Missourians." Yet another Missouri soldier wrote that "we had not a blanket, not a tent, nor any clothes, except the few we had on our backs, and four-fifths of us were barefooted . . . Billy Barlow's dress at a circus would be decent in comparison with that of almost any one, from the major-general [Price] down to the humblest private." Nevertheless, this frontier army of Western Rebels was tough and resilient. General Price's Missouri State Guard would present a stiff challenge for General Lyon's army to eliminate.[8]

Meanwhile, the summer of 1861 quickly passed while Missouri's fate hung in the balance. Like other African Americans in Jefferson City and Cole County, Cathy Williams's life was altered forever by the arrival of the blueclad soldiers of Abe Lincoln's army. Thanks to the Union occupation of Jefferson City, Cathy Williams was now a free woman. The day of liberation had come at last. Cathy's prayers had been answered, or so it seemed.[9]

It is not known if she departed the Johnson farm on her own or with other slaves. Perhaps her former master's family fled with the approach of the Union army. Whatever the circumstances were, she came to Jefferson City, probably with other Johnson slaves. Here, in the town, she could receive food and shelter from Union troops. No doubt she rejoiced at the thought that a lifetime of toil was over.

Unknown to Cathy at the time, the appearance of a new Union regiment from Indiana, which marched into Jefferson City on September 14, 1861, would alter her fate forever. This new command was the 8th Indiana Volunteer Infantry. The 8th Indiana was destined to remain in Jefferson City for barely a week but that period would be long enough to affect Cathy Williams for the rest of her life.[10]

The 8th Indiana was a new regiment, which had been organized at Indianapolis in mid-August 1861, before journeying west by rail to St. Louis to engage in the struggle for possession of Missouri. Then, the Hoosier regiment was officially mustered for three years service at Jefferson Barracks, Missouri, just south of St. Louis on the Mississippi, on September 10, only four days before its arrival in Jefferson City.

The thirty-two-year-old commander of the 8th Indiana was Col. William Plummer Benton. He had recently seen some of the earliest fighting of the war, in today's West Virginia, at Rich Mountain, before becoming the colonel of the newly formed 8th Indiana. Benton was a native Marylander, a Mexican War veteran, and a well-read graduate of Farmer's College in Ohio.

In addition, Colonel Benton was an accomplished attorney and judge by the time he received his commission with the 8th Indiana in the spring of 1861. Indeed, "he showed his devotion to his country by sacrificing a large [law] practice in the wealthy and pleasant town of Richmond [Indiana] to accept the charge of the Eighth." Colonel Benton was a good commander. He was described as "reliable . . . unostentatious and earnest [with] a ruddy hue and rotund form of John Bull." Colonel Benton was destined for a general's rank in barely six months. He would win distinction in the Western theater, including taking part in the campaign to capture Mobile, Alabama, at the war's end.[11]

Rushed westward to meet the growing crisis in the West, the 8th Indiana was hurried to Missouri because the Missouri State Guard was pushing north into the Missouri River country of west central Missouri in a bid to reclaim the state. By the third week of September 1861 and after having unleashed a successful invasion, General Price's Missouri Rebels laid siege to a Federal garrison of around 3,000 men within the strong defenses of Lexington, Missouri.

The unexpected threat from General Price's advance, however, awakened Union authorities to the extent of the crisis in the West. At this time, Lexington was a busy port city on the Missouri River and the county seat of Lafayette County. Alarmed Federal leaders in Washington, D.C., and St. Louis continued to muster strength and concentrate their forces to meet the sudden Rebel thrust north into the heart of the Missouri River country. They had been caught by surprise by the sudden advance of "Old Pap" Price's unpredictable frontier army of farmers, lawyers, and militiamen.

Though they won the siege, the surrender of Lexington during the third week of September and the promise of a winter campaign led to widespread Rebel desertions. Missouri volunteers, or "sunshine patriots," returned to their farms for the fall harvest, deserting the cause. Consequently, General Price was forced to withdraw from his increasingly isolated and vulnerable position in mid-Missouri, marching out of Lexington and heading south.

At Jefferson City, meanwhile, Colonel Benton and the 8th Indiana and other Federal units prepared to take the offensive, after Lexington's capture by General Price. Union authorities now planned to push Price's army from Missouri and into Arkansas. Federal units at Jefferson City, such as the 8th Indiana, made preparations for the next campaign to hurl General Price's Missouri forces from the state's borders. This would be the first military action for the young men and boys of Colonel Benton's regiment from Indiana. A cocky Thomas Melick, Company H, 8th Indiana, would write in December 1861: "[W]e will not have any trouble cleaning Missouri out."

Among the 8th Indiana's preparations for offensive campaigning was the utilization of African Americans from the area around Jefferson City and Cole County. The newly freed slaves from this occupied area of central Missouri, including Cathy Williams, were now considered "contrabands" by Union soldiers. Consequently, these liberated African Americans were considered fair game to be seized and employed to support Union soldiers in the field. Cathy Williams would soon learn that she was no more free as "contraband" than she had been as a slave.

In theory, the Union's contraband policy was based on the legal premise of international law that ex-slaves could be utilized and confiscated by Federal forces because they were formerly employed as property by Confederate forces in supporting the rebellion. Therefore, the African Americans of Jefferson City, Cole County, and other occupied areas of Missouri were now considered contraband of war in Union hands.

In essence, the contraband policy and the Confiscation Acts passed by Congress in 1861 and 1862 allowed for the slaves' freedom from ownership. This strategically significant legislation laid a foundation for President Lincoln's eventual Emancipation Proclamation in September 1862.

And now at Union-occupied Jefferson City, Colonel Benton and his fellow Indiana officers possessed the legal right to seize any ex-slaves who could play a part in helping to suppress the Rebels and assist his regiment in the task of winning Missouri for the Union.

Cathy Williams, recently owned by the wealthy farmer, William Johnson, learned much to her shock that she was now legally contraband of war. Once again, a man-made law made Cathy vulnerable to exploitation because of her color.

Nevertheless, once the liberators had initially occupied the state capital and her mid-Missouri homeland, Cathy Williams gained her first taste of freedom. This was an experience that she would never forget. Acquiring personal freedom for Cathy was probably not unlike that experienced by Linda Brent when she first escaped to the North, after a demeaning life of servitude in the South: "I shall never forget that night . . . and how shall I describe my sensations . . . O, the beautiful sunshine! the exhilarating breeze! and I could enjoy them without fear or restraint. I had never realized what grand things air and sunshine are . . . [after] we had left dear ties behind us . . . ties cruelly sundered by the demon Slavery . . . I verily believed myself a free woman."[12]

Cathy's new status as "contraband" in essence denied freedom to the young ex-slave woman and other African Americans because Union military needs in hostile territory remained paramount. Instead of being allowed to enjoy life as a newly freed woman, a cruel fate intervened to again alter the course of Cathy's life. Just as she began to enjoy freedom, it was suddenly snatched away from her as quickly as it had come.

Against her will, Cathy Williams was now "pressed" into service as a cook for the Hoosier officers of the 8th Indiana. In Cathy's own words: "[W]hen the war broke out and the United States soldiers came to Jefferson City they took me and other colored folk with them . . . Col. Benton . . . was the officer that carried us off." Clearly, Cathy Williams thought none too highly of Colonel Benton, and for good reason.[13]

Cathy Williams was not the only victim. Because of her contraband status, a teenage Georgia slave named Susie Baker was also taken into custody by Union forces. Along the South Carolina coast, she served as the laundress and cook of the 33rd U.S. Colored Troops, originally the 1st South Carolina Volunteers. Susie would remain with the regiment until early 1866, after marrying one of its soldiers.[14]

For Cathy Williams, this enforced service was more than a minor inconvenience or short-term impressment. Cathy's new role with the 8th Indiana would continue for years and take her far away from her mid-Missouri homeland.

Despite her new role Cathy Williams possessed no experience as a cook. As she stated, Colonel Benton "wanted me to cook for the officers." Clearly, Colonel Benton's decisions did not agree with Cathy. No doubt, Benton seemed little different from her former master, William Johnson.[15] Cathy had served for years as a house servant on Master Johnson's farm, and was not assigned to any cooking duties. Nevertheless, this was not sufficient to deter her impressers.[16]

The facts, however, soon spoke for themselves, and she was soon serving as a laundress for the officers of the 8th Indiana. As Cathy explained the situation in which she could not do what was expected of her: "I had always been a house girl and did not know how to cook."[17]

Usually, white laundresses received pay of around five to seven dollars per month. Cathy Williams might not have received any pay. That would have been one reason why the Indiana soldiers acquired these "contraband" who worked as if they were indentured servants paying off their own cost of freedom. The money would not come out of the soldiers' pockets to pay black laundresses, though the women did receive rations and articles of clothing.[18]

This seemingly insignificant role as laundress had broad implications for Cathy, extending beyond that of cook. Like it or not and probably without realizing the fact, Cathy was now part of the military. She would have to adhere to a semblance of some military standards and discipline in the time-honored army tradition of laundress that officially extended back in American military history to 1802.[19]

But the most significant development was in regard to mobility. If the 8th Indiana was suddenly ordered out of Cole County to embark upon a new campaign, then Cathy Williams would be forced to go along with them. As fate would have it, her destiny was now tied to the history of these Hoosiers, and the upcoming offensive to push the Missouri Rebels from their home state. Cathy was about to embark on the greatest challenge and adventure of her life to date.[20]

This would have brought no consolation to an anxious Cathy Williams, who was now even more uncertain about what her future held. Most of all, she did not want to leave her home, family, and friends. In her own words, "I did not want to go."[21] Because she was still unmarried, the fact that she was hesitant to depart the Jefferson City area provides some indication that some of her relatives, perhaps her mother, were living in Cole County at this time. It is also possible she had a romantic relationship in Jefferson City.

With her new status as a contraband of war, Cathy was not only forced into service against her will, she would also have to follow the regiment wherever it was ordered. In the future, this situation would mean that she was destined to become an active participant in numerous military campaigns across much of the South.[22]

Much like the Rebels before them, the Yankees now exploited the available African American labor pool in Jefferson City and Cole County and other newly liberated areas for their own use. Cathy Williams was probably seeing less distinction in regard to white men in blue uniforms or white men in gray uniforms.

To make a bad situation worse, many Union soldiers seemed now to treat African Americans with a prejudice and a disdain that were only too familiar to former slaves like Cathy. And in some ways, this discrimination and exploitation were in fact little different from that of the Rebels. In a strange paradox, the Union's righteous war to free the slaves brought not personal freedom for Cathy Williams, but something similar to the institution of slavery in the form of a new type of indentured servitude.

After having been exploited by Missouri whites for her entire life, Cathy Williams was now about to be exploited by whites from the North. For many African Americans like Cathy, the Civil War brought disillusionment because of what seemed like Northern betrayal. These Yankees displayed a blatant hypocrisy that probably diminished more of Cathy Williams's fast-fading faith in the goodness of human nature, especially among whites. Of course, she was now quite anxious about the prospect of being uprooted from her native homeland and cast into a regiment of strange white men she had never seen before.

At this time, relatively little opportunity existed for Cathy Williams to escape the Union army once she was impressed. Being quite young and on her own for the first time in her life, she was now located in the heart of Missouri, which was heavily pro-Southern. Striking out across country on her own would probably have resulted in capture and reenslavement by the Rebels. In addition, she possessed neither a map, knowledge, or guide to lead her to the nearest free state, either Kansas to the west, Iowa to the north, or Illinois to the east.

Ironically, had she still lived in her native western Missouri, the nearby free territory of Kansas would have provided an avenue for escape. In western Missouri and the western edge of "Little Dixie," the Underground Railroad had for years led Missouri slaves out of Jackson County and west to freedom in Kansas. Here, free populations of ex-slaves, most from Missouri, lived in thriving African American communities.

But now in Jefferson City, Cathy Williams was situated around 150 miles east of the Kansas state line, making escape all but impossible for a young woman on her own and without resources or guidance.

Nor could she escape to the north. Northern Missouri was also heavily pro-Southern even to the Iowa border, which was around 100 miles distant. The chances of escaping eastward were no better for her. Now in the Missouri River country of Cole County, Cathy Williams found herself about 150 miles west of the free state of Illinois and the Underground Railroad towns of Cairo, Godfrey, and Quincy.

Caught amid the confusion and chaos of a conflict raging in Missouri, and with nowhere to escape, Cathy Williams was now permanently attached to the 8th Indiana even if she did not yet realize the fact. Consequently, she grudgingly accepted her new fate because she had no choice. As during her life as a slave, she now would simply have to make the best of it, though she certainly knew that things would not be as difficult as under slavery.[23]

At this time, Cathy Williams's inclination that she "did not want to go," if not some form of subtle resistance to the idea, demonstrated that she was anything but a willing, passive participant with her new lot in life.[24]

Her initial desire to resist the demands for her to join the 8th Indiana proved that slavery had not severely damaged Cathy in psychological terms. She had not been turned into a "Sambo" type, dominated by passivity and fatalistic to the point of easy manipulation.[25]

By this time, she was anything but the docile, childlike, and irresponsible slave the stereotype represented. She had not readily accepted this latest form of manipulation and exploitation by the white world. In addition, Cathy Williams's initial reluctance to serve with the 8th Indiana was an early indication of her sense of independence and healthy self-esteem. This independent streak would remain one of Cathy's most enduring personal characteristics throughout her adult life, and would eventually open the door for her service as a Buffalo Soldier.[26]

Quite understandably, the searing experience of slavery and impressment no doubt left her feeling that she could trust few people, especially whites. In the days ahead, she would be forced to rely even more upon herself and her resources of inner strength.

In time, however, the former slave from Cole County came to accept her new role and life with the soldiers of the 8th Indiana. Cathy's job as a laundress consisted of cleaning and washing the uniforms of officers. For her labor, she probably received a small allowance for necessities, which would have seemed like a fortune to someone who had never been paid before. With this money, she was able to purchase her own clothes and extra food.

In addition, she received the same monotonous and bland rations, usually hardtack and pork, as the men in the ranks. However, this diet was probably superior to what she was fed at the Johnson plantation. And evidently she was allowed some form of tented shelter with other laundresses in the 8th Indiana's encampment if it was available.

During active campaigning, she usually slept on the ground, close to a fire for warmth, like the soldiers. Clearly, it was a hard life for a woman on her own. But Cathy Williams was young and conditioned by the hardships of a life in slavery. Her troubles had only begun, however. Now she would have to endure the same discomforts and deprivations as the 8th Indiana's soldiers, as they began their campaigns across the South.

In fact, as time went on and as she became more acclimated to military life, Cathy perhaps came to view her role in the regiment not only as an opportunity but also as an adventure. Military life was less harsh and demeaning than a slave's existence—even as a house servant. As she would eventually realize, this unusual form of "liberation" gave her cause to be thankful. In fact, Cathy might have rationalized her impressed service with the regiment as perhaps a repayment of sorts to these Hoosier soldiers who in part fought for her own freedom and that of other African Americans. As she soon learned, a laundress's existence with the 8th Indiana was much better than a slave's life.[27]

Nevertheless, the chores of a laundress were demanding, including a good deal of hard work. Cathy needed equipment to fulfill her duties, and this was her responsibility when the regiment was on the move. Her gear included two large wooden tubs of about 25-gallon capacity. Each weighed around thirty to forty pounds, and had to be either carried, if no wagon was available, or moved by her on the march. She also had to transport those items used in washing the uniforms, socks, and underwear of the men: soap, wooden scrub boards and buckets, starch, laundry sticks, and other necessary items.[28]

While Cathy was attached to the 8th Indiana, the Hoosier regiment was part of the Army of the Southwest, which had been organized in December 1861. She would go wherever the army was sent like a soldier in the ranks.[29]

As fate would have it, the Army of the Southwest was about to begin an extensive winter campaign across long distances of rough and rugged terrain in hostile country. Cathy Williams was in for the adventure of her life.

About to unleash a new offensive deep into Missouri to drive out Gen. "Old Pap" Price, the western army of Yankees was poised at Rolla, Missouri. Here, before the big push south, the Federal troops mustered strength, with supplies and munitions pouring in from the railroad line that ran southwestward from the huge supply depot of St. Louis.

But not all was well in the tented encampment of the 8th Indiana. Many unacclimated Hoosier farm boys began to die of disease. At this time and surrounded by more people than had ever visited the Johnson Plantation, Cathy Williams also ran risks of catching something. Already, the ravages of infection had swept through the Indianans' ranks with a vengeance during the late autumn of 1861, taking more young lives than had Rebel bullets. Mercifully, Cathy Williams was spared from the war's greatest killer.

By this time, the 8th Indiana was serving in the 1st Brigade, under Col. Thomas Pattieson. Two other Indiana infantry regiments, the 18th and 22nd Indiana Volunteer Infantry, plus an Indiana battery, made up the Hoosier brigade of the 3rd Division, Army of the Southwest. Colonel Pattieson's 8th Indiana was part of the two-brigade division of Gen. Jefferson Columbus Davis.

This Indiana general was an Old Army soldier and Mexican War veteran. He had been a defender of Fort Sumter in April 1861, serving as an artillery lieutenant. Strangely, he would never kill a Rebel but would single-handedly end the life of another Union general with a pistol shot in a fit of rage during September 1862.

If young Cathy Williams was unhappy with her new role with the Indiana regiment, she was no different from the 8th Indiana's commander, Colonel Benton. From the regiment's encampment at Otterville, Missouri, on December 28, 1861, Colonel Benton, with surprising honesty, requested a leave of absence because "the day after the fall of [Fort] 'Sumpter [sic]' I left a large legal practice, and have not given it an hour [of] attention since. By going home and giving it my personal attention I can secure a considerable amount of money which would otherwise be lost." Attending to his law practice in Indiana proved to be a sufficient reason for his release, and Benton received his leave of absence. Long after the war, Cathy would continue to harbor ill feelings toward the colonel who had forced her from her homeland.[30]

Finally, the Army of the Southwest began its offensive, pushing southward to drive General Price's Rebel army from Missouri's borders. This new campaign was initiated in the dead of winter, and the challenges for Cathy Williams would be demanding. The Army of the Southwest advanced slowly on the town of Lebanon, while marching toward the southwestern corner of Missouri in February 1862. The Yankees planned to push General Price's Missouri army into the wilderness of northwest Arkansas. With banners waving in the crisp winter air, the blueclad soldiers of the Army of the Southwest marched triumphantly into Lebanon, around fifty miles northeast of Springfield and forty miles southwest of Rolla, without meeting serious opposition.

This rare winter campaign had been led by the army's commander, Gen. Samuel Ryan Curtis. Like the lamented General Lyon, who was the first Union general killed in this war at the battle of Wilson's Creek, Missouri, in August 1861, General Curtis was determined to win Missouri for the Union. Settled in for what they expected would be a quiet winter, meanwhile, Gen. Sterling Price's force of about 7,000 Rebels wintered in the area of Springfield, the largest city in southwest Missouri. But now the Rebels were vulnerable by the sudden approach of more than 12,000 Federals of the Army of the Southwest.[31]

In short order General Price's forces evacuated Springfield. The Missouri Rebels then retreated south toward northwest Arkansas in the hope of linking with Confederate forces under Gen. Benjamin McCulloch. While skirmishing and fighting for more than 100 miles during a risky withdrawal, the Missouri

Rebels finally reached the relative safety of northwest Arkansas during the third week of February 1862. Without fighting a major battle, the aggressiveness of General Curtis and his Army of the Southwest succeeded in driving the frontier army of General Price from Missouri and into the remote Boston Mountains of Arkansas.[32]

However, the decisive clash between Generals Price and Curtis to determine Missouri's fate was yet to come. Clearly, it had been far too easy hurling Gen. "Old Pap" Price and his Missouri State Guard and Confederate forces out of their home state without a major confrontation. A rendezvous with destiny was now leading Cathy Williams, the 8th Indiana, and the Army of the Southwest toward the most decisive clash of the Civil War west of the Mississippi River. In Cathy's own words, "[I] was with the army at the battle of Pea Ridge."[33]

The 8th Indiana was destined to play a bloody role in the bitter fighting that would swirl for two days across the wooded hills, deep ravines, and brown fields of Benton County, Arkansas, and an obscure inn called Elk Horn Tavern.

Not long after General Price's Missouri army and General McCulloch's Confederate forces linked in northwest Arkansas, a new Confederate commander, Gen. Earl Van Dorn, arrived from the East to take combined command of the largest concentration of Rebels west of the Mississippi River. A Mississippian and ex-horse soldier of a U.S. Regular cavalry unit who had served on the Western frontier, Van Dorn decided to immediately mount an offensive to reverse the Confederacy's fortunes in the West.

With high hopes for a successful invasion of Missouri, the defeat of General Curtis's Army of the Southwest, and the capture of St. Louis, General Van Dorn's Confederates swung northward, hoping to catch the Federals by surprise. A good opportunity existed for Confederate success because the Army of the Southwest was now spread out for miles in the rugged mountains of northwest Arkansas. However, General Curtis reacted quickly to the new threat from the south, issuing orders for new troop deployments to parry the Rebel advance. Reacting in time, the Union army hurriedly concentrated and took good defensive positions along a high bluff overlooking Little Sugar Creek amid the rough country of Benton County.

It seemed as if General Van Dorn was now checkmated by General Curtis's swift reactions. To counter General Curtis's defensive deployment, however, the Mississippi general developed a new, but risky, plan. By way of a grandiose Napoleonic maneuver that called for a lengthy night march along a small trail hewn through the wilderness—known as the Bentonville Detour—

Van Dorn planned to push his Rebels around General Curtis's right flank to gain the Union army's rear for an attack from the north. The Mississippian then planned to unleash a surprise attack. The battle would begin at sunrise, March 7, 1862.[34]

However, General Van Dorn's effort to gain the Union army's rear was delayed by a series of unexpected difficulties compounded by the nighttime trek through the wilderness and rough terrain. Obstacles erected by Union troops blocked the narrow Bentonville Detour. These barricades effectively impeded the march of the infantry, sabotaging the delicate timetable and the overall timing of the battle plan. With the rising sun of the morning of March 7, General Van Dorn's army was divided by the high ground known as Pea Ridge. Instead of unleashing a concentrated offensive blow, Van Dorn was now forced to launch his attack from the north into the Union army's rear from two widely divided wings—General McCulloch's forces on the west side of the impassable mountain known as Pea Ridge, and General Price's on the east side.

Indeed, the imposing ridge covered in forest and wild peas—for which the elevation was named—now lay between Van Dorn's two separated wings. Such a division of force and the unleashing of two isolated assaults guaranteed an uncoordinated offensive: a recipe for disaster. Yet the Rebels retained the advantage because General Curtis's hastily concentrated Federals were still facing south—and were deployed in defensive position along the high ground overlooking Little Sugar Creek and across the Telegraph Road. Snaking through the wilderness, the Telegraph Road, the main artery connecting northwest Arkansas to southwest Missouri, would soon become a focus of contention.[35]

Despite the shock that they had been flanked and caught by surprise, General Curtis and his troops gamely held their ground against thousands of Rebels who suddenly surged forward out of the thick woodlands to their rear. On the cold morning of March 7, General Curtis successfully reversed his army from south to north to meet the Confederate onslaught. In repulsing General Price's initial attacks toward Elk Horn Tavern, some of the most determined Federal resistance erupted from the 4th Division commanded by Gen. Eugene Asa Carr.

Against the attacking Missouri Rebels, General Carr and his troops held firm in positions around Elk Horn Tavern and along the Telegraph Road. Here, the Yankees defended the open plateau that General Price needed to gain for a high ground advantage.[36]

Ascertaining the extent of the threat against General Carr's battered 4th Division, General Curtis dispatched urgent orders at 12:30 p.m. to hurry forward units of Colonel Davis's 3rd Division from the non threatened defenses along Little Sugar Creek to the south.

These recalled Yankee units now about-faced and swung rearward to confront the rising tide of Rebels from the north. However, by this time, the 8th Indiana was ordered to guard the vital Telegraph Road, in case other Confederate units struck from the south.[37]

The regiment was later recalled and then hurled into the fray. These rookie Hoosiers fought well in their first big battle, holding out against the attacks of General Price's Missouri Rebels who steadily advanced until they had gained an advanced position to outflank the sagging Union line on the right. Here, in defending the area southeast of the Elk Horn Tavern and just south of the Clemon's Field, the 8th Indiana's soldiers fought tenaciously until overwhelmed by superior numbers near the end of the first day's battle.

Back in the 8th Indiana's encampment near Little Sugar Creek, Cathy Williams listened to the most intense fighting that she had ever heard. The crackling guns and booming artillery roaring over this section of northwest Arkansas sounded louder than any Missouri thunderstorm.

After the first day's fighting and as the sun set in the early evening of March 7, the weary soldiers of the 8th Indiana formed in line with the survivors of the 4th Division. The division now held a defensive position across the Telegraph Road and below Elk Horn Tavern from which they would start the second day's fighting on March 8. Elk Horn Tavern itself had been captured by the Missouri Confederates late on the first day.

Here, in a good position, the Indiana soldiers stood immediately to the right of the Telegraph Road and along the southern edge of Ruddick's Field below Elk Horn Tavern. Unlike the fighting of the first day, the second day's struggle would be decided largely by the superior firepower of artillery. In short order, the massed firepower of the long-range and more accurate Federal artillery simply overpowered both the Confederate artillery and infantry, driving the shell-swept Rebel units rearward during the morning hours of March 8.[38]

General Van Dorn's bloodied and disorganized army began to depart the field because of the lack of ammunition, heavy losses, and a failed battle plan. The most decisive battle in the Trans-Mississippi was decided, but not without more bloodletting. The slaughter continued throughout the morning of March 8, long after the Federals had won the contest.

The victorious 8th Indiana then joined in the general advance of the Army of the Southwest, driving the hard-hit Rebels from the field. General

Van Dorn suffered around 2,000 casualties, while General Curtis and his army lost nearly 1,400 men.

The cost of victory at Pea Ridge for the 8th Indiana was five killed and twenty-seven wounded in the two days of fighting. But the price was not in vain. With General Curtis's victory at Pea Ridge, Missouri was won for the Union. Thanks to the sacrifices of men like those from the 8th Indiana, the most strategic state west of the Mississippi would remain under Federal control for the rest of the war.[39]

Both during and after the battle, Cathy Williams might well have helped to attend to some of the wounded soldiers of the 8th Indiana.[40] When not engaged in camp chores, noncombatants attached to the regiment, including drummer boys and women, were often employed in the hospitals to treat the wounded, especially after a major battle.

Black women often served as hospital attendants, which was, in the words of one modern author, "another form of hard labor—albeit one that was a potential source of unusual excitement and adventure—in lives in which such labor was a familiar necessity [in these circumstances] Civil War women had deep wells of both physical and psychological hardiness on which they could draw upon."[41]

Cathy's nursing skills were probably learned during the Civil War years and perhaps first put to use here after the storm of Pea Ridge. Because Pea Ridge was the 8th Indiana's largest battle, Cathy Williams quite likely worked as a nurse or a medical assistant in either the regimental, brigade, or even division field hospital. If so, then she probably helped to bandage wounds, draw and distribute water, wash down operating tables, and carry men on stretchers. Such an experience would have hardened Cathy who for the first time in her life now saw firsthand the horrors of war.[42]

Thanks in part to the Union victory at Pea Ridge, new strategic developments in the vast Trans-Mississippi theater continued in the North's favor. The Union continued to maintain the initiative during its spring 1862 campaigns, which unleashed armies on offensive drives southward on both sides of the Mississippi River.

General Van Dorn's defeated army was soon ordered to join Confederate forces east of the Mississippi River for the concentration in force in northeast Mississippi and a new spring offensive, which would lead to the battle of Shiloh, Tennessee, in early April 1862. In the process, both Missouri and Arkansas were all but abandoned to Union forces, as the Confederate Trans-Mississippi was stripped of its primary defending army because of more urgent geopolitical requirements east of the river. Likewise, the fate of Cathy Williams was to be shaped by these strategic developments.[43]

To the north, meanwhile, Cathy Williams's home state of Missouri would be plunged into a new kind of bitter warfare after the decisive battle of Pea Ridge. The people of Missouri would endure the worst aspects of guerrilla warfare ever to be waged upon Americans in their history. The western Missouri county of Cathy's birth, Jackson, and other counties in this war-torn region, would eventually be depopulated by the infamous Order Number Eleven in a desperate Federal attempt to eliminate the civilian support systems of the Rebel guerrillas.

Among the Missouri guerrillas were women saboteurs and fighters under arms. Not all of the hard-riding Missouri guerrillas, such as Jesse James and the Younger brothers, were men. Cathy Williams would not be the only Missouri woman destined to serve on behalf of her country.

Missouri women such as the Mayfield sisters, Ella and sixteen-year-old Jennie, of Cass County, Missouri, were among the Rebel guerrillas from "Little Dixie." To both friend and foe, these two sisters became known as the "Lady Bushwhackers." In fighting for what they believed to be right, they battled against the bluecoat invaders of their Missouri homeland. Nancy Slaughter Walker and Myra Belle Shirley also fought beside the wild riders of Capt. William Clarke Quantrill's Missouri raiders during the bloody years of guerrilla warfare.[44]

With the advent of spring weather in 1862, meanwhile, General Curtis prepared his army for a renewal of offensive operations. He now planned to invade Arkansas and capture the state capital of Little Rock. Along with Cathy Williams, the soldiers of the 8th Indiana prepared for the next move and a resumption of operations.

When the regiment began their march, Cathy Williams would be beside the Hoosier soldiers to share some of the dangers. From sunrise to sunset, she would march beside the men in the rain, pushing through mud and water like everyone else.

In early April 1862, the 8th Indiana and the Army of the Southwest embarked on their most ambitious campaign to date. The Army of the Southwest now began one of the most difficult campaigns of the Western war, and Cathy Williams would be there every step of the way. During both the Pea Ridge campaign and afterward, Cathy would have a front row seat to the struggle between blue and gray in the Trans-Mississippi Theater. She would view the war close-up and like few other women of the time.[45]

To maintain a blocking position between General Van Dorn's army, which marched eastward in an attempt to cross to the east side of the Mississippi River, and to protect against a Rebel thrust northward toward St. Louis, thousands of General Curtis's Yankees, including Cathy Williams and the 8th

Indiana, marched north across northeastern Arkansas. Then, the Army of the Southwest pushed east into the rugged landscape of the Ozark Mountains in southern Missouri.

Never before had Cathy Williams seen such a mountainous or more forested terrain than the wild Ozarks region. Here, blue-hazed mountains topped the horizon as far as the eye could see. This was unlike Cathy's native counties of Jackson, a prairie region, or Cole, which had low hills.

For these Yankees of General Curtis's army, the difficult march continued eastward through the mountains of the Ozarks and across ice-cold streams swollen by spring rains toward West Plains, Missouri. This small town in south central Missouri nestled in the Ozarks immediately above the Arkansas line.[46]

Finally, the Army of the Southwest reached West Plains on April 27. Then, after a brief rest, the Union march went on. For what seemed like an eternity, the weary and hungry Union soldiers, with rations now cut out of necessity because of logistical breakdowns, continued to toil over the seemingly endless forests, hills, and valleys of the Ozark Mountains. All the time, Cathy Williams continued to march forward beside the ranks of the 8th Indiana. Like the Hoosiers, Cathy probably hated the mountainous terrain—the rugged Ozark Highlands. Marching up and down these heavily wooded hills along narrow dirt roads made feet and legs sore.

So critical did the supply situation become for the Army of the Southwest that General Curtis described that from his men, "the cry is for shoes (horse mule and men) and pants." If the average Federal soldier suffered so severely from the want of footwear, pants, and other clothes, the plight of individuals attached to the army, like Cathy Williams and other former slaves, was even more severe. Cathy now ran an even greater risk of catching an illness or disease and becoming injured, while campaigning under deplorable conditions that shocked even General Curtis.

Fortunately for her, Cathy's years under slavery had hardened her for such a challenge. In fact, she may have been even more hardened than many of the citizen-soldiers of the 8th Indiana, especially those who had led sheltered lives as businessmen, clerks, students, and storekeepers.

By comparison, Cathy Williams had existed on inferior rations and inadequate medical treatment, and wore at best secondhand clothes throughout most of her life as a slave. For her, suffering and deprivations were nothing new, and she accepted them simply as a part of life. In fact, Cathy's existence as a slave probably could not have been much more difficult than what she now experienced while campaigning with the Union army. For the most part, a laundress's life in the Union army was much better than the existence of the average Deep South slave.[47]

From the forested mountains of southern Missouri, the Yankees of the Army of the Southwest, had become now almost an army lost in the wilderness. The situation became even worse when General Curtis's men turned south to enter the seemingly endless woodlands of north central Arkansas on April 29.

The severe hardships and trials for General Curtis's army and Cathy Williams were only beginning. Now, the arduous trek continued as the long-suffering Federal soldiers kept moving southward and ever-deeper into the wilderness of north central Arkansas. As usual, Cathy suffered beside the men of the 8th Indiana. Despite the adversity and harsh conditions, Cathy endured as well as the men in the ranks. All the while, she was gaining confidence by accomplishing what she thought impossible for a woman in an army of soldiers: a lesson not soon forgotten by her.

General Curtis's soldiers now captured the town of Batesville in north central Arkansas. Then, the army's relentless advance continued farther into Arkansas and deeper into the Confederacy. However, the depths of the southward penetration resulted in a greater breakdown of the army's fragile supply line: a line already stretched to the limit in reaching more than 300 miles from Batesville, Arkansas, to Rolla, Missouri. Now General Curtis's soldiers, including Cathy, suffered as never before. They became increasingly destitute and half-starved with supply and forage wagons breaking down and rations becoming scarce in what was becoming a logistical fiasco. In fact the support systems broke down and failed so miserably that the optimistic springtime offensive designed to capture Little Rock was canceled.

Now, the weary Union army was forced to backtrack and concentrate. General Curtis's forces consolidated at an advanced position around Batesville in order to survive in hostile country as best they could. If anything, Cathy Williams was becoming even more of a master of survival during this hard campaigning in the wilderness.[48]

Just when the 8th Indiana believed that things could not possibly get any worse, they of course did. By this time, General Curtis decided to undertake an even more audacious gamble to redeem a failed campaign. He now made the unprecedented decision to completely sever what little remained of his tenuous supply line link with Rolla in order to resume the advance across eastern Arkansas in an attempt to reach the Mississippi River.

When and if he gained the west bank of the Mississippi, then General Curtis's troops could be supplied by the Union navy, which controlled most of the river's length. From now on, the 8th Indiana Yankees, Cathy Williams, and the Army of the Southwest would have to live off the land. This move was made long before Gen. William T. Sherman's famous March to the Sea utilized the same logistical strategy of survival in 1864.[49]

During the last week of June 1862, General Curtis's troops swung out of Batesville. They then marched along the White River, which led south to the "Father of Waters," the muddy Mississippi. Not unlike Gen. Winfield Scott's march that resulted in the capture of Mexico City in 1847, General Curtis's forces embarked upon a gamble by an isolated army operating independently and without a supply line deep in enemy territory. This, of course, meant greater hardship on the men in the ranks, and especially those individuals attached to the army like Cathy Williams.[50]

But this campaign in the Arkansas wilderness was not simply one of deprivation and suffering. It was important to lift the morale of the weary soldiers and fulfill their role as liberators. As they marched, the Yankees in Arkansas became a magnet for hundreds of African Americans from the plantations and farms. As in the case of Cathy Williams, the first sight of the blue uniforms of Union troops meant liberation from slavery, if not from service with the Union army.

The long-suffering Army of the Southwest had suddenly become an army of liberation to hundreds of blacks. As the Yankees pushed southward and ever-deeper into Arkansas northeast of Little Rock, great numbers of slaves left their plantations and joined the troops of Mr. Lincoln's army, basking in their newly gained freedom.

The mere "presence of the Army of the Southwest sounded the death knell of slavery in Arkansas's premier agricultural region." Desperate planters attempted to hide their slaves in the swamps, hollows, and thickets, but such efforts were usually in vain. Long before President Lincoln's Emancipation Proclamation, freedom was in the air when the blue troops drew near.

Hundreds of African Americans departed their Arkansas plantations and owners to begin a new life as freedmen and freed women. One slave never forgot the moment that had been dreamed of for so long: "Every time a bunch of No'thern sojers would come through they would tell us we was free and we'd begin celebratin'."

While far from home for the first time, Cathy Williams was certainly inspired by the sight of these newly freed people. Free from the shackles of slavery, these liberated blacks sang religious songs, danced, and shouted in joyous celebration. Seeing the former slaves follow General Curtis's army, this young woman from Missouri must have felt a measure of pride in the liberating roles of the 8th Indiana and the Army of the Southwest. If any single event made Cathy Williams see the righteous side of military life and convince her that a blue uniform represented moral good, it was probably the liberation of slaves.

Week after week, ever-increasing numbers of blacks from north and central Arkansas, whose numbers would eventually swell to thousands by the campaign's conclusion, followed behind this hard-marching army of liberation. Like herself, they could now look forward to a better life and brighter future, after linking with the Union army. By this time, hundreds of African Americans, enjoying freedom for the first time in their lives, continued to reach the army in droves. They were "wandering around the camp as thick as blackberries," wrote one soldier who was amused by his role as a liberator.[51]

Perhaps the knowledge that she was now part of a liberating army helped to give Cathy Williams the idea of one day wearing the blue uniform. Much like the cross to Christianity, the blue uniform served as an enduring symbol of freedom and liberation for the ex-slaves of both Missouri and Arkansas. The emotional sight of hundreds of black people receiving their long-desired freedom was probably an emotional experience for Cathy Williams, and one that she certainly never forgot.[52]

Watching as hundreds of the former Arkansas slaves flooded to the army no doubt brought back fond memories of her own day of liberation in Jefferson City not so long ago. This liberating role was perhaps a primary reason why Cathy continued to faithfully serve with the 8th Indiana and the Army of the Southwest rather than deserting the command despite the many opportunities to do so.

The campaign progressed and General Curtis continued to march away from the White River and southeast across country towards Helena, Arkansas, and the Mississippi. Now the march, which seemed to have no end for the worn participants, continued day after day. Without meeting opposition and with more excited slaves flocking to them, the first Yankees struggled onward to finally reach the west bank of the Mississippi and Helena on July 12, 1862.

Throughout this grueling campaign, the soldiers and camp followers of the army suffered from the intense heat and humidity, choking clouds of dust, insufficient rations, various illnesses, and poor drinking water. The long, hot trek to gain the port town of Helena on the Mississippi was made "with only filthy, slimy water from the swamps to drink," complained one soldier. Such dirty drinking water resulted in more disease, which steadily took young soldiers from the ranks, including sending additional 8th Indiana men to early graves in Arkansas.

At Helena, one of the most demanding campaigns of the Civil War finally came to an end. Here, General Curtis's worn soldiers encamped around the town and along the banks of the Mississippi. The men of the 8th Indiana finally enjoyed a respite. Now they began to recuperate from their hard march across hundreds of miles of Missouri and Arkansas.

Even though the campaign had ended, the possibility of death actually increased in the tented encampment. Disease flourished even more when an army remained stationary than when it was on the move.

In addition, the unhealthy location of Helena, the low-lying area of the encampments, and the poor drinking water from the Mississippi spread sickness. It is not known if Cathy Williams became sick during this period but it is quite likely. Importantly, she had survived one of the longest and most demanding marches of her life. Still only a teenager, the hardships of slavery and her own sense of determination had already allowed her to accomplish what few other women had achieved.

For the soldiers of the 8th Indiana and Cathy Williams, the respite along the Mississippi allowed some much-needed time for recuperation. Likewise, this was also journey's end, at least for the moment, for the thousands of ex-slaves who had followed the army to the west bank of the Mississippi. But with a Union army encamped so deep in Confederate territory even more runaway slaves poured into Helena, after they learned of the army's location. Here, hoping to start a new life, "thousands of refugee Negroes who came looking for the Jubilee [gathered] in the squalid contraband camps around Helena."[53]

By this time, no other Federal army had advanced so deeply into the Confederacy or across a greater expanse of Rebel territory as the hard-marching Army of the Southwest or accomplished so much in a relatively short time. What is more, General Curtis's campaign deep into Arkansas had continued well into the hot and humid months of the summer. This was at a time when many generals, both North and South and including Gen. Robert E. Lee, believed that the severity of Southern summers would make active campaigning in the South an impossibility for Northern troops.

In pushing so deeply into the Confederacy, more than 500 miles were traversed by the Army of the Southwest, the 8th Indiana, and Cathy Williams. They had marched across southern Missouri and northern and eastern Arkansas in less than three months, and had fought a victorious battle—against the odds—in the process.[54]

All the while, Cathy Williams demonstrated considerable endurance by simply managing to keep up with the command and enduring the same ordeals as the men of the 8th Indiana. Merely reaching journey's end at Helena with the army was an amazing feat. Cathy had shown that she had a fortitude, determination, and physical endurance equal to the most hardened soldiers of the Army of the Southwest.

In the camp at Helena, Cathy could probably count her closest friends among the other black laundresses of the 8th Indiana. These women were perhaps former Missouri slaves from the Cole County area and Jefferson City. Even in the military, these African American women continued the maternal and kinship tradition that existed under slavery. In addition, she probably also had friends and acquaintances among the regimental cooks, who probably were also African American women. It is not known if the situation of the 8th Indiana and the women attached to it applied, but sometimes the laundresses of Union regiments found lovers among the white soldiers—one legacy of slavery. Some white officers forced themselves on the black cooks and laundresses, committing rape. Other more enterprising females sold their bodies to the soldiers to make extra money to buy the things that they needed.

Some men of God in blue were not immune to this vice. One Protestant chaplain of an Illinois cavalry regiment was found sleeping with an ex-slave woman when captured by Missouri Confederates, from Cathy's own native "Little Dixie" region, in eastern Louisiana during April 1863.

So extensive was the abuse of African American women by white troops during the Civil War that angry black soldiers openly complained to authorities over the gross injustice. One soldier, for instance, took the trouble of having his complaints printed out for all to see: "[W]e have a set of [white] officers here who apparently think that their commissions are licenses to debauch and mingle with deluded freedwomen." It is not known if Cathy Williams was exploited in this fashion because of her vulnerable position but such might well have been the case.[55]

While General Curtis and the Army of the Southwest recuperated at Helena, the lightly defended Confederate city of Little Rock became a political and military target of Union authorities. Consequently, Union troops under Gen. Frederick Steele, who would soon replace General Curtis as the Army of the Southwest's commander, pushed westward and toward the Arkansas state capital during the second week of August. Among the soldiers of this expedition were hundreds of black troops in blue uniforms. These were the first African American soldiers that Cathy Williams would have ever seen, and no doubt it left a deep impression on her.

Almost certainly, this young ex-slave from Missouri felt a surge of pride. Such an experience probably kindled a desire within her to have the opportunity one day to put on a blue uniform herself. And why not? Fighting in a blue uniform was viewed by blacks as a holy crusade and righteous struggle sanctioned by God. For the men and women of African descent, this was most of all a holy war of liberation that would bring a new and brighter day for all African Americans. Here, on the banks of the Mississippi, the genesis of Cathy Williams's future role as a Buffalo Soldier was taking shape.[56]

Fearing another entrapment as at Vicksburg, Mississippi, General Price would eventually order his Rebel army to evacuate the capital of Arkansas without a fight. One disgusted Missouri Rebel wrote that "the capital of Arkansas was abandoned without a blow." Shortly afterwards, U.S. flags were flying once again from the public buildings of Little Rock.[57]

A strange fate now suddenly intervened to take Cathy Williams away from Helena and her long-time companions of the 8th Indiana. Quite suddenly and unexpectedly, Cathy was ordered from the regiment and dispatched to Little Rock to learn the art of cooking.[58]

Cathy must have been shocked to receive the order. She had probably assumed that all plans to transform her into a cook had long since been abandoned. Now she learned that such was not the case. No doubt, this news was not well received. By this time, she might well have considered the 8th Indiana as her home. And after just going through such a rough campaign, she probably desired to stay put for a time.[59]

Since the 8th Indiana was not ordered to Little Rock, she evidently was sent with other African Americans to learn new skills. Perhaps she even accompanied some black troops on the march to the state capital, getting a close look at these new soldiers of Lincoln's armies.

Here, at Little Rock on the wide, brown Arkansas River, Cathy Williams learned how to cook. In her own words, "I learned to cook after going to Little Rock."[60]

Then, after gaining her culinary skills, she spent some time cooking for the occupation forces in the city, where hundreds of other ex-slaves provided menial service to the Union soldiers. For the first time, she now engaged in an occupation that she had never known before.[61]

During the summer of 1863, the 8th Indiana participated in the Vicksburg campaign on first the west side and then the east side of the Mississippi River, evidently while Cathy remained in Little Rock as a cook. However, she might well have been with the 8th Indiana for this campaign because she stated that after she learned to cook at Little Rock, "the command moved over various portions of Arkansas and Louisiana."[62]

By this time, the 8th Indiana's first commander, Colonel Benton, now a general, commanded an Indiana and Illinois brigade of Gen. Eugene A. Carr's 14th Division, XIII Corps, of General Grant's Western army during its attempt to capture Vicksburg.

Under the command of Col. David Shunk, after moving south through eastern Louisiana to cross the Mississippi below Vicksburg, the 8th Indiana won distinction in the battle of Port Gibson, Mississippi, on May 1, 1863, capturing an Arkansas battleflag and artillery. Then, the regiment fought in the decisive battle of Champion Hill, Mississippi, on May 16, 1863. After the Rebels retreated westward to the fortifications of Vicksburg, the 8th Indiana was engaged in the forty-seven-day siege of the city, which eventually choked the life out of the encircled Confederate army of Gen. John C. Pemberton.

More than thirty Missouri slaves—many of whom were from "Little Dixie" and Cathy Williams's native Jackson and Cole Counties—now served with a brigade of Missouri Confederate troops defending Vicksburg. Quite possibly, Cathy Williams might have known some of these African Americans. Vicksburg finally surrendered to General Grant on the Fourth of July, 1863, and the North took a giant step toward winning control of the Mississippi River.[63]

If life was too difficult in the regiment or Union officers of the 8th Indiana abusive, why had not Cathy Williams deserted while on the march or in camp or even from Little Rock? Cathy evidently possessed good reason for serving the 8th Indiana. By this time, she evidently had taken a liking to military life. Or perhaps she had a lover who was a servant to one of the officers. Or perhaps a relative served as a cook, blacksmith, or nurse with the Indiana regiment.

Because Cathy Williams was destined to enlist one day in the Buffalo Soldiers partly to be beside a cousin and a "particular" friend, the possibility exists that this relative and friend also might have been with the 8th Indiana.

It is not known but perhaps Cathy Williams, without resources and especially if she was on her own and without relatives back in Missouri, planned to eventually return to Indiana with the Hoosiers after the war's end. At this time and perhaps thanks to the influence of abolitionists in the regiment, Indiana might have been viewed by her as a place where she could make a home as a free woman. Perhaps some Indiana soldiers promised her land or assistance if she settled down in the Hoosier state. Whatever the reason, Cathy evidently possessed a strong desire to follow the regiment for the remainder of the war.

By this time, however, the 8th Indiana was no longer stationed at Vicksburg. After having been assigned to the Department of the Gulf, the Indiana soldiers had boarded steamboats at the Vicksburg wharf on August 20, 1863, to embark on a new assignment. They had then been taken, with the rest of XIII Corps to Carrollton, Louisiana, several miles north of New Orleans, in preparation for a new campaign in the Deep South.

In the sprawling encampments of white tents around the low-lying town of Carrollton, the newly arrived soldiers of the Department of the Gulf prepared for a new challenge. [64]

Cathy Williams was with the 8th Indiana during what would become known as the Red River campaign. She continued to fulfill the role of a cook for the regimental officers. In addition, Cathy probably also continued to work as a laundress.[65]

This new Union offensive would be led by Gen. Nathaniel Prentiss Banks. A general through political connections, Banks had captured the fortress of Port Hudson, Louisiana, to ensure the winning of the Mississippi River in July 1863 only days after Vicksburg's fall.

As urged by President Lincoln, the Red River campaign of 1864 was designed to place Union troops on Texas soil to remind Emperor Maximilian and the French in Mexico of the nearby presence of U.S. forces. Such a military presence would be a strong hint of President Lincoln's desire to uphold the Monroe Doctrine—by force if necessary.[66]

Thousands of Yankees advanced into south-central Louisiana through the Bayou Teche country of swamps, cypress forests, and canebrakes. During the first phase of the Red River campaign in the spring of 1864, the 8th Indiana and Cathy Williams campaigned through the swampy wilderness. This was a guerrilla-infested, disease-ridden Rebel haven, which was far from civilization. As in the Army of the Southwest's 1862 campaign in Arkansas, Cathy continued to risk the dangers from both the ravages of disease and the attacks by Rebels during this campaign west of New Orleans.[67]

Despite the dreadful conditions, this was an overpowering Union offensive. Indeed, Federal authorities planned for the occupation of all Louisiana by the end of 1864. In the spring, Cathy Williams was part of the advance up the Red River to capture Shreveport—a springboard for the invasion of Texas. Among the Union forces were the black troops of the 73rd, 75th, 84th, and 92nd U.S. Colored Troops.[68]

The advance of the Union troops up the Red River and through rich countryside of central Louisiana yielded many captured supplies, including a great deal of cotton. These bales were either confiscated or destroyed. In Cathy's own words: "I saw the soldiers burn lots of cotton."[69]

Not clear on the strategic situation or geography of a complex campaign—not unusual for a regimental cook—it is not surprising that Cathy Williams was in error when she described what she saw during the campaign: "I . . . was at Shreveport when the rebel gunboats were captured and burned on Red River."[70]

The vessels Cathy had seen burning were in fact Union gunboats of Adm. David Porter, who acted in concert with the advancing Federal infantry. In early May 1864, Confederate cavalry destroyed five of Porter's boats on the

Red River. It is also apparent that she was not present at the capture of Shreveport, which was not seized by General Banks whose forces retreated before gaining their objective. Cathy's memory had dimmed more than a dozen years after the Red River campaign in regard to the advance upon, instead of the capture of the town.[71]

After Shreveport, Union operations continued. On November 12, 1864, the 8th Indiana was dispatched from Berwick City, Louisiana. Berwick City was located on the Lower Grand north of Atchafalaya Bay in the Gulf of Mexico southwest of New Orleans. The 8th Indiana were bound westward for Texas.

By this time, General Banks was striking at isolated points along the sprawling Gulf coast of Texas, including at Aransas Pass which was just northeast of Corpus Christi. In mid-November, the 8th Indiana was part of the force that captured a Confederate fort on Mustang Island, and then took Fort Esperanza near Aransas Pass, about half way between Galveston and Brownsville, Texas.

After these Union successes on Texas soil, the Hoosier regiment marched to Indianola, Louisiana. Here the men of the 8th Indiana reenlisted for the war. As a cook and laundress, Cathy Williams did not sign any enlistment papers or reenlist. She was serving on her own free will by this time.

But a price had been paid by these long-marching men from Indiana. By the end of 1864, nearly 140 soldiers of the regiment had died of disease. From beginning to end, disease remained the greatest killer of this conflict.[72]

After reenlisting and traveling on to New Orleans, the Indiana soldiers prepared to return north to Indianapolis for a month furlough. In Cathy's words, "we afterwards went to New Orleans." The Hoosiers traveled by steamboat up the Mississippi and past the fallen Confederate fortress of Vicksburg, and then northeast up the Ohio River to their Indiana homeland.

Ready to resume their crusade against the Confederacy after the short respite, the men of the 8th Indiana traveled south for more action, reaching the port of New Orleans by way of steamboat. It is not known if Cathy Williams went to Indiana with the regiment, but probably not. Most likely, she remained in the South. Nevertheless, she was once again with the regiment at New Orleans at some point either before or after the Indianians' month-long furlough.[73]

On July 27, 1864, and after the failure of the Red River campaign, the 8th Indiana embarked by steamboat north and steamed up the Mississippi for Morganza, Louisiana, around thirty miles north of Port Hudson. Then, after disembarking, the Hoosier unit swung several miles north to the town of

Morganza. The following day, the 8th Indiana marched west from Morganza to the Atchafalaya River. Here, amid the low-lying bayous and swamps, they skirmished with defending Rebels.

The next day, the Indiana regiment returned to Morganza, where Cathy Williams remained at the regimental encampment. As in many such operations in the Rebel country of Louisiana, Cathy watched as the Yankees burned more cotton. Cotton was "white gold" because the bales were used by the Confederacy to purchase weapons, munitions, and supplies, which were being transported across the Rio Grande River to Mexico before the final journey to European markets.[74]

CHAPTER THREE

New Challenge
in the Eastern Theater

THE 8TH INDIANA WAS NOW REASSIGNED TO THE EASTERN THEATER. THIS meant that Cathy Williams was about to depart the Mississippi Valley for the first time in her life. This journey would take her far, and she would face many new challenges in the months ahead.[1]

From Morganza Bend, Louisiana, the 8th Indiana and Cathy Williams traveled south down the broad stretches of the brown Mississippi to New Orleans. Then, the steamboat pushed into the sprawling waters of the Gulf of Mexico for the trip east then north up the Atlantic coast. Cathy Williams was now traveling farther from her native homeland of Missouri than ever before. The steamboat carrying the Indiana regiment pushed up the Atlantic coast, entering the Chesapeake Bay and the Potomac River, which led to the nation's capital, Washington, D.C.[2]

Cathy saw new sights and a new land that she had never before known existed. Already, Cathy had experienced so much that the nightmare of Missouri slavery probably seemed to have been part of a different lifetime.

On August 12, 1864, the 8th Indiana reached Washington, D.C., and the Hoosier soldiers and Cathy Williams disembarked from the steamboat.[3] On the move east, Cathy Williams simply stated how, "Finally I was sent to Washington City."[4]

Here, she saw the nation's capital for the first time, viewing the recently completed U.S. Capitol dome and the yet uncompleted Washington Monument. Both projects had begun construction with the help of slave labor and the city itself had long served as a major slave trading center: an appropriate symbol that mirrored the fundamental contradiction of slavery in the world's greatest democratic republic. Antislavery societies had printed broadsides that denounced Washington, D.C., as the "Slave Market of America." Ironically, slavery had only been outlawed in the District of Columbia in mid-April 1862, while Cathy Williams was serving with the 8th Indiana in Arkansas not long after the battle of Pea Ridge. [5]

From Washington, D.C., the men of the 8th Indiana marched west to Berryville, Virginia. Here, the Hoosiers joined the units of the XIX Corps under Gen. William H. Emory. The 8th Indiana now became part of the 4th Brigade, under Col. David Shunk who had been promoted from regimental to brigade commander, of General Cuvier Grover's 2nd Division, Army of the Shenandoah.

By this time, the 8th Indiana was commanded by Lt. Col. Alexander J. Kenny. In an interesting twist of fate, General Grover would be a senior officer of the Buffalo Soldiers of the 38th U.S. Infantry, in which Cathy Williams would serve during the postwar period.[6]

On August 12 the veteran 8th Indiana became part of the army of a pugnacious little Irish general named Phil Sheridan. He was busily gathering forces for a new campaign, in response to Gen. Jubal Early's recent raid on Washington, D.C. Early's attack had shocked the capital, President Lincoln, and all the North, resulting in what would be General Sheridan's retaliatory strike. By this time, General Sheridan, another tough Westerner had developed into one of the most aggressive leaders in the Eastern theater.

As the commander of the newly established Middle Military Division, a post he assumed as of August 7, Sheridan's mission was to sweep the Shenandoah Valley clean of Rebel forces, specifically General Early's troublesome army. In addition, he was determined to deny the vital supplies and resources of the fertile Shenandoah to Gen. Robert E. Lee's Army of Northern Virginia, the principal Confederate army in the East and defender of the Confederacy's capital of Richmond, Virginia.

In September 1864 with the leaves on the trees beginning to turn red and yellow, General Sheridan's confident army advanced from the Berryville area. As usual, Cathy Williams traveled with the men of the 8th Indiana. The lengthy columns of Yankees marched through the grain fields and belts of woodlands of the Old Dominion, while surging up the Shenandoah Valley with the intent of defeating General Early's Rebels.

When General Sheridan struck, he hit hard. This newly formed army was a good one, winning September battles at Opequon Creek, Winchester, and Fisher's Hill, and driving General Early's outgunned defenders from the field on each occasion. Believing that Early's army was effectively eliminated by these series of victories, a confident General Sheridan withdrew to consolidate his gains.

Basking in his valley successes, Sheridan then took an advanced defensive position in the Valley and held his ground. Here, the general awaited the expected orders to dispatch troops to General Grant's Army of the Potomac, which was now engaged in the vicious struggle with the Army of Northern Virginia for possession of Richmond.[7]

It now appeared that General Sheridan had succeeded in his mission of making Washington, D.C., and the Shenandoah Valley secure by defeating General Early's army and sending its scattered remnants into the wilderness of the Blue Ridge Mountains.

During the respite and after a job well done, Sheridan was ordered to the nation's capital to discuss strategy with President Lincoln and other leading officials and commanders. At age thirty-three and after his victories in the Valley, General Sheridan had solidified his reputation as one of the youngest and most successful major generals of the Union.

As if somehow ordained, the life of the ex-slave Cathy Williams now became strangely linked with that of the promising West Pointer from the West, General Sheridan. After more than two years of service with the regiment, Cathy now departed the 8th Indiana when she was unexpectedly assigned to serve as cook and laundress for General Sheridan and his staff at the headquarters of the Army of the Shenandoah.

Her duties with Sheridan's staff were the same as those with the officers of the 8th Indiana. It is not known but perhaps other African Americans were also selected for duty at General Sheridan's headquarters.[8]

In her own words, years later: "[A]t the time Gen. Sheridan made his raids in the Shenandoah Valley I was cook and washwoman for his staff." Cathy Williams was probably shocked by this development that forced her to leave the 8th Indiana, her longtime home.[9]

The tranquillity that had settled over Sheridan's encampments in the Valley was merely the calm before the storm, however. General "Old Jube" Early planned to gamble everything on one roll of the dice. He prepared to launch a desperate bid to regain the initiative in the struggle for possession of the rich Shenandoah. Early devised a surprise attack on Sheridan's army, which had remained inactive after its recent victories, and which by the early autumn of 1864 had become vulnerable.

Eager to strike his unwary opponent, General Early moved his troops forward to exploit the opportunity. Easing as silently as possible along the base of Massanutten Mountain, around 17,000 Rebels advanced under the cover of darkness on General Sheridan's sleeping army of about 30,000 men. Around

the Shenandoah Valley town of Middletown just above the north fork of the
Shenandoah River and along a small stream called Cedar Creek, General
Sheridan's tranquil encampments, including that of the 8th Indiana and the
general's own personal headquarters, were about to be struck by a Confederate avalanche.

By this time, General Sheridan's headquarters included Cathy Williams.
Once again, Cathy had been left without a choice. And as fate would have it,
she was about to find herself in the eye of the storm that was about to descend
upon Cedar Creek.[10]

At 5:00 A.M. in the half-light of October 19, thousands of howling Rebels
suddenly attacked the sleeping Federals. With battle flags flying and weapons
firing in the near darkness of early morning, the Confederates charged
through the Union encampments.

Hit hard, the Yankees were caught by surprise by the sudden Rebel onslaught that surged out of the thick blanket of foggy, dense woodlands. Some
Union officers were eating breakfast when General Early's assault struck. Half-
dressed Union soldiers spilled from their tents, and grabbed muskets in the
confusion. The Federals attempted in vain to organize a solid defense against
the surging Rebel tide.

Despite being seasoned veterans, many of the surprised Federals fled to
the rear during that chaotic morning. The rout was on, and seemingly nothing in the world could stop the panic or the steamrolling Confederate assault
that was pushing aside all before it. One Confederate recalled the Yankee encampment, where endless rows of "tents whitened the field from one end to
the other [while] the country behind was one living sea of men and horses—
all fleeing for life and safety."[11]

Caught in the turmoil of the Rebel assault, Cathy Williams was now at
the general's own headquarters. She could not have been at a more dangerous
location at a more inopportune time. The headquarters was a prime target of
the attacking Rebels.[12]

Cathy was taken by surprise like everyone else in General Sheridan's hard-
hit army, which was now dissolving under the Rebel pounding. During the
first phase of the attack, she was at Sheridan's headquarters at the Belle Grove
House, nestled between the Valley Turnpike, to the south, and Meadow
Brook, to the north. This was soon overrun by the rising tide of Confederates,
who raced forward with Rebel Yells and the confidence that a complete victory was at hand.

Along with the retreating flood of Yankees, Cathy Williams joined the
demoralized throng of panicked Union soldiers who now fled for their lives. If
she was captured by the Rebels, she knew for certain that a life of slavery lay

in store for her. Then, she might have been fated to endure the horror of sale on the auction block, ending her days laboring on a cotton plantation in the Deep South. Given such motivation, Cathy probably outdistanced a good many Yankee soldiers in her flight from what for her would have been the worst of all possible fates.

Just south of Belle Grove, the 8th Indiana's encampment was also overrun by the screaming Rebel hordes. Almost all of the headquarters of senior Union officers were likewise captured during the Confederate assault. At Gen. William H. Emory's headquarters, one African American servant who served the general's staff, a former slave named Patrick, attempted to save the staff's milk cow in the confusion. However, along with Cathy Williams, he was soon forced to join the retreating mob of defeated Federal soldiers as the yelling Rebels closed in behind.[13]

Losing two dozen artillery pieces, its encampments, and more than 1,300 men as prisoners, not to mention the piles of dead and wounded, the battered Army of the Shenandoah was already crushed by the Confederate attack by the time the sun rose high into the morning sky. Instead of immediately following up on his amazing success, however, an over-confident Jubal Early paused his attack.

Meanwhile, General Sheridan—who had not been at his headquarters— on his way back to rejoin his army after sensing trouble at his Valley encampment, was shocked to learn of disaster at Cedar Creek. He then rapidly rode back to assist his reeling army, rallying the defeated throngs of troops along the way. Cheering the unexpected sight of their general riding into action, these veteran Yankees suddenly took heart. They turned and followed their fiery commander back into the fray.

Incredibly, during "Sheridan's Ride," the general's sudden appearance electrified the entire army before midday, including the beaten soldiers of the 8th Indiana, which likewise turned around to engage the Rebels. With the irrepressible General Sheridan leading the way and providing invaluable leadership during the moment of crisis, the rallied Yankee troops charged upon the Confederates, who were now in turn caught by surprise by the late afternoon counterattack and beaten from the field.

Quite unexpectedly, by the force of leadership and power of personality, at Cedar Creek General Sheridan turned a disaster into another surprising Union victory. In the process, "Cedar Creek was a personal as well as a national triumph for Sheridan . . . from the lonely moment on the Winchester turnpike when he deliberately chose to return to the battlefield, thus wedding his fate to that of his army, he had accomplished something very much like a miracle, rallying a beaten . . . army, reinvigorating it with the force of his own tornadic personality, and sending it forward to an eleventh-hour victory, the likes of which had seldom if ever been seen in American military history."[14]

Clearly, by this time, Cathy Williams was in association with one of the most dynamic military commanders on the Union side, General Sheridan. What is more, some meager and largely undocumented evidence exists that this link would continue on the Western frontier in the years following the Civil War.[15]

Interestingly, as if to foreshadow the fact the Cathy Williams would one day serve under the general as a Buffalo Soldier, Sheridan learned of women disguised as men during the Civil War years. In January 1863, the general discovered two women serving as men in his command, and personally dismissed them from service. He even provided them with proper women's clothing.[16]

Such female ambitions were not restricted to the Union army. On the Confederate side, two young farm girls from Pulaski County, Virginia, served in General Early's army until the fall of 1864.[17]

After the battle of Cedar Creek, additional duties were assigned the 8th Indiana. As a result, Cathy now took leave of General Sheridan's headquarters after a brief, but eventful, association. It is not known but perhaps she requested to go back to the 8th Indiana regiment.[18]

On the other hand, she might have simply slipped away from General Sheridan's headquarters when she learned that the 8th Indiana was preparing to move out. If so, then this would indicate that she might have had a family member or lover with the regiment. Certainly by this time, she would have considered the Indiana unit to be her adopted home because she evidently now had none back in Missouri. Either way, Cathy was with the 8th Indiana for its next assignment.

On January 6, 1865, the Hoosiers departed the Shenandoah Valley never to return, traveling northeast to Baltimore, Maryland. Then, the Indiana soldiers embarked on a steamboat for a trip down the East Coast, taking them south to Savannah, Georgia. In her conversation with a St. Louis newspaper reporter in late 1875, Cathy Williams told him: "[W]e afterwards went . . . by way of the [Atlantic] to Savannah."[19]

Cathy was seeing a lot of the United States during her service with the far-roving Indiana regiment. For a young woman, she had come a long way from her humble life as a house slave on the William Johnson plantation.[20]

With the 8th Indiana, Cathy Williams reached the Atlantic port city of Savannah, which General Sherman had captured in December 1864, on January 16, 1865. Here, in southeast Georgia, the regiment remained on occupation duty until August 28, 1865, when the unit was mustered out of service.[21]

After four years of bitter fighting, the Civil War was finally over for Cathy Williams and the soldiers of the 8th Indiana. Both Cathy and the Western regiment had seen plenty of campaigning and adventures across the South. Compiling a lengthy record of faithful service on both sides of the Mississippi and as far east as Virginia, Cathy had served with Union armies for nearly three and a half years. But this was only the beginning of the military service of the young ex-slave named Cathy Williams.[22]

CHAPTER FOUR

Triumph of the Spirit:
First Female Buffalo Soldier

AFTER FINALLY WINNING ITS WAR OF ATTRITION AGAINST THE CONFEDERATE nation and after four years of bloody fighting, the victorious Grand Army of the Republic was dismantled. Now tens of thousands of seasoned veterans returned to peaceful pursuits to enjoy life once more. A million and a half Union soldiers took off their blue uniforms during the massive demobilization of a huge military machine that had crushed the South and its armies.

However, the rapid dismantling of the Union's great war machine left the American nation weak militarily, especially on the Western frontier. A new army was now needed for frontier duty in the West. The safety of the frontier had been neglected during the Civil War because an all-out effort was directed toward defeating the Rebels.

Not surprisingly, the Native Americans had taken advantage of the absence of Federal troops during the war years to resume the offensive after Western garrisons were either reduced or transferred eastward to confront the Confederates. Despite the pressing requirements of frontier service throughout the expansive West, the U.S. Army was about to resume its former prewar strength of around only 16,000 troops.

Other legacies of the bloody years of Civil War remained. The successful Civil War service of more than 200,000 African Americans won for blacks a permanent place in the Regular army during the postwar period. Having earned "an opportunity to play a major role in the settlement of the West" from a thankful American nation, despite considerable political and domestic resistance to the concept of black troops in the postwar army, these African

Americans of both cavalry and infantry regiments would become known as the Buffalo Soldiers.

As during the years of civil war, the American military would remain segregated. African Americans would continue to serve in all-black units under the command of white officers. Paternalism and the slavery's bitter legacy continued to exist for black soldiers during the postwar period. Despite the important role played by African Americans in the Civil War, almost as if the bloody sacrifices at Milliken's Bend, Louisiana, Fort Wagner, South Carolina, the Petersburg Crater, Virginia, and Olustee, Florida, had been already forgotten, military and government leaders in Washington, D.C., still considered the use of black troops in the frontier West "as something of an experiment." In reality, the opposite was the case, because no "experiment" in fact existed. A distinguished black role in the American military had been demonstrated time and again in all of America's wars, beginning with the American Revolution.[1]

Embarking on another attempt to begin a new life after years of Civil War service, Cathy Williams was once again on her own. She now probably traveled by rail to Indiana with the returning 8th Indiana, which ended its service at Indianapolis on September 17, 1865. Here, Cathy evidently concluded her association with the soldiers of the regiment, after it was mustered out of service. No doubt, this separation was not without some emotion because the Hoosier regiment had been her only home for nearly the last four years.

Indeed, by this time, she had become thoroughly militarized as a person. After her years of faithful service, Cathy was now almost as completely acclimated to military life as any hardened veteran in the ranks. Plenty of good reasons existed to explain such a transformation since she had been first forced into service during the fall of 1861. One of the foremost of these was that military service was better than the life she had experienced under slavery.

On her own for the first time in years, Cathy Williams now continued west from Indiana and traveled across the wide prairies and farmlands to Iowa. In her own words, "I was sent from Virginia to some place in Iowa."[2] Her words seem to indicate that either she or the soldiers of the 8th Indiana purchased her ticket to continue the journey west toward her native Missouri.

A short time thereafter, Cathy then journeyed south and arrived in St. Louis. From St. Louis, as Cathy stated, she "afterwards [traveled a short distance south] to Jefferson Barracks."[3]

Perhaps one reason why she returned was to link up with at least one family member, a cousin, or others, because she had "relatives" at this time in the state.[4] In addition, her mother might have still been living in Jackson County, Cole County, or even St. Louis. Reuniting with family members was certainly an explanation for Cathy Williams's return to her native state, where she had known only slavery.

By the summer of 1865, Cathy was living a short distance south of St. Louis close to the old French community of Carondelet on the Mississippi. Here, she stayed in the vicinity of Jefferson Barracks "for some time," in her own words.[5]

Besides readily available menial employment in the area, Cathy Williams settled down around Jefferson Barracks evidently because her cousin or her "particular friend" either worked at or close to the nearby military installation on the Mississippi River.[6] In this way, she also remained close to the military life she had known.

Other explanations for Cathy's movements might be these—Cathy and her cousin and "particular friend"—might have traveled to Missouri together because they all served together in the 8th Indiana during the war years. Or she might have joined them after returning to Missouri.[7]

Cathy Williams remained in the vicinity of Carondelet and Jefferson Barracks until the next summer and fall of 1866.[8] She may have found employment as a cook, though probably not for U.S. troops at Jefferson Barracks, because this was where she would eventually enlist in the U.S. Army. It is more likely that she might have worked as a cook or laundress for white families either in Carondelet or perhaps even south St. Louis.[9]

While in the vicinity of Jefferson Barracks and while probably in contact with workers from the military installation, Cathy first learned of the astounding news that black soldiers were being enlisted in the U.S. Regular Army.[10]

Now, for the first time and unlike the situation in the Civil War, African Americans could exercise their rights as newly franchised citizens of the United States by serving in the Regular army. This ground-breaking news must have brought a surge of pride and new hope for the future to her. No doubt the thought of black troops rekindled fond memories of the many young African American soldiers that she had seen marching with pride and discipline during the war years.

At this time, Jefferson Barracks served as a primary recruiting depot for the postwar army. Cathy Williams now suddenly found herself near the exact location where a great dream of African Americans was taking shape and becoming a reality: thousands of African Americans were now being given the opportunity of serving as professional soldiers.

Only after much heated debate in Congress during the summer of 1866 was the opportunity given for ex-slaves and former Union soldiers of African American heritage to enlist in the Regular army. This was not gained easily. It involved yet another struggle to overcome racism and discrimination among some of the highest-ranking leaders of the land.

As throughout American history, the decision to enlist African American troops was based more on pressing military requirements and urgent national self-interest than genuine enlightened concern for African Americans. At this time after the mass demobilization, the United States was now virtually without a military, while simultaneously facing two potentially volatile situations that could explode into open warfare at any time: conflict with France in Mexico and with the Native Americans across the frontier West.

Valid moral reasons also existed for the American nation to utilize black troops in the postwar army. As Pres. Abraham Lincoln had emphasized during the Civil War, African American troops repeatedly "demonstrated in blood their right to the ballot" and citizenship. However, President Lincoln's words were quickly forgotten by many whites after the war was won: the tragic dilemma for African Americans after all of America's wars.

During the late autumn of 1866, Cathy Williams made the most momentous decision of her life. Despite entailing considerable risk, she decided to make the audacious attempt to enlist in the U.S. Army.

Why would this young African American woman make such a decision, after years of hard service during the Civil War? First, she was an adventurous type and possessed a free spirit, especially after witnessing the end of slavery. In a moral sense, Cathy probably also desired to serve on behalf of the country that had fought a great civil war and lost dearly in order to free African Americans. In addition, she may have wanted to continue to live the life that she had known for three and a half years with the 8th Indiana.

Other factors existed to explain her decision to enlist in the Buffalo Soldiers. One was that little opportunity existed even for white women of the times, except year after year of servitude as a wife and a life as little more than a domestic. For a single African American woman with a slave past, future prospects were far more grim. By this time while living in Carondelet, Cathy realized that only one avenue of opportunity now lay open for her to succeed in life, to gain economic independence, and achieve a life worthy of respect and dignity: possibilities so unfairly denied her because of both her sex and race.

Cathy, therefore, carefully orchestrated and developed a plan that was as innovative as it was bold: disguising herself as a man in an attempt to enlist in the army. Cathy Williams was determined that neither her sex nor race nor even her slave past would stand as an obstacle to deny her future success in life.

Despite the fact that it was illegal for a female to enlist in the U.S. Army, a higher moral calling beckoned this resilient ex-slave from the Missouri River country. She wanted to make the most of the opportunity that was offered to African American men. Cathy now saw a chance to not only exercise the right of an American citizen—though it was reserved only for males—but also to serve her country.

In a practical sense, Cathy's decision to attempt to enlist in the Buffalo Soldiers was hardly unreasonable under the circumstances. In fact, it made perfectly good sense for a variety of reasons. By this time, Cathy Williams was a seasoned veteran of years of hard military campaigning, having marched hundreds of miles with the regiment. She had become used to an exciting and adventurous life and by the summer of 1866 had been through more hardships and difficulties than most women in America.

The fact that she was not a man was not a sufficient reason to deter her from attempting to join the army in disguise. This was not an uncommon practice. In fact, hundreds of white women had recently served in Union and Confederate armies during the Civil War disguised as men.

This fact, however, was probably not known to Cathy Williams at the time, and therefore provided no source of inspiration. By all accounts and according to her own words, Cathy based her decision to join the Buffalo Soldiers upon an original idea. She was not following by example.

Not only white females, but many black women served in military roles during the Civil War. Besides having been an abolitionist and conductor on the Underground Railroad, ex-slave Harriet Ross Tubman, whose birth name was Araminta "Minty" Ross, was one such African American woman. The irrepressible Tubman served in a military role during the war years. She was inspired by this conviction: "I should fight for my liberty as long as my strength lasted."

Most of all, Cathy Williams, in her own words, decided to become a Buffalo Soldier because she "wanted to make my own living and not be dependent on relations or friends." After the Civil War, Cathy discovered that enjoying freedom was a challenge because life for ex-slaves was rough and making a living was difficult. Prejudice and discrimination flourished, and both Missouri and the St. Louis area were still very much Southern in attitude. White soldiers returned home to take jobs formerly held by free blacks or slaves. Economic times were hard for a former slave, especially a female. Cathy Williams needed a steady income to survive.

But the decision to enlist in the U.S. Army was much more than economic. Becoming a Buffalo Soldier would be a logical course of action by her, offering solutions to previously unsolvable problems. Hardened by life and war, Cathy Williams was an independent, open-minded, and free-thinking woman by this time. Like many veterans, she probably experienced some difficulty in resuming civilian life and the mundane realities as a lowly domestic. As throughout the past, she continued to think for herself and act on her own. In many ways, therefore, Cathy's decision to enlist was an easy one for her.

But choosing to serve in the disguise of a man in the American military would not be easy, embodying considerable risk that would never diminish. Cathy would have to pass herself off as a man to enlist in the first place, and then perhaps for years while in service. Successfully maintaining this imposture as a soldier would be the most difficult, complex, and demanding challenge of her life. Presenting herself as a man and imparting false information at the time of enlistment would be the first test for her to pass.

In regard to the morality of Cathy Williams's decision to present herself as a man to ensure enlistment, perhaps Ruth Flowers, a black woman born in Colorado, stated it best in regard to Cathy's attempt to escape a dependent existence and to create a better life for herself: "[T]o make a life you endure most anything, women do." Clearly, Cathy's decision to enlist in the U.S. Army involved simple survival in a world that discriminated against her for no more reason than her color and her lowly social status.

Cathy now laid careful plans and developed a well-conceived strategy. Her objective was to join the newly formed 38th United States Infantry, which began to organize at Jefferson Barracks in August 1866. In addition, she chose to attempt to enlist in this regiment because her cousin and a "particular friend" were members.

Cathy Williams already shared a common experience with these men of the Buffalo Soldier regiment. Many soldiers who served in the 38th Infantry were Civil War veterans. Cathy Williams elected to serve in an infantry regiment rather than a cavalry regiment for good reason. For one, she probably did not know how to ride a horse, as neither slave life nor her Civil War experiences would have afforded her such an opportunity. Quite possibly her cousin and "particular friend" enlisted in the 38th Infantry to accommodate her need to serve in an infantry rather than a cavalry unit. This made good sense. Service in an infantry regiment was essential not only in concealing her sex and true identity, but also ensured that the ruse could be continued long term.

During the Civil War, most women soldiers served in infantry regiments for many of these same reasons—avoiding service in both cavalry and artillery units, where a female could be more readily exposed. In this regard, therefore, Cathy made a wise decision to join the infantry.[11]

To successfully enlist in the U.S. Army, Cathy would have to first conceal her sex with a clever disguise that would arouse no suspicion not only at the time of enlistment but also for years to come. No doubt, in her life as a slave and while campaigning with the 8th Indiana, she probably wore men's clothes out of necessity. Cathy probably felt comfortable in both military and male clothing. In her case, this experience would work to her advantage. There were also the cultural norms of the time. Anyone who wore pants was assumed to be a male without question, according to the strict gender codes and traditional values of American society.[12]

In addition, this enterprising young woman would have to act, move, and speak much like a man to fool the veteran army recruiters at Jefferson Barracks. Years of close association and interaction with Union soldiers, both backward farm boys and educated officers; freed slaves; and many other types of people across the country gave her worldly experience and keen insights into human nature and psychology that she could now utilize to her benefit. Because female enlistment in the U.S. military was an illegal act, Cathy would have to be smart, enterprising, and resourceful.

Without exaggeration, one unnamed woman who successfully served in the Civil War disguised as a man for a lengthy period was bestowed a compliment for intelligence by a journalist who described her story: "She must have been very shrewd to have lived in the regiment so long and preserved her secret so well." Now Cathy Williams would have to do the same to make her ambition come true.[13]

By this time, Cathy must have reasoned that she was sufficiently smart to successfully conceal her sex not only from the recruiters but also from her fellow soldiers. This required a high degree of intelligence and cleverness to perpetuate the ruse and to fool countless numbers of people, both black and white.

It is not surprising that an ex-slave would have the resourcefulness to design a clever plan that involved a great deal of secrecy and cunning. As a slave in Missouri, and even when she was with the 8th Indiana, she would have found it necessary for her own well-being, and perhaps even personal survival, to hide her thoughts, feelings, and emotions while serving whites, both slave masters and military officers.

Certainly, Cathy's survival as a slave in Missouri probably depended occasionally upon a clever and judicious use of concealment, secrecy, and acting ability that had to be convincing. The capacity to disguise her innermost thoughts and feelings would have been especially useful as a means of survival for a young female slave. Such skills prevented not only punishment but also her own possible sale downriver to the cotton plantations of the Deep South.

Cathy's survival skills learned in coping with white men as a slave and in the Civil War would have been well honed by this time. These could be employed in dealing with white officers of the 38th Infantry, helping to maintain her disguise. Such skills would certainly be put to good use in her military service as a Buffalo Soldier. First, however, she would have to fool the recruiters.[14]

On November 15, 1866, Cathy Williams embarked upon her task to join the military and to undertake a new life. On her own, she walked into the recruiting office at Jefferson Barracks with the hope of enlisting for three years service.[15]

It was a promising beginning for her at the Jefferson Barracks recruiting office. Both Cathy's demeanor and appearance—which betrayed no sign of femininity—and sudden entry into the enlistment office aroused no suspicion among the officers at first glance. But the process of a successful enlistment would require much more skill, artful tact, and luck. Standing before the white recruiters, Cathy Williams informed the enlistment officials that she wanted to become a soldier in the 38th U.S. Infantry. It was a good start. Fortunately, Cathy was taller at five feet, nine inches than the average man of the day. No one noticed or even suspected that she was a female.

Consequently, the process of completing the lengthy paperwork for enlistment began without a hitch. Her disguise as a man caused no suspicion, while she began to answer questions posed by the recruiting officers. Eager to gain a new recruit especially without having to do the work of finding one themselves, the recruiters apparently felt like they were fortunate to have acquired the healthy-looking young man who now stood before them.

Cathy Williams would have to fool more than the recruiters at Jefferson Barracks, however. She continued the process of enlistment in the presence of Maj. Henry C. Merriam. He was formerly the commander of the 73rd U.S. Colored Troops during the Civil War, and won distinction during the attack on Fort Blakeley, Alabama, outside Mobile, on April 9, 1865. Major Merriam was now the third highest ranking officer of the 38th Infantry Regiment. Merriam, who would occasionally command the unit and serve as the major for the regiment until March 15, 1869, was not suspicious about the tall and physically fit African American youth standing before him. To Major Merriam, this new recruit—dark, slim, tall, and athletic—merely looked much like one of the many ex-slaves who came to Jefferson Barracks to enlist.

Cathy had chosen the name of William Cathay, and this she gave to the recruiters. Her decision to invert her first and last names was not only effective but also symbolically meaningful. Such a calculated decision reveals that she possessed a healthy measure of self-respect and pride in her name and in herself. It also confirms that she retained a positive self-image, despite the lingering psychological scars of slavery. The name "William Cathey" was now written (spelled incorrectly) on the enlistment form. Before the ink was dry, this young woman from the Missouri River country had officially become "Bill" Cathay.

Cathy Williams was most likely illiterate. Throughout the antebellum period, slave-owners feared the revolutionary potential of slaves who could read and write and think for themselves. Consequently, the repressive slave codes of the antebellum South, including Missouri, had forbidden the education of slaves. The vast majority of former slaves were illiterate in the years immediately following the Civil War.

In addition and as required, she also gave her age to the recruiting officer. She was listed as twenty-two years of age on the enlistment form. In addition, Cathy also stated that her occupation was that of cook. Her personal experience and years of faithful service in the Union Army now paid dividends, enhancing her chances for a successful enlistment.[16]

So far, her clever disguise was working to perfection. She probably now wore her hair short to make her look more like a William than a Cathy; in addition she evidently wore baggy and oversized clothes to conceal her feminine shape. Cathy also probably used a large slouch hat to conceal her face as much as possible.[17]

At this time, Cathy was tall, thin, and fit, which also assisted in concealing her sex. Like many other slave women toughened by a hard life, Cathy Williams was physically robust, muscular, and athletic. In this sense, her physical presence alone defied the socially accepted notion of the weaker sex. Her exceptional physical condition would play a key role in the success of her disguise as a man.[18]

Young Cathy Williams certainly looked the part of a thin but physically fit young black male, beardless and smooth-faced. And thanks to her service in the Union army, she now convincingly acted and talked like a soldier as well. She was smart, articulate, and quick-thinking. Perhaps she virtually talked her way into enlistment, speaking rapidly as if to keep any suspicions from the minds of her recruiters. In her enlistment papers, she was described simply as "black" in regard to three features and physical characteristics: eyes, complexion, and hair—as if there were no individual distinctions.

Fortunately for Cathy, the majority of whites generally possessed little experience of blacks on a personal level. In general, this fact tended to cause whites to take an overall uncritical appreciation or little keen notice of the varying, intricate physical characteristics of African Americans. The racist generalization that all blacks looked much alike might well have applied to these recruiters at Jefferson barracks.

At this time, many whites actually found it hard to distinguish a black man from a black woman. For example, in October 1858 during a speech in Indiana by an abolitionist African American woman named Isabella Van Wagener, a former New York slave who had renamed herself Sojourner Truth, the white audience who turned up to hear her lecture suspected that she was a male. They demanded immediate proof that Isabella was in fact a woman. Thin, tall, very dark, small-breasted, and with short hair, Sojourner had to publicly bare her breasts before a large audience to demonstrate that she was not a man posing as a woman.

Without suspecting that this young African American might be a woman, Major Merriam signed the enlistment papers as the principal witness to the enlistment of William Cathay. So far, so good. Everything was going according to Cathy's plan. Her disguise, clothing, demeanor, and acting ability had successfully concealed her sex from perhaps as many as a half dozen whites: veteran recruiters and officers of the 38th.[19]

Despite her success up to this point, considerable risk still remained for Cathy Williams. Even the slightest hint of femininity could disclose her deception. Only a few years before in St. Louis, a young woman named Lizzie Cook attempted to enlist in the Union army with her brother. Her disguise as a man was successful, but her refined manners at the dinner table betrayed her as a woman to the men around her.[20]

In fact, the signing of the papers was only the beginning of the lengthy enlistment process at Jefferson Barracks. The most serious obstacle for a successful enlistment still lay ahead. Before she officially became a U.S. soldier, "William Cathay" would have to pass a medical exam by an army surgeon. Despite her disguise, Cathy Williams was no doubt apprehensive about what was the greatest threat to her successful enlistment, the physical examination.

Fortunately, however, the army surgeon gave anything but a thorough exam to this new recruit. It seemed as if the army was only concerned if she could march for miles and fire a musket. Cathy was athletic, slim, young, and healthy. Consequently, she looked to be excellent material for the new regiment. As in the Civil War years when hundreds of women served in both blue and gray, the brief, cursory examination all but ensured Cathy Williams's successful enlistment.[21]

Probably with much relief but without expressing any sign of elation that might betray her, Cathy Williams was no doubt surprised that the army surgeon gave her no thorough physical exam. Consequently, she easily passed, overcoming her greatest potential obstacle. Army physician C. M. Powers, now the acting appointed surgeon of the 38th Infantry, had failed to discover that Private Cathay was a female.

With the name of "William Cathay" now signed on the enlistment papers, Cathy Williams's bid to become a soldier was a success at last. Cathy had long possessed the dream of a better life filled with self-respect, pride, and a measure of equality, and now that dream was turning into reality by her own initiative and intelligence.

The newly signed enlistment papers stated: "I CERTIFY, ON HONOR, That I have carefully examined the above named recruit, agreeably to the General Regulations of the Army, and that in my opinion he is free from all bodily defects and mental infirmity, which would, in any way, disqualify him from performing the duties of a soldier." Now the ex-slave and Civil War veteran known as Pvt. William Cathay was an official member of the U.S. Army. This resourceful young woman had already accomplished what few women dared to contemplate much less to achieve on their own. The former house servant of a Missouri master, and laundress, cook, nurse, and attendant of the 8th Indiana was now a Buffalo Soldier![22]

Cathy's new name was now permanently inscribed on the official enlistment papers of the 38th U.S. Infantry, which stated:

> I, William Cathay born in Independence in the State of Missouri, aged twenty-two years, and by occupation a cook do hereby acknowledge to have voluntarily enlisted this fifteenth day of November 1866 as a Soldier in the Army of the United States of America, for the period of THREE YEARS, unless sooner discharged by proper authority: Do also agree to accept such bounty, pay, rations, and clothing, as are, or may be, established by law. And I, William Cathay, do solemnly swear, that I will bear true faith and allegiance to the United States of America, and that I will serve them honestly and faithfully against all their enemies or opposers whomsoever; and that I will observe and obey the orders of the President of the United States, and the orders of the officers appointed over me, according to the Rules and Articles of War.

Then, in the DECLARATION OF RECRUIT, the name of William Cathey appeared in the following statement:

> I, William Cathey desiring to ENLIST in the Army of the United States, for the term of THREE YEARS Do declare, That I am twenty-two years and two months of age; that I have neither wife nor child; that I have never been discharged from the United States ser-

vice on account of disability or by sentence of a court-martial, or by order before the expiration of the term of enlistment; and I know of no impediment to my serving honestly and faithfully as a soldier for three years.

The two different spellings of her name in the enlistment documents are simple to explain given the general levels of literacy at the time. Her new name that included an "e" in Cathy to form the name Cathey in her papers was written down by her enrolling officer who spelled the name "Cathay" the best way he could. However, her discharge papers included the correct spelling of Cathay with an "a" instead of an "e." Despite the exact spelling in the enlistment forms, she was now Pvt. William Cathay. Further confusion resulted later when a St. Louis journalist wrote down her first name in the mid-1870s article as "Cathy" Williams and that she was discharged as William *Cathy*.

Other than that joyous, unforgettable day of liberation in the late summer of 1861, certainly the proudest moment in Cathy Williams's life came on November 15, 1866. On this day she put on the uniform of the nation that she was now sworn to serve with her life.

What Cathy Williams now wore with pride was the standard issue blue infantry uniform of the Civil War. This uniform consisted of a dark blue blouse and lighter blue trousers. It may have looked smart, but it was more suitable for the parade ground than active campaigning in the field. Ill-suited for the harsh weather conditions on the Western frontier, the thick wool uniforms felt like ovens in the heat of summer but barely kept out the harsh winds and snows of winter. Cathy Williams also strapped on the issue Model 1866 cartridge box, which was unpopular with the men in the ranks. Her other accoutrements included the brass oval "US" belt buckle and brass "eagle" plate on the shoulder belt.

In addition, the buttons on her uniform were the brass "eagle" type stamped with a small shield located in the button's center beneath the outstretched wings of the American eagle.

Pvt. William Cathay was also issued a rifled musket. The Model 1866 was a modified Springfield rifle-musket from the Springfield arsenal in Massachusetts. Lightweight and splendidly balanced, these fine weapons were modified after the Civil War to fire a metallic cartridge. This meant that the Springfield could be loaded at the breech instead of at the muzzle. In 1867, General Grant described this modified breechloading weapon, also known as the "Allin Conversion" rifled musket, as "simple, strong, accurate, and not apt to get out of order."

With her successful enlistment on November 15, 1866, Cathy Williams certainly underwent a profound psychological and spiritual transformation by becoming Pvt. William Cathay. In one stroke, she had succeeded in winning a greater measure of equality for herself than at any other time in her life.

At least one other woman was known to have eventually followed in Cathy Williams's footsteps before the end of the nineteenth century. A white woman and Civil War veteran named Sarah Emma Edmonds served in the Regular army in the late nineteenth century. Previously, Edmonds has been mistakenly recognized as the first woman to serve in the Regulars.

But in truth, Cathy Williams has the honor of being the first woman and the first black female to serve as a Regular in the U.S. Army. By becoming the private soldier William Cathay, she was breaking new and uncharted ground. On her own and defying convention, Cathy shattered stereotypes of both sex and race while embracing a sense of both adventure and patriotism. Cathy Williams as William Cathay had boldly embarked upon a path that would lead the way for future generations of American women, both black and white, in the U.S. military. To date, Cathy Williams remains the only documented black female to have served in the U.S. Army, before the integration of blacks and women into the armed forces after World War II.

Beyond purely psychological factors, economic considerations played a role for Cathy's enlistment in the Buffalo Soldiers. For an ex-slave and especially a black female, U.S. Army service was an extremely good deal, ensuring financial security and stability. Unlike the world outside the military, this was a stable way of life that she could only envy as a lowly cook and laundress with the 8th Indiana. While a large percentage of white soldiers at this time viewed the Regular army as merely "a refuge . . . to the black man it offered a career," and ample opportunity to advance in life. And to Cathy Williams, such military service offered what she craved, an adventurous and rewarding life that would have been impossible for her to obtain as a woman in civilian life.

Despite its risks, for former slaves military service on the Western frontier guaranteed shelter, regular meals, clothing, a steady income, medical care, and even an opportunity for education. This was far more than Cathy had ever received during her years as a slave or would probably have gained while struggling to survive as a freewoman, especially in either Missouri or the South. The regular pay of $13.00 per month for military service was much better than this young former slave woman could have earned in the St. Louis area, in a country dominated by prejudice, sexism, and racism.[23]

As in her time with the 8th Indiana, her new regiment, the 38th Infantry, would serve as a secure home for Cathy Williams. This Buffalo Soldier regiment now provided a relatively safe haven and support system for Cathy and also served as a friendly transplanted African American community. Much like the role of the slave community during the antebellum period, a regiment of African Americans would provide a spiritual, psychological, and emotional refuge in a white dominated world. This was still vitally important, because many harsh realities still remained for African Americans, especially women, as the promise of equality was shown to be a hollow dream after 1865.

But the 38th U.S. Infantry was much more than simply a safe haven from a meager, day-to-day existence. Cathy Williams realized that if she were only given the opportunity she could soar and accomplish what no one, black or white, believed that she could possibly achieve on her own. Thanks to the tragedy of her slave past, she may have understood that nothing in life would be handed to her or could be won without sacrifice. Such realizations would have provided sufficient motivation for her to become a Buffalo Soldier and risk conditions on the frontier.

Much like Cathy herself, the 38th U.S. Infantry was no ordinary regiment of volunteers. This fine unit was created only because the U.S. Congress had out of necessity opened the door to the formation of African American regiments in the postwar U.S. Army. At this time, these U.S. Regular units carried the highest level of status and prestige in the U.S. military. In reality, however, what those doors opened was perhaps the most demanding and harsh frontier service experienced by any U.S. troops after the Civil War.[24]

Interestingly, another African American by the name of Williams had served in a Regular unit, the 38th U.S. Infantry, which was the lineage unit of Cathy's regiment during the War of 1812. U.S. Regular units had opened their ranks to black recruits, once again as the result of the lack of white recruits in an unpopular war, this time against the British. One of the black men who stepped forward was Pvt. William Williams, age twenty-two and an ex-slave from Maryland who, like Cathy, changed his name to enlist. As a member of the 38th U.S. Infantry, Private Williams was mortally wounded during the British attack on Fort McHenry in 1814.[25]

CHAPTER FIVE

A Distinguished Legacy Perpetuated

CATHY WILLIAMS'S SERVICE IN THE MILITARY WAS NOT WITHOUT PRECEDENT. In fact, Cathy's role in the 38th Infantry was only the perpetuation of a distinguished tradition of women's service in the American military. Women have possessed a lengthy military tradition throughout history, not only in the United States but also throughout the world. Like Cathy Williams, many of these women concealed their sex and disguised themselves as men by donning uniforms to serve faithfully beside their male comrades.

For example, a Missouri woman also by the name of Williams had "donned the breeches" during the Civil War. A nineteen-year-old woman, whose identity remains unknown, enlisted under the name of John Williams in the 17th Missouri Volunteer Infantry in October 1862, when Cathy was with the 8th Indiana. Unlike Private Cathay, the true sex of Private Williams was soon discovered. She was then officially discharged from service because she "Proved to be a Woman."[1]

The historical record has been compiled almost exclusively by male historians. Therefore the military roles of these early women of courage have been largely obscured and forgotten. This unfortunate situation has been particularly pronounced in American culture. In the words of author Antonia Fraser: "Almost every culture throughout history has had its Warrior Queen or Queens either in fact or in fiction, or in some combination of them both. The U.S. is so far one of the significant exceptions."[2]

Negative stereotypes fostered by prejudicial societies that have historically promoted solely male-dominated militaries, not unlike racism directed toward

80

African Americans, have long attached negative stereotypes to women warriors, categorizing them as either "sexually suspect, or neurotic."

Nothing, however, could have been farther from the truth. The historical record, including the remarkable story of Cathy Williams, proved that the opposite held true. Like their male counterparts, women warriors have long demonstrated the valued characteristics of honor, courage, and loyalty in serving their country, nation, clan, or tribe throughout the military annals of both America and the world.

The role of black warriors, much like the role of women warriors in world history, embodied a lengthy martial tradition. But this integral role has been largely ignored by historians, even in the most highly studied aspects of European military history. For instance, blacks served with distinction in Napoléon's Grande Armée. Napoléon took pride in his mulatto general, Thomas-Alexandre Dumas. The general was known for his compassion, saving citizens in the Reign of Terror during the French Revolution by dismantling the local guillotine in one town for firewood. The mulatto general's son was Alexandre Dumas, the celebrated author of *The Three Musketeers*.

Napoléon's overseas armies in the West Indies included a large number of black troops. Inspired by the spirit of equality spawned by the French Revolution and slavery's abolition in the French islands of the Caribbean, black and mulatto officers commanded black units of revolutionary French troops across the West Indies.

Among Napoléon's Grande Armée in Europe, three battalions of pioneers consisted entirely of black soldiers. Two of these battalions, known as the *"pionniers noirs"* and the *"pionniers blancs,"* were composed mostly of Haitians captured by the French who had attempted in vain to crush the slave revolt on the island of Haiti, leading to the first black republic in world history. These blacks of the Grande Armée served under a mulatto commander named Col. Joseph Domingue, or Hercule, who won distinction as an officer in the Imperial Guard and during Napoléon's bloody campaigns in Italy and Egypt.

One of Napoléon's black battalions was later transformed into a Neapolitan infantry regiment. Later it became known as the "Royal Africa" and was stationed for a while in Germany.

The tradition of black pioneers was widespread in European military history. For instance, the British formed a Black Pioneer Company in New York in the spring of 1776 during the American Revolution.

The first major military role of African Americans was during the American Revolution. Even before the firing of the "shots heard round the world" at the small town of Lexington, outside Boston, Massachusetts, Crispus Attucks, an ex-slave and black seaman of Boston, was the first colonial to fall mortally wounded during the infamous "Boston Massacre" in March 1770.

Symbolically, these black colonials who fought against the British chose last names that indicated their unquenchable thirst for freedom, such as Pomp Liberty and Dick Freedom. Many New England blacks came forward to fight at the opening clash of arms at Lexington. In fact, during the initial show-down at Lexington when the minutemen from Massachusetts stood firm against the British Regulars, an African American named Prince Estabrook fought beside the New Englanders of Capt. John Parker's militia company.

Throughout the eight years of the American Revolution and despite the initial opposition of both Gen. George Washington and the Continental Congress, hundreds of African Americans served in integrated units during the colonies' struggle for independence. With surprise, one of General Wash-ington's officers wrote in a letter that there "are in the Massachusetts Regi-ments some Negroes [and] such is also the case with the Regiments from the other colonies [such as] Rhode Island [which] has a number of Negroes." The numbers are significant. More than 800 African Americans, an estimated 7 to 8 percent of Gen. Washington's forces, fought at the battle of Monmouth, New Jersey, in late June 1778.

In some cases, colonial military companies consisting entirely of African Americans were organized for service against the British invader. Like the white colonists, African Americans in rebellion struggled against the Redcoats at great risk to protect their homes and families, while fighting to gain a greater measure of equality in the land of their birth. Meanwhile, hundreds of other blacks, ironically, found liberty by fighting for the British Army against the Americans. These African Americans struggled for both the Crown and their freedom in the red uniforms of the Ethiopian Regiment and other British units.[3]

Despite the shortage of white volunteers and British successes throughout the dismal year of 1776, colonial resistance to black participation in the strug-gle for liberty lingered—a situation destined to be repeated both during and immediately after the Civil War. Of course, this resistance was especially strong among Southerners, including initially General Washington and slave owners who viewed armed African Americans as a serious potential threat, which would cause their slaves to rise up in revolt.

During the darkest days of the American Revolution, however, and not unlike the period of greatest national crisis during the Civil War, enthusiasm for the war among whites declined. The lack of widespread desire by whites to fight for their own freedom, ironically, opened the door for a greater black role in the war. At an early date, hard-pressed recruiters for colonial armies sought to fill their ranks with black soldiers.

The majority of African Americans served in the crack Continental regiments of Gen. Washington's army. Zealous members of the free black society of New England responded with overflowing patriotism, enlisting in large numbers by 1777. By 1779, consequently, a full 15 percent of Gen. Washington's Continental Army consisted of black patriots, who continued to fight while the majority of white colonials remained either neutral or pro-British.

In total, perhaps as many as 10,000 African Americans served in colonial armies during the American Revolution. A French officer, who was more open in expressing the truth than his American hosts in regard to blacks fighting for white freedom, was impressed by the sight of so many fine-looking black soldiers in the colonial armies. In 1781, this officer wrote that he encountered a disciplined Rhode Island regiment in which "the majority of the enlisted men are Negroes or mulattos; but they are strong, robust men, and those I saw made a good appearance." So widespread was African American enlistment and service in Washington's army that an incredulous Gen. Philip Schuyler of New York asked in some disbelief: "Is it consistent with the Sons of Freedom to trust their all to be defended by slaves?"

White colonial women, including Mary Ludwig Hays McCauley, who fought at Monmouth; Nancy Hart; Jemima Warner, who was killed in battle; and Margaret Cochran Corbin, known also as "Captain Molly," won lasting fame in American history by fighting beside their husbands as "Molly Pitchers." The distinguished role of both black men and women in the American Revolution, however, was quickly forgotten by an ungrateful nation. In fact, some of the more unfortunate African Americans were actually returned to slavery.[4]

The tradition of fighting women was so strong that enemies of George Washington claimed that he was "even a woman in disguise." The fact, therefore, that some women disguised themselves as soldiers must have been a reality to the revolutionary generation or such a rumor would not have surfaced.[5]

A martial and revolutionary tradition also existed for generations in the African American community, though not in the U.S. military. Widespread black defiance and resistance to white authority were evident by the long record of slave revolts across the South. To quote historian Herbert Aptheker who placed the extent of slave insurrections throughout American history in their historical perspective: "[T]he uprisings and plots came in waves, as though anger accumulated and vented itself [and these] waves were the rule, with clearly defined periods, as: 1710–1722, 1730–1740, 1790–1802, 1819–1823, 1829–1832, 1850–1860."

The distinguished names of the greatest African American revolutionaries of the antebellum period include Jemmy of South Carolina; Denmark Vesey of Charleston, South Carolina; Gabriel Prosser of Richmond, Virginia; and

Nat Turner of Southampton County, Virginia. These committed black revolutionaries were motivated by a grim resolve: "If I die, I die free." These desperate bids for freedom were righteous crusades and holy wars of liberation for African Americans in slavery.[6]

By far, the largest participation of African Americans in the American military came during the Civil War. More than 200,000 African Americans, or 12 percent of the Federal forces, served in the Union armies and navy. As during the American Revolution, the overall war effort had first to falter before the nation allowed widespread black participation in the conflict. This tapped a vital manpower resource, which became all-important for the North at a crucial time during a lengthy war of attrition, playing a part in the Union's ultimate victory.

Even the Confederacy organized black units in the capital of Richmond, Virginia, during the last year of the war when defeat was all but inevitable. Before 1865, however, thousands of Southern blacks served in Confederate armies across the South, and even took fighting roles on the battlefield.

The black contribution to the Northern war effort, however, was far more extensive. Sixteen black soldiers, including Union seamen who fought on the rivers of the South and the high seas, won the Medal of Honor for heroism under fire during the last half of the Civil War.

The tradition of African American soldiers winning Medals of Honor during the Civil War continued into the later years of the nineteenth century with the heroics of the Buffalo Soldiers during the Spanish-American War. The hard-fighting Buffalo Soldiers garnered a total of twenty-three Medals of Honor during service in both the Indian and Spanish-American Wars.[7]

But by far, the most forgotten players in American history have been those African American women who participated in America's struggles from the American Revolution to the Civil War and beyond. The long-overlooked role of black women often included the participation in military action not on behalf of but against the U.S. military.

Some military efforts of African American females came in opposition to the expansion of the United States. Early in the nation's history, black women, along with men, allied themselves with Native Americans, who also possessed a lengthy tradition of women warriors, to fight against the invading swarms of white European soldiers and settlers.

In the words of historian William Loren Katz: "[T]housands, welcomed by or born among Native American nations, tried to help stave off the march of white 'manifest destiny.'"

Perhaps one of the best examples of the effectiveness of these female warriors came in the Seminole War during the 1830s and 1840s. Future president and Mexican War hero, Gen. Zachary Taylor, a Virginia planter and slave owner who possessed around $50,000 worth of slaves, was stunned to discover that the Seminole women "fought so long that they were more defiant than the men."

But the military tradition of women Indian warriors far predated the Seminole Wars. As early as the American Revolution, for example, colonial soldiers discovered women warriors among the Cherokee. But the Creek of Georgia and Alabama possessed a strong women warrior class, and this martial tradition was continued by the Seminole people, who were derived from the Creek. To his shock, even Davy Crockett, while serving as a scout under Gen. Andrew Jackson, learned as much during the Creek War, when he encountered a hard-fighting female warrior. For generations, ex-slaves intermingled with the Creek people of Georgia and Alabama, uniting against white imperialism and encroachment in the wilds of Florida.

By the time Cathy Williams served as a Buffalo Soldier on the Great Plains, Cheyenne braves, who first bestowed the name Buffalo Soldiers upon the black troops, often rode into battle with women warriors by their side. These female warriors, such as a Cheyenne woman named Ehyophsta, were dressed, armed, and fought like men. The Crow tribe of the Missouri River country could claim the prowess of the "Woman Chief," who likewise fought beside male warriors in raids on the Great Plains. In addition, the Blackfoot tribe of the Upper Missouri possessed respected female fighters, including such warriors as "Manly Hearted Woman," "Hate Woman," "Brave Woman," and "Brown Weasel."

Continuing the legacy of the American Revolution, the active participation of black women in conflict continued in the Civil War. In the early days of the war, for instance, African Americans in Boston—where the famous 54th Massachusetts Infantry, which won fame for its assault on Fort Wagner, was raised—passed a resolution for active black participation in the struggle. This resolution made a special allowance for New England black women to serve as seamstresses, laundresses, and nurses, and "warriors, if need be."

Like Cathy Williams during these years, thousands of African American women supported the Union army in a wide variety of noncombat roles. They served as nurses, spies, couriers, seamstresses, cooks, laundresses, and laborers. These African American female soldiers included former "contraband" Susie King Taylor of the 1st South Carolina Colored Volunteers, while from the eastern shore of Maryland came Harriet Ross Tubman: known as "Black Moses" for her effort in leading slaves to safety along the Underground Railroad. Tubman also worked for the Union as a spy and scout, and more significantly led "black troops on several forays into Confederate territory" in South Carolina in 1863.[8]

As the rich cultural traditions of West Africa played a role in influencing the vibrancy of the slave community in America, so the tradition of women warriors in African societies helped to lay a foundation for the participation of black women in the U.S. military. In ancient times, "the existence of warlike women's nations" were known in West Africa. Legendary black female leaders, known as *kentakes,* defended the nation of Ethiopia against the Macedonians, led by the world's greatest conqueror, Alexander the Great, and later fought against the disciplined Roman legions.[9]

Throughout Africa, the women warrior tradition flourished. African tribes such as the Beja, possessed "a corps" of female lancers. And a battalion of spear-carrying women fought neighboring tribes. Other African tribes possessed military units consisting of female archers, and later, of women riflemen. The West African tribes such as the Yoruba, the Kpelle, and the Hausa also possessed a strong tradition of female warriors.[10]

The martial legacy of black women warriors continued in Africa for centuries. For instance, in the nineteenth century, Shaka Zulu, chief of the Zulu tribes of South Africa, created a women's army of Bantu females, while in North Africa, Muslim women, including slaves and females of the desert bedouin, took part in a jihad, or holy war, against the French forces led by Napoléon, who attempted to conquer Egypt and the Middle East in 1799. Ironically, in Napoléon's invading army, "the Army of the Orient," French women served in the ranks disguised as men. In the 1850s, the army of the African kingdom of Dahomey consisted of 12,000 warriors of which nearly half were women.[11]

One of the best historical examples of the widespread participation of black women in battle came during the Haitian Revolution of the 1790s. Striking back in righteous indignation at their French masters, thousands of oppressed slaves rose up on the Caribbean sugar island to fight and win their freedom, establishing the world's first free black republic. In the tradition of female martial roles throughout African history, Haitian women played a part in what was the most successful slave revolt in history.

During the people's wars of liberation that freed Latin and South America from Spanish rule in the 1820s, black women fought for their own and their country's freedom. On the Atlantic coastal region of Colombia, for example, black slave women, known as *Las Cimarronas,* battled to liberate their country, and another black rebel, Mariana Grajales of Cuba, fought for Cuban independence against the Spanish. She became a national heroine who is still revered today by the Cuban people.

In addition, both women and blacks fought at sea as pirates. Female pirates included such women as Grace O'Malley, Maria Lindsey, and Granny

Wale, who sailed in the Caribbean and elsewhere. Here, on the high seas, an equality for blacks existed, which was nonexistent at home. Blacks were welcomed into this strangely egalitarian—but criminal—society.

In addition, New England women served with American privateers during the War of 1812. Lucy Brewer served aboard the famous USS *Constitution,* or "Old Ironsides," while on the other side, one black woman, under the name William Brown, fought aboard the British warship, *Queen Charlotte.*[12]

Rather than providing an isolated example of African American participation in the military, the story of the Buffalo Soldiers merely perpetuated a rich historical military legacy of black service throughout American history. After the Buffalo Soldiers, the Tuskegee Airmen of World War II fame continued the tradition of the distinguished service of African Americans in struggling against two foes: the enemy on the battlefield and racist American society at home.

The best example of this historical lineage was in the case of Gen. Benjamin O. Davis, Sr., a Buffalo Soldier and the first African American general in the history of the U.S. Army, and his son, the first commander of the Tuskegee Airmen, Gen. Benjamin O. Davis, Jr. Ironically, the roots of the Davis family military tradition was with the grandfather of Gen. Benjamin O. Davis, Jr., Louis Patrick Henry Davis, who was a servant of Civil War general, John A. "Black Jack" Logan of Illinois.[13]

In a coincidental twist, the place where Cathy enlisted for service as a Buffalo Soldier, Jefferson Barracks, was destined to become the location of one of the first black Officer Candidate Schools for Tuskegee Airmen during the Second World War.[14]

As demonstrated throughout the annals of American history, the distinguished service of African American troops in the post–Civil War army was certainly no "experiment." In this sense, there was in truth nothing for African Americans to prove or demonstrate in terms of their fighting qualities because they had already proven themselves throughout America's military history.

But if any example influenced Cathy Williams, it might have been the service of the many women who served disguised as men during the Civil War years. Almost certainly she never encountered one, even though some served in General Grant's army, but she might have heard camp talk about them. In fact, one woman of the 66th Indiana Volunteer Infantry—a sister regiment of Cathy's 8th Indiana—was discovered disguised as a man.[15]

And during the Red River campaign of 1864 in which Cathy participated, Sarah Rosetta Wakeman served with the 153rd New York Volunteer Infantry in the guise of a man. Unlike the more robust Cathy Williams, Private Wakeman died of disease while serving her country.[16]

Quite possibly, Cathy Williams might have learned the story of a Confederate general's wife, Mary Lucretia Kennerly-Bowen, who was a resident of Carondelet. When her husband Gen. John Stevens Bowen died and her brother was killed in battle, she joined the 1st Missouri Confederate Brigade after Atlanta's fall to serve beside her surviving two brothers because she "had no home but the regiment." As a soldier in the ranks, she was wounded at the battle of Allatoona, Georgia, in early October 1864. After the war, Mrs. Bowen returned to her home in Carondelet.[17]

Cathy Williams and Mrs. Bowen both lived in Carondelet in the last half of 1866, until November, when Cathy joined the Buffalo Soldiers. Had Cathy Williams heard of Mary's exploits in the Civil War? Had they met at some point in Carondelet, or might Cathy have cooked, washed clothes, or did domestic work for Mrs. Bowen? Probably not, but still a slim possibility exists.

The exact number of women who served as soldiers during the Civil War is unknown but it was likely in the hundreds. Usually, after enlistment, the only way that a female soldier was detected was if she was wounded or killed on the battlefield or was hospitalized.

What was the motivation of these women who went to war disguised as men? Certainly, a sense of duty and adventure, patriotism, and a taste of equality were primary motivating factors. Another factor was that some of these women followed in the footsteps of either lovers or husbands for the chance to serve with them. It is not known but perhaps even Cathy Williams was in this category. She stated that her cousin and "particular friend . . . were partly the cause of my joining the army."[18]

This largely unrecognized role of women, both black and white, in the Civil War may have created an important precedent for Cathy Williams's enlistment on November 15, 1866. After all she became a Buffalo Soldier, in her own words, because "I wanted to make my own living and not be dependent on relatives or friends."[19]

Clearly, Cathy Williams desired a measure of equality, pride, and respect that she had not yet experienced in her life. And this could only be obtained by army service on the Western frontier.[20]

CHAPTER SIX

The Buffalo Soldiers

ONE FUNDAMENTAL REASON WHY THE STORY OF CATHY WILLIAMS IS IMPORtant and meaningful today is because it illuminates not only an African American's and a woman's struggle against the odds, but it also reveals new insights into the lives of the forgotten Buffalo Soldiers, the black infantrymen of the frontier West.

Despite compiling an impressive record, the African Americans of the Buffalo Soldier infantry units have remained largely absent from the pages of history books. Although the legendary African American cavalrymen have been the subject of many books, novels, histories, and even movies, the African American "grunt" has been ignored, fading away in obscurity in the historical record.

Compared with the dashing black cavalrymen who have endured in romance and legend, "no such plaudits have been accorded the infantry, though they followed hard on the heels of the cavalry . . . their story has received little attention and our history is poorer for it."[1]

What were the forgotten contributions of the Buffalo Soldiers, especially the infantry? During the post–Civil War period, the Buffalo Soldiers were the roughest riders as cavalry and hardest marchers as infantry on the Great Plains. From beginning to end, these African Americans fought harder, longer, and against greater adversity than white troops. In this sense, "the experiment begun in 1866 with Negro Regulars proved a success."[2]

The early foundation for the historical legacy of the Buffalo Soldiers was first laid by Africans Americans who fought in the bloody battles of the Civil War. In the late spring of 1866 and barely a year after the victorious Army of the Potomac marched in triumph through Washington, D.C., during the two-day Grand Review in late May 1865, the Buffalo Soldiers were organized for service on the Western frontier. In the process, "the most historically significant change in the composition of the Regular army" after the Civil War resulted in the enlistment of African American soldiers.[3]

Despite thousands of black troops having served in the Army of the Potomac, however, the African American soldiers were not part of that famous victory parade and celebration in Washington, D.C. Despite the distinguished service—and sacrifice—of blacks in the war, discrimination had raised its ugly head before the guns of North and South had hardly ceased firing.

This symbolic negligence signified the lack of appreciation by the victorious nation for the important role of black troops during the Civil War. Such a lack of official recognition played a role in placing the postwar recruitment of the Buffalo Soldiers, many whom were Union army veterans, in an "experimental" phase by many authorities and politicians.

The Civil War's end unleashed hundreds of thousands of veterans, both black and white, into a new world. This postwar society was becoming more mechanized and modernized as an agrarian nation began to grow without the roadblocks of sectional friction and division. But in this changing world, black veterans were in the worst position, left without either a fight or a job. While thousands of white veterans returned to their homes, the ex-slaves, including Cathy Williams, often had no homes to return to, after slavery's death and four years of brutal warfare.

Faced with these harsh realities, many African American veterans joined the U.S. service, after Pres. Andrew Johnson overcame initial resistance in both Houses. He signed the bill authorizing the formation of more than sixty regiments for Regular service on July 28, 1866. To bolster the 16,000-man Regular army, the bill called for the formation of six regiments of African American troops to meet the urgent requirements of the frontier defense and westward expansion. This was the first time in American military history that African Americans were permitted to enlist in the Regular army in separate units: an opportunity that Cathy Williams exploited at the first opportunity.

Two of these newly authorized black units were cavalry regiments and the other four were infantry regiments. From the beginning, the number of Buffalo Soldiers in the infantry exceeded the number in the cavalry.

One of these newly formed African American regiments was the 38th Infantry, which was now the home of Pvt. William Cathay. Compiling an impressive record of endurance and performance, the troops of the 38th Infantry were destined to garrison numerous forts and camps across a wide stretch of the Western frontier. In addition, they would perform duty in guarding hundreds miles of major roads and trails that snaked through Indian country, the sprawling prairies of the Great Plains, and the deserts of the Southwest.

In the dramatic story of the winning of the West, the Buffalo Soldiers' mission was among the most difficult and challenging of any service in the American military at this time. These soldiers served in the most remote and desolate parts of the Western frontier, patrolling and guarding large sections of a seemingly limitless land, while battling the fiercest warriors on the Great Plains.

The Buffalo Soldiers, nevertheless, would accomplish a great deal against the odds and certainly more than anyone, especially whites, expected. Engaged on two hostile fronts, they fought against both a superior Native American adversary, and discriminatory white military personnel, including officers, and American society in general. Nevertheless, the Buffalo Soldiers persevered to serve with honor in an undermanned postwar Regular army, while undertaking the formidable task of holding down the Western frontier.

How undersized was the postwar army in the West? A large percentage of the Regular army's strength was serving on occupation duty in the South during the Reconstruction period. Other Regulars served in Texas along the Rio Grande River as a deterrent to the French in Mexico. Only a relatively few undermanned regiments of the Regular army were stationed in the West after hundreds of Civil War volunteer regiments were demobilized.

All in all, what the Buffalo Soldiers would achieve on the Western frontier exceeded the accomplishments of white troops who faced only a single opponent in a struggle on only one front. In Gen. Colin Powell's words: "The Buffalo Soldiers [are] an everlasting symbol of man's ability to overcome, an everlasting symbol of human courage in the face of all obstacles and dangers."

Historian William Leckie has also placed the distinguished role of the Buffalo Soldiers in a proper historical perspective: "[T]he thriving cities and towns, the fertile fields, and the natural beauty [of the West] are monuments enough for any buffalo soldier." The accomplishments of these black soldiers would have to serve as enduring monuments because, tragically, "prejudice robbed them of recognition and often of simple justice."

At best, life for the average Buffalo Soldier on the remote Western outposts and isolated forts was not only primitive but also harsh. Far from homes and families, these young black soldiers lived a Spartan, dangerous existence.

During Pvt. William Cathay's term of service, the 38th Infantry embarked on a lengthy tour of duty that would take them across the breadth of the Great Plains. Cathy Williams and her male comrades were destined to serve across a wide expanse of the Western frontier, including the sun-baked prairies of Kansas, the mountains of Colorado, the parched mesas of New Mexico, and the unforgiving deserts of the Southwest.

As during the Civil War, the African American troops were commanded by white officers, many of whom were veterans, possessing years of hard-won experience. Like any group of individuals of any race, these Caucasian officers consisted of various types of men. Some were enlightened toward blacks, while others were prejudiced. However, in general, the officer corps of the Regular army during the postwar period was generally considered to have been inferior overall compared with the Civil War officers who had volunteered out of patriotism and duty rather than for economic gain.

When Cathy Williams passed the test for enlistment in mid-November 1866, the 38th Infantry was stationed at Jefferson Barracks. At this time, Jefferson was the largest military installation west of the Mississippi. Here, on the banks of the river and immediately south of St. Louis, the new regiment had existed for only a few months before the time of Cathy's enlistment.[4]

Having joined the regiment, the question now was how would she continue to disguise her sex when in the close proximity of so many men, especially in the beginning of her service. First, an emphasis on learning drill and marching was the main feature of training, and this Cathy accomplished as well as any man.[5]

Sturdy and toughened from both life as a slave and her years marching with Union armies, Private Cathay found no difficulty in carrying either her Springfield on her shoulder or a heavy pack on her back, consisting of about forty to fifty pounds of equipment. In her own words, she was "a good soldier," excelling at any challenge of military life.[6]

To ensure that she gave no hint of her sex, Cathy probably kept her uniform blouse buttoned to the top. She also no doubt kept her hair cut short. In addition, Private Cathay probably adopted masculine habits of drinking, talking about sex with women, smoking, chewing tobacco, cursing, etc., as other women who fought as men during the Civil War had successfully employed to enhance their disguise.

Clever ruses were necessary because some disguised females during the Civil War were discovered by their comrades at the faintest evidence of feminine characteristics or mannerisms. The least clues included the manner in which shoes and socks were put on, or even an "unmistakable twist to the dishcloth in wringing it out that no masculine [sic] could ever successfully counterfeit."

The only advantage that young Private Cathay possessed at this time was the element of surprise, because no Buffalo Soldier of the 38th expected a young woman—who did not look that much different from other young ex-slaves in an ill-fitting and baggy uniform—to be among them. Their unwariness, however, would not have been enough. Her ruse was complicated by such feminine hygiene concerns as her monthly menstrual cycle. Private Cathay would have to be as careful as a spy and flawlessly perform her male role on a 24 hour-a-day basis in order to fool her new comrades.[7]

One of the enduring myths about women who disguised themselves as men to serve their country in the Civil War was that they were perceived by men to be what they called "Amazons."[8] But Cathy Williams would have to ignore any natural urges and forgo sex because her military career would end abruptly if she became pregnant—which is how some women soldiers were discovered during the Civil War.

To make her dream of an independent and self-sufficient life come true, Cathy willingly made the sacrifice of love and family to obtain her goal of serving as a soldier. At this point, she would let nothing get in her way or allow anyone to destroy that cherished dream that she so passionately embraced. In the words of one woman of the Civil War who was caught during the initial physical examination and was not deterred from attempting to enlist elsewhere: "[She was] bound to be a soldier or die."[9]

In these first weeks of enlistment, Private Cathay's stay at Jefferson Barracks would either make her or break her. If she aroused no suspicions among the African Americans—who would be more aware than the white recruiters in regard to both physical demeanor and mannerisms—then she would have a chance at succeeding in her plan.

Already thirty-five years old by the time of the brothers' war, Jefferson Barracks was named in honor of Pres. Thomas Jefferson, as was Cathy Williams's hometown of Jefferson City. Near the little French village of Carondelet on the west bank of the Mississippi, the barracks stood on high ground overlooking the river. Its elevated position on the bluffs, which, dominated the "Father of Waters," offered a fine panoramic view to the east and south.

Here, at the bustling military post, the cavalry regiments of the Regular army were organized in 1855. At that time, the legendary 1st and 2nd U.S. Cavalry, which contained many future Civil War greats, were first established. Now at Jefferson Barracks, the 38th Infantry was in the process of completing its organization during the fall and winter of 1866–67.

After the Civil War, many Western volunteer regiments returned to Jefferson Barracks before mustering out of service. But now it was the birthplace of the new Buffalo Soldier regiment, the 38th Infantry. Here, on the soil of her home state, Cathy Williams was taught the duties and requirements of a private soldier. With new-found pride and enthusiasm, she trained in the open air of the parade ground of Jefferson Barracks along with her comrades of Company A.

Throughout the winter of 1866–67, she learned the ways of soldiering, and performed with success regular duties with the regiment for several months.

At this time, only two people in the 38th knew that Private Cathay was a woman, her cousin and her friend.[10] These two were key cohorts who played roles in helping Cathy successfully perpetuate her ruse. As she stated, they were the only ones who "knew that I was a woman." And they kept Cathy's secret.[11]

Cathy Williams proved to be a model soldier. In her own words: "I was a good soldier . . . I was never put in the guard house; no bayonet was ever put to my back. I carried my musket and did guard and other duties while in the army."[12]

Unknown to her at this time, a host of stern challenges loomed for William Cathay and the men of the 38th. Even though differences between North and South were now settled, troubles with the Native American peoples continued on the Western frontier. At this time, the task facing the small Regular army was simply "overwhelming." These frontier defenders, "faced problems of staggering proportions, one of which was the vast land area that they were responsible for protecting and pacifying."[13]

Morale and *esprit de corps* were especially high among the Buffalo Soldiers. For many of them, including Cathy, a life of slavery was now only a haunting memory. As during the Civil War, these African American soldiers felt that the eyes of all blacks and the nation were upon them. A Buffalo Soldier chaplain, George Gatewood Mullins of the 25th U.S. Infantry, described the mind-set of these African Americans in the ranks: "They are possessed of the notion that the colored people of the whole country are more or less affected by their conduct in the army."[14]

General Sheridan explained that the mission of the frontier Regulars was the formidable task of "controlling the Indians west of the Missouri River, they having become very restless and troublesome because of the building of the Pacific railroads through their hunting-grounds, and the encroachments of pioneers, who began settling in middle and western Kansas and eastern Colorado immediately after the war."

This meeting between migrating whites and Native Americans on the vast stage of the Great Plains resulted in a highly combustible and violent mix that offered no peaceful solution for their differences. The clash of two competing cultures and civilizations ensured additional years of bloody warfare across the Western frontier. Into the vortex of this cultural clash, the newly enlisted Buffalo Soldiers were about to be hurled to try to remedy a host of complex cultural and racial problems that had no solutions.

Two of the republic's most esteemed military leaders would tackle this most vexing of all problems for the postwar army. During Cathy Williams's term of service with the 38th Infantry, the Civil War hero and future president, Ulysses S. Grant, would team up with his close friend and top lieutenant from Civil War days, General Sheridan. Reestablishing the formidable team that conquered the Confederacy, Grant would hand "Little Phil" the mission of quelling the escalating Indian trouble by any force necessary, making him commander of the Division of Missouri.[15]

On February 13, 1867, meanwhile, the 38th Infantry finally completed its organization at Jefferson Barracks. Cathy Williams now served in the ranks as a proud member of the newly formed 75-man Company A. From the beginning, Company A was commanded by Capt. Charles Edward Clarke, a distinguished Civil War veteran. Cathy was fortunate to serve under Clarke who was a good officer. He treated the Company A soldiers with respect and fairness.

At the beginning of the Civil War, Clarke served as a captain of the 6th Michigan Volunteer Infantry, which was organized at Kalamazoo, Michigan, in August 1861. Consisting of tough soldiers from "the farm lands" of southwestern Michigan, this hard-fighting Western regiment became known as the "Bloody 6th." The Michigan regiment served for the war's duration in the Department of the Gulf, as the 8th Indiana had done for a period of its service. Interestingly, the 6th Michigan's first commander, Col. Frederick William Curtenius, resigned after he refused to obey a general's order to return slaves to bondage, after they linked up with the 6th Michigan, because of the order's immorality.

Captain Clarke won promotion, becoming the unit's major by June 1862. Earning distinction on August 5, 1862, Captain Clarke, the senior commander at this time, led the 6th Michigan in a successful counterattack that recaptured lost artillery and helped to thwart Gen. John C. Breckenridge's offensive effort to capture New Orleans. Here, the 6th Michigan won its sobriquet, "Bloody 6th," thanks in part to Captain Clarke's aggressive leadership and bold tactics.

Later during the struggle for possession of the Mississippi River and the Confederate bastion at Port Hudson, Louisiana, Clarke gained distinction for heroics during the assault on the massive fortifications along the river. At the same time, hundreds of eager black troops demonstrated their mettle in the bloody frontal assaults on Port Hudson's defenses. Young Clarke became the lieutenant colonel of the 6th Michigan in May 1864, serving until the war's end. Returning to his regular rank of captain after the war, Clarke was breveted major on March 7, 1867.

To conceal her sex from her comrades of Company A and especially from her commander, Captain Clarke, Private Cathay probably remained relatively quiet and aloof around the other soldiers before she gained their confidence in accepting her as a man. In addition, she probably wore a blue uniform that was baggy and over-sized to disguise her feminine shape. Fortunately, she was slim, aiding her disguise. From beginning to end, Cathy's slender but athletic physique assisted her in her successful ruse. She probably did not even have to bind up her breasts, which were small.

In addition, Cathy might have deliberately worn a wide-brimmed slouch hat instead of a kepi—which the soldiers generally disliked because it offered little protection from the heat, rain, and snow—to conceal her face as much as possible. Many soldiers serving on the Western frontier exchanged the French-inspired kepi of the Civil War period for the more popular wide-brimmed slouch hats. These were more durable and practical especially during active campaigning and in the harsh weather of the Western frontier.

Both training and active duty continued unabated for Pvt. William Cathay until the arrival of the spring of 1867, when Cathy's active service was interrupted when she was struck down with illness. Located along the Mississippi River and despite being positioned on high ground, Jefferson Barracks was vulnerable to the ravages of disease, especially cholera. Deadly epidemics of the disease had long swept the South and Upper South communities and cities along the Mississippi River. For instance, Nathanial Lyon, who was stationed at this busy outpost before the Civil War, was concerned about the lingering affects of a recent cholera epidemic, complaining that Jefferson Barracks was "a most unhealthy place."

Not surprisingly, Cathy became seriously ill at Jefferson Barracks. She was stricken with a high fever and began vomiting, indicating the first symptoms of a more serious illness. Then, some pustular eruptions appeared on her body, and then more developed. These spread over her skin. She was infected by an acute, infectious virus.

Private Cathay had contracted smallpox. In her own words, which matter-of-factly explained her predicament: "I was then taken with smallpox." As indicated by her service records, Pvt. William Cathay contracted her case of smallpox at Jefferson Barracks, *after* enlisting in the Buffalo Soldiers and not before: a controversial point that arose after her service in the U.S. Army.

In mid-February 1867, an ailing Cathy Williams, with small red blisters on her body and face, was transported a short distance across the Mississippi. Here, she was hospitalized in an infirmary at East St. Louis, Illinois. Cathy Williams stated that she "was sick at a hospital across the river from St. Louis." This was probably the first time in her life that Cathy was hospitalized for an illness, and received regular medical attention.

As Cathy Williams stated, the small Illinois community of East St. Louis was located directly across the Mississippi River from the thriving port city of St. Louis and just northeast of Jefferson Barracks. At East St. Louis, however, the immediate area along the east bank of the Mississippi was situated on much lower ground than Jefferson Barracks. Hence, this swampy location was more unhealthy and vulnerable to the spread of disease. Rising waters from the winter melt and spring rains annually flooded the level Mississippi flood plain around East St. Louis, serving as a breeding ground for disease, especially during the summer months.

During this period, Jefferson Barracks was a hub of hectic activity, with soldiers and government contractors and civilian employees from across the nation mingling together. Falling victim of smallpox in this environment was not unusual for an ex-slave from rural Missouri, where she had relatively little contact with large numbers of people from other areas, especially urban areas and overseas. Even during the Civil War, she had served for years with the Indiana soldiers, who were mostly farm boys from rural Indiana and Westerners like herself. Being a rural Missouri female slave working around country boys from the West had kept her relatively free from the illnesses spread by a major urban population.

By this time, Private Cathay would have been quite vulnerable to the ravages of disease. After her slave life and years of hard service with the 8th Indiana, Cathy's health might have been fragile by this time even though no record indicates as much. Ironically, smallpox was one of the primary diseases that often swept through the slave population during the antebellum period. In fact, smallpox perhaps killed more slaves than any other illness.[16]

Clearly, Cathy's luck was holding up. She was a member of the U.S. Army and therefore good medical care was available when she was stricken. So far, Cathy Williams continued to lead a charmed life, defying the odds. To her, no doubt it seemed that God was on her side.[17]

Cathy's hospitalization in East St. Louis was as lengthy as her case of smallpox was severe. Only months after her successful enlistment in the army, Cathy remained on her back in a hospital bed in an East St. Louis infirmary. Here, she had to make an extra effort to keep her sex concealed from the hospital physicians, nurses, and staff.

Many women who had enlisted as men in the Civil War were discovered during hospitalization. In fact, hospitalization was the primary cause of their discovery. To date, therefore, this was Private Cathay's greatest challenge in keeping her secret. Certainly, this period of hospitalization was not only one of illness but also one of considerable anxiety for her, demanding a large measure of resourcefulness and cleverness to escape the discovery of her sex.[18]

At the East St. Louis hospital, Cathy learned that her company was ordered west for duty. General Sherman was now distributing his newly organized Regular army units to protect the frontier. At varying intervals from March to June 1867, reassigned companies of the 38th Infantry traveled west from Missouri to Kansas. In mid-March 1867, Captain Clarke and the Buffalo Soldiers of Companies A and B marched out of the gates of Jefferson Barracks. These soldiers now embarked upon a new challenge in the West.

Captain Clarke led his black infantrymen toward a new assignment at Fort Riley in east central Kansas. Evidently both Cathy Williams's cousin and "particular friend" were also members of Company A. If so, then they now marched out of Jefferson Barracks with Captain Clarke's column, leaving a lonely Private Cathay in the East St. Louis infirmary.

During the entire period at Jefferson Barracks, these two friends, evidently ex-slaves from Missouri like herself, had never revealed the secret of her sex in anyway or at anytime. In Cathy's own words, which indicated a measure of respect for them because they had faithfully kept her precious secret for so long: "[Even though they] knew that I was a woman, they never 'blowed' on me."[19]

After boarding a train at the main St. Louis station, the Buffalo Soldiers of Company A now headed west, generally parallel to the Missouri River and toward the frontier.

Who were these resilient and hardy African Americans who marched in the ranks of the 38th Infantry? Where did they come from and what were their personal motivations? Were the past lives and experiences of these former slaves similar to Cathy Williams's past? Who were these "invisible" black soldiers who have been long absent from the pages of history and ignored by both black and white historians?

Not only were these African Americans of the 38th mostly ex-slaves who had endured the horrors of slavery but many were also veterans of USCT (U.S. Colored Troop) regiments from the Civil War. Other African Americans who served beside Pvt. William Cathay were free blacks from the North. Compared with the ex-slaves and Civil War veterans of the 38th Infantry, these free blacks initially underwent a more difficult period of readjustment to the harsh discipline and strict rules of military life.

In the 1860s, an observant white sergeant, Harry H. McConnell, of the 6th Cavalry, described the African Americans of the 38th with admiration, while emphasizing these soldiers' high spirits, which partly indicated their soaring hopes for the future: "[I]t seemed to me they were well adapted to the life and duties of the soldier[, and] their volatile, devil-may-care characters fitted them for the ups and downs of the army." [20]

At this time, the Indians of the Central Great Plains were causing trouble in General Sheridan's Department of the Missouri. As throughout American history, besides the clash of cultures, the principal root of the Indian troubles was over the insoluble issue of land ownership. White settlers coveted what the Native Americans had worshipped and possessed for centuries: their ancestral homeland of beauty and inestimable natural wealth.

Quite understandably, the Indians believed that there was no land ownership issue, because it was their ancestral homeland and it could not be sold or bartered away by mere mortals. No matter what the odds, the Great Plains Indians were not willing to give up their land without a fight.

Nor were the tribes of the Great Plains willing to relinquish their nomadic way of life. This, of course, was tied to the vast expansiveness of their western lands and the migrating buffalo herds. Kiowa chief Satanta, who would commit suicide in prison rather than submit to white domination, expressed his great love for the ancestral homeland in 1867: "I love the land and the buffalo and will not part with it . . . I don't want to settle [on a white man's reservation.] I love to roam over the prairies [and] there I feel free and happy . . ."

As a tragic fate would have it, the Native Americans of the Plains now stood squarely in the path of a relentless white migration, a barrier to the republic's progressive vision of a transcontinental nation. The conclusion of the Civil War's bloodletting now unleashed the pent-up energies of the American people. They now resumed their great push to conquer the West and fulfill what was believed to be their nation's special destiny. In the minds of white settlers, politicians, and soldiers, a justifiable, if not moral, reason existed for them to force the Native Americans from their ancestral lands. They believed that expansionism, the fruits of progress, and national greatness were ordained upon them by a smiling providence, which had turned its back on the Native Americans.

Consequently, the vast expanse of the Great Plains, once known as the "Great American Desert," now became the dramatic stage for the republic's westward expansion. Unlike the story usually described in American history books, this was not entirely a white migration, however. The forgotten players of the republic's expansion were the large numbers of African Americans who also went west across the Great Plains to begin a new life on the frontier.

These were in fact "wagons of opportunity" for black men and women, who joined the wagons trains that journeyed to the new lands of Oregon and California during the 1840s. One African American migrant who traveled to California in 1849 was a Missouri slave named Alvin Coffey, who mined gold in the Sierra Nevada. Like white Americans, hundreds of African Americans now continued their push toward the setting sun to find a better place.

Between 1860 and 1870, more than a million whites poured west like a flood; traveling along the Santa Fe, the Smokey Hill, and the Oregon-California Trails. This great exodus, however, ensured that these migrants pushed through the sacred hunting, burial, and religious grounds of the Native Americans. Thousands of migrants crossed the Indian lands without either respect, concern, or understanding toward a dissimilar culture, especially one they considered inferior. While the Buffalo Soldiers protected the seemingly endless swarms of white settlers from the angry Indians, ironically, these same whites, including former slave owners, also despised African American culture and traditions.

As could be expected, the Native Americans of the Great Plains fought to defend their homeland rather than submit to domination by this interloping "foreign" culture from the East. The Indians were determined to save their way of life at all costs. Despite their valiant efforts, however, no amount of Indian defiance could resist the advance of technology, progress, and the white man's civilization.

Most recently, the Native Americans were aroused by an offensive strike by the U.S. forces under Gen. Winfield Scott Hancock. In an ill-advised attempt to teach the Indians a lesson, General Hancock's forces burned a Cheyenne and Sioux village at Pawnee Fork on the Arkansas River, near Fort Larned in central Kansas.

General Hancock's punitive expedition of spring 1867 was in retaliation for a Sioux victory, the Fetterman Massacre. Here, in northeast Wyoming near Fort Phil Kearny in December 1866, Capt. William Fetterman and eighty bluecoat soldiers were wiped out by an ambush that exploited the overconfidence and naïveté of the "Long Knives."

General Hancock's expedition included George Armstrong Custer's 7th Cavalry and seven companies of a sister unit of the 38th Infantry—the white 37th Infantry. Instead of awing the Indians with brute force, however, General Hancock's ill-fated expedition merely sparked a full-scale conflict, "Hancock's War."

Hancock's offensive action was destined to unleash an Indian rampage across the Central and Southern Great Plains, including an area around Fort Harker on the Kansas River in central Kansas.

As Pvt. William Cathay soon learned, service on the Western frontier was a tough tour of duty. In the words of Capt. Charles King who was not guilty of exaggeration: "[A] more thankless task, a more perilous service, a more exacting test of leadership, morale and discipline no army in Christendom has ever been called upon to undertake than . . . was the lot of the little fighting force of Regulars who cleared the way across the continent for the emigrant and settler." This point of view was echoed in the words of another embittered officer on the frontier, who moaned that "honest and arduous service in the western posts is unrecognized and unrewarded."[21]

In general, the Western army of U.S. Regulars consisted of a motley force of frontier fighters. They were now saddled with the almost impossible task of making the frontier safe for the flood of migrants surging westward. In addition, their mission included protecting the mail service, roads, and telegraph lines, and guarding the railroad that was pushing toward the Pacific.

In overall terms, the Regular army's role was to safeguard the uncontrollable force of humanity that fueled the westward movement. In this way both cavalry and infantry served as the vanguard of Western settlement and economic development, which ensured the destruction of Native American culture.

Ironically, playing a part in pushing aside the Native Americans were Regular army regiments of ex-slaves who themselves had been victims of "western economic development," only a few years before. As ordered, the Buffalo Soldiers would have to dispossess the Native American peoples of their ancestral homelands.

Other enemies of the Buffalo Soldiers during service on the Western frontier were isolation and monotony, which were endemic at the small garrison outposts across the remote West. Serving in the West was a lonely experience that had even caused Ulysses S. Grant to take to the bottle before the Civil War. In contrast to the white troops on the frontier, however, the Buffalo Soldiers, both the cavalry and infantry regiments, for the most part thrived in this Western environment.

Black solidarity, which made for a high-spirited and resilient soldiery, was partly the legacy of the close-knit kinship system and familial environment of the slave community of antebellum days. Then, slaves bonded together under a repressive regime that required unity for survival. And now, the Buffalo Soldiers forged strong bonds with each other for much the same purpose.

Quite unlike white troops in the West, frontier duty for the Buffalo Soldiers was an experience that continued to forge a stronger bond and sense of solidarity. This experience increased the Buffalo Soldiers' level of camaraderie, unit pride, *esprit de corps,* and morale, which soared to heights unseen in white regiments serving on the frontier. Even the discrimination within the military, which included demands for the disbandment of black units and hostility from white officers, played a role in cementing a stronger bond among these African Americans.

When compared with the days before the Civil War and even an impoverished sharecropper's life in the Reconstruction South (that was not unlike slavery) service on the Western frontier was not as difficult for these former slaves as it was for white soldiers. Relatively few whites, unless perhaps recent Irish immigrants, had led more difficult lives. For African Americans who had been hardened by life in slavery and Civil War service, duty on the frontier offered "a rare 'safety valve,'" and a chance for a relatively good life in the West.

Despite often being issued inferior equipment, weapons, and "broken down" horses rejected by white commands—continuing an army practice of discrimination from Civil War days—the epidemics of deadly disease that steadily took men from the ranks, the harsh frontier climate, and arduous service in an untamed land, the Buffalo Soldiers' morale remained generally higher than that of white regiments year after year. This reality helped to earn the Buffalo Soldiers a well-deserved reputation for having the lowest desertion rate of all U.S. Army units on frontier service.

From beginning to end, the Buffalo Soldiers also shone in other areas. Unlike white cavalrymen in the West, alcoholism—for which the post–Civil War army was legendary—was relatively uncommon among the black troops. Like Cathy Williams, these tough African Americans were intent on proving their worth for all to see. Racist stereotypes could only be shattered by good conduct and discipline in camp and heroics in action. They believed that the eyes of not only the black community but also the white world were upon them and for the most part they acted accordingly.

The situation of the Buffalo Soldiers was not unlike that of the Tuskegee Airmen of World War II, some eighty-five years later. The Buffalo Soldiers could proudly claim the lowest desertion rates in the frontier army because most of these men wanted to make careers out of the service and, perhaps most of all, prove a point.

Compared with white soldiers in the West, not only was the desertion rate among the Buffalo Soldiers low but reenlistment remained high despite the poor rations, insufficient pay, and discrimination. As a further sign of unit discipline, and to the shock of white officers and other observers, "very few buffalo soldiers missed roll call."

The Buffalo Soldiers "excelled in discipline, morale, patience and good humor in adversity, physical endurance, and sobriety [and] above all, they performed well on campaign and in combat." Despite his well-known preference for white soldiers, General Sherman was complimentary toward his African American troops. Paying a rare tribute, "Old Billy" wrote that the Buffalo Soldiers "are good troops, they make first-rate sentinels, are faithful to their trust, and are as brave as the occasion calls for."

During active campaigning in the West, the great Western artist Frederick Remington was impressed by the unmatched camaraderie, fortitude, and boundless humor of the Buffalo Soldiers. Remington paid a glowing tribute when he described that the black soldiers "occupied such time in joking and in merriment as seemed fitted for growling. They may be tired and they may be hungry, but they do not see fit to augment their misery by finding fault with everybody and everything [and] they are charming men with whom to serve. Officers have often confessed to me that when they are on long and monotonous field service and are troubled with a depression of spirits, they have only to go about the campfires of the Negro soldier in order to be amused and cheered by the clever absurdities of the men." Remington was equally impressed by the noble bearing and physical presence of these African Americans: "[T]he physique of the black soldiers must be admired—great chests, broad-shouldered, upstanding fellows."

Most of all, this high morale and irrepressible spirit resulted in superior performances by Buffalo Soldiers when fighting the Indians. From near the Canadian border to the border of Mexico and from Missouri to the Far West, the Buffalo Soldiers constantly "saw harder service than the white regiments." As evidence of their fighting prowess during their campaigns against the Native Americans, eighteen Medals of Honor were won by the Buffalo Soldiers during the Indian Wars.[22]

During the early springtime of 1867 and while Private Cathay remained in the East St. Louis hospital, military developments on the Western frontier continued. The Buffalo Soldiers of Companies A and B, 38th Infantry, continued to travel westward by train during the journey from eastern Missouri to eastern Kansas. Only four days after departing Jefferson Barracks, Captain Clarke and his infantrymen of Company A disembarked at Fort Leavenworth, Kansas. The railroad had been completed to the Kansas fort on the eastern edge of the Great Plains, precluding a more lengthy march.

Fort Leavenworth was located in northeast Kansas, near the Missouri River, on the Missouri-Kansas border. During the antebellum period and in the Civil War years, Fort Leavenworth loomed as a safe haven for hundreds of Missouri slaves who fled west to escape to free territory across the Missouri-Kansas line.

In fact, the first black regiment that saw combat during the Civil War, the 1st Kansas Infantry, was composed of many African Americans, including ex-Missouri slaves, from Fort Leavenworth. Eager for revenge, these ex-slaves initially fought against the Rebels at Island Mound, Missouri, in late October 1862. Although largely forgotten, this was the first engagement of black troops in the Civil War.

In addition, a large black population, with the majority consisting of ex-slaves from Missouri, existed in nearby Leavenworth, Kansas. Nearly 2,500 African Americans were living at Leavenworth by 1865. Here, at Fort Leavenworth, the 10th Cavalry had recently been formed, continuing the tradition of the 1st Kansas Infantry. The 10th Cavalry was destined to become perhaps the most famous Buffalo Soldier unit in the West.

The stay for Private Cathay's Company A at Fort Leavenworth was brief, however. Once again, Captain Clarke ordered his men aboard the train. After following the course of the Kansas River and the Smoky Hill Trail west, and after disembarking from the railroad cars of the Union Pacific Railroad, Eastern Division, Captain Clarke led his black infantrymen into Fort Riley, Kansas, on March 24, 1867.

These men of the 38th Infantry completed the more than 400-mile journey by rail from Jefferson Barracks in eastern Missouri to eastern Kansas. For the first time, these former slaves and Civil War veterans found themselves on the edge of Indian country at Fort Riley, which had been built in 1853.

Private Cathay, however, had not yet caught up with Captain Clarke and the men of Company A. Once she had recovered from smallpox at the East St. Louis hospital, Cathy Williams received orders to report to Fort Riley. She then took the train from Carondelet to St. Louis, and then traveled westward across the woodlands and fields of central Missouri. Private Cathay next traveled west to link up with her company, following the same route as Captain Clarke's command.

Ironically, in journeying westward by train to rejoin Company A and just before reaching Kansas City, Missouri, Private Cathay passed through Jackson County, Missouri. Jackson County was where she had been born a slave in a world of slavery that was no more. No doubt, Cathy reflected on her slave past during the journey west to face her greatest challenge to date: active service as a Buffalo Soldier on the Western frontier. For Cathy Williams, who was now proudly wearing a blue uniform, that slave past now must have seemed more far away and remote than ever before.

Near the confluence of the Kansas and Republican Rivers in northeast Kansas, and about 130 miles west of Independence—Cathy Williams's birthplace—stood Fort Riley. The frontier fort nestled amid the sprawling prairies and was situated along the Smokey Hill Trail that ran immediately north of the Santa Fe Trail. Dominating the wind-swept high ground and grasslands of a wide, commanding plateau, Fort Riley served as the gateway to Colorado, the Far West, and the Pacific Coast.

In the push toward the Pacific, the iron rails of the Eastern Division of the Union Pacific had been laid to Fort Riley in September 1866. From Fort Riley, the Union Pacific continued west to eventually cross the Great Plains before reaching Denver, Colorado, and the most imposing natural barrier on the North American continent, the Rocky Mountains.

At Fort Riley after a 120-mile train ride west from Fort Leavenworth, a recovered Cathy Williams, with her face still marked by smallpox scars, reported for duty in early April 1867, four days after departing Jefferson Barracks. Ironically, some unexpected benefits to her came with the smallpox. These lingering pockmarks now helped to mask some of the lingering traces of a clear complexion and smooth skin that betrayed feminine beauty, assisting in her disguise as a man. After rejoining Company A, and reporting to Captain Clarke, Pvt. William Cathay was now ready for duty on the Western frontier.

Here, at Fort Riley on the north side of the Kansas River, Private Cathay might have been surprised by what was the typical fort on the Western frontier. Like almost all Western frontier forts during this period, Fort Riley was distinguished by neither fortifications, walls, or timbered stockades to protect the isolated garrison from Indian attack. In fact, the typical frontier fort, including Fort Riley, was nothing more than a group of buildings with a parade ground in the center of surrounding structures, including the barracks, officers' quarters, and headquarters buildings. At this time, the soldiers of Company A were probably encamped just outside the fort because of limited accommodation and space, or perhaps because of racism. As General Sherman described the typical Western fort of this period: "[S]ome of what are called military posts are mere collections of huts made of logs, adobes, or mere holes in the ground, and are about as much forts as prairie dog villages might be called forts."

Consequently, not everyone, especially if they came from the East, liked what they saw at Fort Riley, which was situated amid a wilderness of the seemingly endless prairies. One individual who did not like the look of forlorn Fort Riley was the aristocratic and pretty daughter of a Michigan judge. Libbie, as she was called by her husband, was the wife of a dashing cavalry commander who would win immortality for a last stand against the Plains Indians at a place in southern Montana called Little Big Horn in June 1876: George Armstrong Custer.

Forgotten by most historians, among the slain of Lieutenant Colonel Custer's 7th Cavalry troopers was one African American, Isaiah Dorman. He was known as "Custer's 'Black White Man,'" and the "black Wasichu" by the Indians. Standing Bear, of the Ogalala Sioux, described his discovery when checking the enemy dead: "[T]he fourth one was a black Wasichu [white soldier]." Also forgotten by historians was the fact that at least one female warrior of the Sioux, "Moving Robe," was present at the fighting against Custer's hated bluecoats at Little Big Horn.

Detesting Fort Riley's isolation on the bleak prairies of northeastern Kansas, Elizabeth Bacon, or Libbie Custer, to use her married name, was living with her husband who was stationed at the post during this period. While working for General Sheridan's staff, Cathy Williams no doubt saw Libbie's dashing husband, the "boy general" of the Civil War, when he fought beside Sheridan during the Shenandoah Valley campaign of 1864.

Ironically, after turning down a lieutenant colonel's commission to lead black troopers of the 9th Cavalry, perhaps because of racism and a giant ego, Custer was commissioned a lieutenant colonel in the newly organized 7th Cavalry in late July 1866. Fort Riley now served as the headquarters of the regiment. Lieutenant Colonel Custer was convinced that his white troopers of the 7th Cavalry were far superior in almost every way to the Buffalo Soldiers. In reality, the opposite was closer to the truth as the historical record indicates.

At least by words rather than actions, Custer expressed an open mindedness toward the idea of black troops, but only to a point. He explained: "I am in favor of elevating the negro to the extent of his capacity and intelligence, and of our doing everything in our power to advance the race morally and mentally as well as physically, also socially. But I am opposed to making this advance by correspondingly debasing any portion of the white race." Consequently, at this time, Custer no doubt looked down upon African Americans in blue uniforms, including the men of the 38th Infantry.

Despite his public protestations, and much like the rumors concerning Thomas Jefferson and Sally Hemings, Custer was reported to have slept with African American women during Civil War and Indian War campaigns, according to Capt. Frederick Benteen, of the 7th Cavalry. During the Indian Wars, Custer was known to have had two black cooks, Lucy and then Mary Kercherval, who traveled with her son Charles, by the time of the Little Big Horn fiasco.

Probably much like Cathy Williams's initial impression when she had first arrived at Fort Riley to rejoin her company, Libbie Custer was disappointed first by the fort's appearance and then by the dreary existence of life there. She found it hard to believe that such a collection of "storey-and-half buildings about a parade ground constituted a fort on the plains." Indicating a certain amount of racism and harboring the typical prejudices of an upper class Eastern lady of the day, Libbie at this time was served by "her colored swain Henry."

Also indicating a lack of personal association with African Americans (except as servants), Mrs. Custer felt uncomfortable around so many black soldiers, whose distinctive cultural behavior and rich camaraderie she did not understand. These blacks included soldiers of the 38th Infantry. One could easily understand how the sight of African Americans wearing the same color uniform as her idolized husband would have been a blow to Mrs. Custer's pride and vanity. She complained with a measure of contempt that the black troops of the 38th, when the 7th Cavalry was absent, were "boisterous, undisciplined creatures."

Encountering various forms of discrimination both inside and outside the U.S. Army, which merely reflected the overall prejudices of American society in general, was all too commonplace for the Buffalo Soldiers. Some racism was even forthcoming from the commanding officers at key Western outposts where the black soldiers were stationed, including Fort Leavenworth. During their years of distinguished frontier service, "the only obstacles [that the Buffalo Soldiers] could not overcome were those of prejudice and discrimination." As was so often the case the black infantrymen of the 38th Infantry were sometimes assigned to the worst possible quarters: dirty, poorly ventilated, too small for the number of men assigned, insect-infested, and disease-ridden.

Libbie Custer's negative impressions of Fort Riley can be understood because they were comparable to the reactions of many other equally romantic and idealistic wives of white officers. Many such women, nevertheless, became enchanted by the West's beauty and even military life itself.[23]

During this period, many officers' wives found military life exciting and challenging. These women often viewed the Western frontier and the military with a romantic idealization more rooted in novels than reality. For instance, after a tour in Europe and by way of marriage to an army lieutenant, Martha Dunham's greatest desire upon returning to the United States was to continue a "military existence." As she wrote, "I concluded the only thing to do was to join the army myself." Cathy Williams had felt much the same in the months immediately following the Civil War.

One of the personal ambitions of Teresa Griffin, another officer's wife, consisted of "joining the army." After marriage to an army lieutenant, Teresa described that "no recruit ever entered the service with more enthusiasm than I did or felt more eager to prove himself a soldier." Like Cathy Williams, many of these women fell in love with the mild climate, awe-inspiring picturesque views, the reinvigorating sense of independence in the wide open spaces, the vast prairie lands that rolled endlessly to the horizon, and the beautiful mountains of the West.

Despite the lingering memories of her husband's death in the Fetterman Massacre, Frances Carrington remained mystified by the stirring "grandeur" and beauty of the Great Plains. In much the same way and as the course of her life demonstrated, Cathy Williams loved the West and its raw beauty and wide open spaces. But most of all, Private Cathay probably revered the inspiration of what the West had to offer her both as a woman and an African American: a liberating sense of freedom and a feeling of equality never experienced before.[24]

The frontier West was an untamed and seemingly boundless land of the big sky. Like other Buffalo Soldiers and officers' wives, Private Cathay was no doubt enchanted by what she saw around her, surpassing anything that she had seen in her native Missouri. In every direction around Fort Riley, the seemingly endless expanses of broad prairies flowed in every direction, possessing a beauty that could not be forgotten. Josiah Gregg, who lived in Jackson County, Missouri, at the same time that Cathy Williams toiled as a slave there, described the majestic grasslands along the Santa Fe Trail as "the grand prairie ocean [which was] as level as the sea."[25]

This bountiful land that was the home of the Native Americans captivated women like Mary Maguire Carr. She was the wife of Gen. Eugene Asa Carr who won a Medal of Honor for his defense of the Elk Horn Tavern at Pea Ridge, where Cathy had heard the battle rage in March 1862. Like many old army officials who supported the status quo and looked unfavorably upon this so-called "experimental" use of African American troops on the Western frontier, General Carr was so antiblack that he chose to take a lower rank rather than command African Americans. "I had reached 'the plains' [and now] understood what that comprehensive word meant [because] it was like the sea. As far as the eye could reach, vast stretches of vacant land" in every direction, wrote an enchanted Mrs. Carr.[26]

This vast unspoiled land provided the ideal natural setting for the nurturing of a new sense of freedom and independence, which contradicted those man-made things that Cathy Williams most detested in life: racism, prejudice, and injustice, which had been the cornerstones of slavery not that long ago.

One traveler to the frontier West, Robert Louis Stevenson, caught the exhilarating sense of freedom on the Western frontier by explaining how European immigrants and Easterners, "who shall have grown up in an old and rigid circle, following bygone fashions and taught to distrust [their] own fresh instincts" were transformed by the Western experience, successfully living and prospering for "themselves [while] far from restraint and tradition."

Clearly, this was a free land that was worth fighting to possess. Certainly the Native Americans believed so, explaining why they fought so tenaciously in defending the land that they loved. But, the Indians at first had tolerated the whites and their relentless encroachment, believing that a mutual coexistence was still possible despite the wide cultural differences. By the late 1860s, however, that naive belief and early tolerance were destroyed forever by events that neither the white settlers nor this land's indigenous inhabitants could either control or stop.

Instead of peaceful coexistence, the Indians were now fighting the soldiers to preserve their own freedom in the land that they had possessed for centuries. In the 1867 words of Ten Bears, a Comanche, who explained the sense of freedom that emanated from the beauty of this vast land, "I was born upon the prairie, where the wind blew free and there was nothing to break the light of the sun. I was born where there were no enclosures and where everything drew a free breath."

While Private Cathay loved the soldier's life, she may well have experienced some pangs of conscience over the U.S. Army's mission of conquering the Native Americans. These indigenous peoples desired only to continue their way of life unhindered, but like African Americans before them, it was now their turn to suffer the wrath of Anglo feelings of superiority and domination over all things.

In many ways, Pvt. William Cathay was now a minority member fighting a white man's war for white, but not black, progress. One historian viewed Western expansion as a catalyst that led to "the spread [of the] metaphysics of Indian-hating." Even at this time, harsh white attitudes toward African Americans were much the same.

A bitter irony now existed for the Buffalo Soldiers, generally hated by whites, who were fighting to suppress the Native Americans who were equally detested by Anglos. The only difference was that the Indians could offer resistance against white domination, unlike blacks. Despite the moral complexities of westward expansion and its deep racist roots, the Buffalo Soldiers' role still served as an inspiring model for black communities across America.

A certain moral dilemma probably existed for Private Cathay, especially if she was of partial Indian ancestry, like other Buffalo Soldiers. In historical terms African Americans taking up arms against the Native Americans was not unlike blacks battling fellow blacks to deny them freedom. Throughout the annals of American history, it was common for African Americans to intermarry with native peoples, in a tradition that historian William Loren Katz aptly described "as old as Thanksgiving." Beginning in the colonial period, the blending of Native Americans and African Americans along the Atlantic Coast was so extensive as to create a distinctive biracial people with a separate heritage.

In terms of resistance to enslavement and white domination, the best example of the phenomenon of Indians and African Americans combining as one were the Black Seminoles. In the wilderness of Florida, ex-slaves from Georgia and South Carolina escaped south to join the Seminole peoples. Here, the two peoples eventually merged into one, presenting a united front against white domination. A combined alliance of blacks and Seminoles offered stiff resistance to U.S. forces during the Seminole Wars.

When the united force of ex-slaves, Black Seminoles, and Seminoles rose up as one in revolt in 1836, they possessed sufficient strength to ravage the settlements of northeastern Florida along the St. John's River. This bitter conflict—America's first guerrilla conflict and first "racial war," which became known as the Second Seminole War—has been viewed by American historians as solely an Indian war.

In reality, however, this conflict was in fact a "Negro War," as one frustrated general, Thomas Sidney Jesup, who knew only too well the disturbing truth, expressed it. Even as early as 1818 when he marched an army into Spanish Florida to strike the Seminole and black towns during the First Seminole War, Gen. Andrew Jackson described the Florida conflict as "this savage and negro War." Fear existed that the spread of news of a "Negro War" in Florida would spark the slaves across the South to rise up in rebellion against their white masters.

To counter this threat, thousands of U.S. Regulars and volunteers from Western states rushed to Florida to put down the Indians and African Americans before this lethal combination incited the slaves to a war of liberation. Among the volunteers of 1836 were those from Cathy's native homeland of Jackson County, Missouri, and other counties of "Little Dixie." Col. Richard Gentry's Missouri regiment was destined to meet former slaves in battle amid the Florida wilderness.

In a climactic battle that was the largest of the Seminole Wars, the U.S. Regulars and Colonel Gentry's Missourians led by Brig. Gen. Zachary Taylor clashed with the Black Seminoles, ex-slaves, and Native Americans on a bloody Christmas Day in 1837 at the battle of Lake Okeechobee. Here, on the banks of the huge lake on the northern border of the Everglades, in a cleverly conceived defensive position amid a hammock of oak, palmetto, and hickory, the combined force of Indians, Black Seminoles, and ex-slaves made their stand. From this defensive position, they inflicted more casualties on a U.S. force by Native American peoples than in any other Indian War encounter up to that time.

Winning additional acclaim for his fighting prowess and leadership skills on this bloody Yuletide in south central Florida, the principal African American war chief was John Cavallo, or John Horse. He was the product of a slave mother and a Spanish master. Cavallo was raised in the Seminole tribe, winning respect among the Seminole peoples for his fighting prowess and leadership skills. He became known far and wide by the war-name of Hokepis Hejo, or Crazy Breast, because "his heart is recklessly brave." John Horse had demonstrated leadership ability and tactical skill at the earlier Florida battles of the Withlocoochee Crossing and the Wahoo Swamp.

The battle of Lake Okeechobee was fought less than five years before Cathy Williams's birth in western Missouri. During the Seminole Wars, the formidable alliance of Seminoles, ex-slaves, and Black Seminoles thwarted the military might of the United States for more than forty years, tying up and frustrating the professional soldiers from West Point in a seemingly endless guerrilla war.[27]

Laying the foundation to a moral dilemma for the African American soldiers on the Great Plains, ex-slaves in blue uniforms, in a reversal of roles, now attempted to suppress the Native Americans. This conflict on the Western frontier has been seen by some modern historians as racial genocide. At this time, the Buffalo Soldiers were an armed force of colored people fighting under the U.S. flag, led by white officers, battling against another people of color on behalf of the future development of an Anglo nation.

Since colonial days, whites had successfully conquered one native people after another in part by utilizing a clever strategy of employing Indian allies to escalate the self-destructive process of in-fighting among Native American tribes: an effective policy of divide and conquer.

While serving under veteran white officers on the frontier, this realization of the irony of people of color battling against another people of color for the economic and political advantage of white industrialists, railroad men, greedy settlers, and miners may well have caused former slaves like Private Cathay some concern. This contradictory situation was now quite unlike anything that Cathy Williams had experienced before. Now, perhaps for the first time, the lines between right and wrong, good and evil were blurred for this young black woman.

Indeed, her past experiences had been uncomplicated in terms of morality. Cathy Williams's past military experience had been in service of the liberating Union armies during the Civil War, which swept across the South and freed thousands of slaves along the way in a righteous moral crusade. But now the situation was not only much different but also largely reversed. For obvious moral reasons, this conflict—a white man's war—against the Native Americans to dispossess them of their ancestral homelands was quite different from any conflict that young Cathy Williams had known before.

In addition, the brutal manner in which the conflict was waged against the Native American peoples, including men, women, and children, was also perhaps a cause of concern for Cathy Williams, who might still have been haunted by the cruel memories of slavery. This type of internal conflict was not unusual for former slaves. In New Mexico, for instance, one Buffalo Soldier named Robert Ball Anderson, a former slave and a Civil War veteran, defiantly refused orders to kill an Indian woman and her baby. He stood firm on moral grounds against orders. If placed in a similar situation, would Private Cathay act differently?

As a young woman and ex-slave, Cathy Williams would probably have been more sensitive than the average male, black or white, to the Indians' tragic plight and hopeless situation. The Indians' dilemma might well have reminded Cathy Williams of what black people had suffered and endured for years under the blight of slavery not so long ago.

In fact, Northern liberals, who had once espoused the cause of black freedom and the Emancipation Proclamation, now turned their attention to deploring the sad plight of the Indians. In brutal fashion, this war against the Native American peoples was about to be waged ruthlessly by modern warriors who were masters at winning decisive victory. The heroes of the American nation and the South's conquerors would be as merciless as they were successful in employing the sword of the republic. These modern warriors included Generals Grant, who became president in 1868, William T. Sherman, Phil Sheridan, and George Armstrong Custer. All Civil War heroes, they would soon take the brutal art of waging total war that had decisively crushed the South and unleash it on the Great Plains.

As in destroying the willpower of the Southern people to resist and in devastating the Confederacy's ability to fight, these capable modern soldiers would soon wage total war on the Native Americans' support system. These targets of the republic's finest included the villages and cornfields, the vast herds of buffalo, which were the staple of the Plains Indians, and even the Indians' horses, which were essential to their nomadic way of life. As demonstrated during the Civil War, this brutal type of modern warfare knew no mercy or bounds. Not surprisingly, Wendell Phillips declared in 1870 that "I only know the names of [these] savages upon the plains . . . General Custer, and at the head of all, General Sheridan."[28]

This merciless brand of total warfare that would be waged upon the Indians roused a greater degree of sympathy among military wives than in their officer-husbands. With a clear understanding of the meaning of morality after her experiences in slavery, Cathy Williams also might well have been sympathetic to the Indians' plight. This young woman and former Missouri slave may have harbored sympathetic opinions about the harsh realities of racial warfare, despite having been sworn to perform her duty as a U.S. soldier. In many ways and much like the African American experience, the Native American peoples now struggled for survival in a world where whites seemingly crushed everything that stood in their way.

Like many other Western women, a sympathetic Frances Carrington admired the valiant efforts of the Native Americans, who struggled to preserve their homeland and way of life. She wrote that the Indians' brave attempt to protect their homes and families "with spirit [was] akin to that of the American soldiers of our early history." And Teresa Viele found inspiration in the Comanches' heroic struggle against the hated American interlopers "whom they considered to be the aggressors" and with ample justification, especially in regard to the Texans.[29]

On April 10, 1867, and not long after her arrival at Fort Riley, Cathy Williams's lingering illness—an ailment known during the nineteenth century as the "itch"—once again reappeared. She might have allowed the illness to progress, fearing an examination at the infirmary would betray her sex.

On that date, nevertheless, the illness became so pronounced that she was admitted to the post infirmary at Fort Riley. The "itch" was also known as scabies or psora. This ailment was caused by an infection of the skin, resulting in scabs. In nineteenth century terminology, however, the "itch" was a loose term applied to skin conditions that produced irritation and formed a scab. It is not known but Cathy's condition might have been a legacy of an illness from slave days or Civil War service.

Here, at Fort Riley, Pvt. William Cathay remained in the post hospital for some time. Probably, this was a welcomed respite from the boredom and discipline of military duty. At the infirmary, she was able to get much-needed rest. Cathy recuperated as best she could under what by today's standard must have been primitive and unsanitary conditions. On April 30, 1867, she was officially listed as sick at the Fort Riley hospital with more than a dozen other privates.

Private Cathay remained at the Fort Riley infirmary until May 14, after a period of hospitalization that lasted more than a month. Meanwhile, the Buffalo Soldiers of the 38th Infantry basked in the balmy weather of springtime.

The advent of the new season brought bright sunshine and warm breezes to the Kansas prairies. Day after day, the black troops drilled on the parade ground of Fort Riley in neat uniforms and with ever-growing precision. Along with *esprit de corps,* discipline was getting better all the time.

Even after their required duties and assignments were completed, the men of the 38th remained active and in high spirits. Feeling frisky, these feisty African Americans performed physical feats that impressed observers. One spectator at Fort Riley included Libbie Custer. In the words of Mrs. Custer, who must have viewed the antics of the free-spirited African Americans from the wives' quarters with some disbelief, the men of the 38th found physical relief and exercise on the sprawling parade ground of Fort Riley by "turning hand-springs all over the sprouting grass."

Despite her initial first impressions of the lonely Kansas outpost, Libbie Custer gradually took a liking to Fort Riley. In a letter of September 1867 she wrote that "this post is almost perfect as a garrison [and] no place could be cooler or more agreeable as a summer residence . . . it is considered the third best post in the U.S. and Genl. Sheridan and his staff will be there."[30]

Cathy Williams's recovery at Fort Riley was timely because new orders were received by the two companies of the 38th. Now, on May 13, Private Williams and her comrades were ordered to report to Fort Harker, Kansas. Soon, the Buffalo Soldiers of Companies A and B marched to the railroad depot, and after traveling west for two days parallel to the Smokey Hill Trail and the Kansas River, they arrived at Fort Harker in central Kansas on May 15.

The men of the 38th Infantry departed Fort Riley not long before the famed 10th Cavalry was headquartered there in August 1867.

At this time, the various companies of the 38th Regiment were on the move. Companies A and B would join Companies C, E, I, and G, which had departed Jefferson Barracks on May 12, at Fort Harker on May 17. Companies C, E, I, and G, however, would depart Fort Harker, west for Fort Hayes, before the end of May. Meanwhile, Cathy Williams and Captain Clarke's Company A remained at Fort Harker, settling into military life at the outpost in central Kansas.

Fort Harker, though still under construction, served as a primary supply depot for the military installations farther west. However, the fort, just southwest of Fort Riley and farther west up the Kansas River on the Smokey Hill Trail, was also a breeding ground for cholera. As the Buffalo Soldiers now learned, cholera could take a soldier's life more easily than an Indian arrow or bullet. In fact, the cholera epidemic of the summer of 1867 would take far more lives than the Native Americans. As fate would have it, the hardest hit and most affected area of the epidemic was where the 38th Infantry now served, Kansas.

Pvt. William Cathay, 38th U.S. Infantry. MARTY BRAZIL

Jackson County Courthouse, Independence, Missouri, 1845. STATE HISTORICAL SOCIETY OF MISSOURI, COLUMBIA

African-American laundresses and their children during the Civil War. AUSTIN HISTORY CENTER, AUSTIN PUBLIC LIBRARY

Newly freed laundresses of the Upper South. COLLECTION OF THE ONONDAGA HISTORICAL ASSOCIATION

Battle of Pea Ridge, Arkansas, March 7–8, 1862. STATE HISTORICAL SOCIETY OF MISSOURI, COLUMBIA

Helena, Arkansas, during Union occupation, September 1864. ARKANSAS HISTORY COMMISSION

Gen. Henry C. Merriam. WILLIAM G. MUELLER, *THE TWENTY-FOURTH INFANTRY: PAST AND PRESENT* (FORT COLLINS, CO: OLD ARMY PRESS, 1972)

The 7th U.S. Cavalry on the parade ground of Fort Riley, Kansas. U.S. ARMY MILITARY HISTORY INSTITUTE

Officers' quarters at Fort Union, New Mexico, 1867. U.S. ARMY MILITARY HISTORY INSTITUTE

9th Cavalry on parade in Sante Fe. U.S. Army Military History Institute

Town of Trinidad, New Mexico, c. 1881. Colorado Historical Society

The cholera epidemic that swept through the Western frontier with such deadly vengeance in fact began in North America when English immigrants landed at Halifax, Nova Scotia, the year before. The disease then spread to the major Eastern cities of the United States, including army garrisons, until cholera would take more than 1,200 soldiers from the army's ranks by the end of 1866.

It was only a matter of time before the cholera epidemic struck Forts Riley and Harker as the disease spread west, hitting one frontier outpost after another. The first cases of cholera appeared at Fort Riley on August 30, thanks to the arrival of diseased recruits from Carlisle Barracks, Pennsylvania. The migrants and their long trains of wagons, which were especially devastated by the cholera epidemic, were the principal carriers of the disease. In this subtle way, cholera was now transferred to the grassy plains of central Kansas from a large urban area, St. Louis.[31]

Even in regard to the cholera's spread, racism and prejudice came into play to negatively affect the Buffalo Soldiers' reputation, saddling them with yet another racial stereotype. A medical officer began an unfounded rumor that would stain both the image and reputation of the men of the 38th Infantry. Without sufficient evidence, he incorrectly concluded that "a regiment of U.S. troops [the 38th Infantry] from that post [Jefferson Barracks]—at which they had been organized and from which they were equipped for service—occasioned a most disastrous outbreak of cholera on the high, dry plains of western Kansas," during the summer of 1866.

This early, hasty assessment of who caused the disease's spread was based more upon fiction than fact and damaged the Buffalo Solders' reputations because, thereafter, "every account which mentions the cholera epidemic of 1867 in Kansas accepts without reservation the argument that three companies of the 38th Infantry spread the cholera across the Plains as they traveled from Jefferson Barracks, Mo., to Fort Union, New Mexico."

Indeed, historian Evan S. Connell wrote in his popular book, *Son of the Morning Star: Custer and the Little Bighorn*, in 1984 that "the principal carrier [of the cholera epidemic] seems to have been the Thirty-eighth Infantry, which was afflicted at Fort Leavenworth." However, such was *not* the case. Had the regiment been infected with cholera at Fort Leavenworth, the command certainly would not have been allowed to travel across the West from Jefferson Barracks to outposts in Kansas and then on to forts in New Mexico.

Typical of the prejudice held against black soldiers were the words of one white physician at the time who believed that the Buffalo Soldiers were "naturally more prone to disease of an epidemic type than white men." Unfortunately, Western writers and historians have perpetuated the mythology that this deadly epidemic was spread by the Buffalo Soldiers of the 38th Infantry, which was not the case.[32]

In truth, civilians either from the wagon trains or railroad workers who laid the tracks across the prairies to Fort Harker most likely spread the epidemic west. Again, the soldiers of the 38th Infantry would not have been allowed to depart Jefferson Barracks in the first place had these troops been infected with cholera, which in any case struck Jefferson Barracks nearly a month *after* the Buffalo Soldiers departed St. Louis. As Major Merriam of the 38th later explained: "[T]here had been no case in the companies at or before reaching Fort Harker."

Whatever the source, the cholera descended upon Fort Harker, when Cathy Williams and her Company A were part of the garrison there. Rather than serving as the disease's carriers, the Buffalo Soldiers of Company A now risked becoming victims of cholera. As fate would have it, Fort Harker would be harder hit by the disease than any other fort on the Western frontier. Meanwhile, additional Buffalo Soldiers, who were suffering more severely from an epidemic of diarrhea than cholera at this time, began to reach Fort Harker, when Companies D, F, and K, 38th Infantry, arrived at the fort in late June.[33]

As Companies A, B, D, F, H, and K assembled at Fort Harker, they were hit by the cholera epidemic. The deadly chain reaction that first began with the civilian population now ravaged the Fort Harker garrison. The first cases of cholera appeared just after mid-June, bringing panic with them. After having only recently recovered from smallpox, Pvt. William Cathay now faced a second serious threat, risking death from cholera. But in fact, Cathy faced a double danger: not only death but another period of hospitalization that might reveal her sex, resulting in an early exit from the military. At Fort Harker, Cathy's anxiety would certainly have been high at this time.

No one was safe from the disease at Fort Harker. While Companies A, B, and K of the 38th remained in an encampment around the fort, another detachment of the regiment, Companies D, H, and F under Major Merriam, was located at a campsite on Plumb Creek. The Plumb Creek encampment was situated eighteen miles from Fort Harker to escape the ravages of the epidemic.

Despite these precautions, the threat from the disease was ever-present. One soldier wrote without exaggeration in a letter that Fort Harker was "the most unhealthy place I ever saw [and] I believe the cholera was amongst us for most every one of us was taken with diarrhea, vomiting, and griping in the stomach."

On June 28, Pvt. George Groom of Company H, 38th Infantry, was the first Buffalo Soldier to die of cholera at Fort Harker. Before the fatal epidemic subsided, almost thirty soldiers would fill a large plot of lonely graves at the post. In addition, another twenty-nine civilians connected with the fort would also be fatally cut down by the disease.

It was not long before a number of women at Fort Harker began to die. Cathy Williams must have been especially alarmed to learn that two of the post's surgeons lost their wives to the cholera. Asst. Surgeon George McCall, who was attached to the 38th Infantry, also died.

Meanwhile, additional cases of severe diarrhea continued to break out among the Buffalo Soldiers, indicating the disease's early stages and cholera's rapid spread. A good chance existed that Private Cathay would also be stricken by the epidemic. Perhaps she exhibited some early symptoms of the disease. Nevertheless, she remained on duty for three weeks, while the cholera epidemic swept through Fort Harker's garrison and took more victims.

Not every Buffalo Soldier who was sent to the post infirmary with cholera died. Many stricken African Americans were fortunate, recovering at the camp hospital. Diligent medical men took aggressive action to combat cholera's spread.

For example, as has been noted, campsites were transferred away from the fort to new locations. In addition, sanitation, never good to begin with, was improved to combat the deadly contagion. The black soldiers were also ordered to only drink water after boiling. Personal cleanliness among the troops was also emphasized, latrines were improved, overgrown weeds around the fort were cut down, and the entire area—which suffered from neglect and served as a breeding ground for the epidemic—in and around Fort Harker was cleaned-up and sanitized.

Groups of Buffalo Soldiers were detailed to work in the hospitals as orderlies. One of these might well have been Cathy Williams. A white surgeon who was impressed by the heroic work of these African Americans wrote: "I was very much surprised at their fidelity . . . the [men] placed great faith in disinfectants, and after their use they seemed to have no fear of the disease." Relentless efforts were made by competent medical men in uniform to combat the cholera and halt its spread at Fort Harker.[34]

As if the cholera epidemic was not enough, Indian problems also swept across the Great Plains in June 1867. That month, the soldiers of the 38th Infantry finally got their first chance to fight Indians. The opportunity to face the Native Americans first developed when Lieutenant Colonel Custer and his 7th Cavalry departed from Fort Hays, located on the Kansas River and the Smokey Hill Trail between Forts Riley and Wallace, on June 1, 1867. As directed by General Sherman, Custer and his 7th Cavalry rode toward the Republican River country to attack the Cheyenne and their Sioux allies.

Custer and his men rode eighty miles west across country from Fort Hays and the Platte River country to Fort Wallace, west of Fort Harker, farther up the Kansas River and near its source. At this time, Fort Wallace was the last outpost in western Kansas, and was located not far from the Colorado border.

Here, near Fort Wallace, an element of the 7th Cavalry escorting Custer's wagons was attacked. Indicating the high spirits and morale of these African Americans in their first Indian fight, a detachment of the 38th Infantry came to the rescue in stirring fashion.[35]

Mrs. Custer described the contest outside Fort Wallace in which the men of the 38th rose to the challenge, demonstrating the mettle of the Buffalo Soldiers: "[A] dozen negro soldiers, who had come with their wagon from an outpost of supplies, were placed near the garrison on picket duty. While the fight was going on, the two officers in command found themselves near each other on the skirmish-line, and observed a wagon with four mules tearing out of the line of battle. It was filled with negroes, standing up, all firing in the direction of the Indians. The driver lashed the mules with his black snake, and roared at them as they ran. When the skirmish-line was reached, the colored men leaped out and began firing again. No one had ordered them to leave their picket-station, but they were determined that no soldiering should be carried on in which their valor was not proved."[36]

At Fort Wallace throughout the scorching hot days of July, meanwhile, the ravages of cholera continued to take a toll upon the garrison, including the 7th Cavalry. The spread of disease throughout the outposts—including Fort Riley where Mrs. Custer expressed concern for her welfare—combined with General Sherman's recall orders to protect the forts along the Kansas River and in the Smokey Hill Valley, caused Custer to return. Then, without permission and against orders, Custer, brother Tom Custer, and the 7th Cavalry troopers pushed east nearly a hundred miles to Fort Harker, where the 38th Infantry was stationed on the journey to reach Fort Riley and Libbie.[37]

Here, at Fort Harker, Private Cathay might have reflected on the sight of the "Laundresses' Row." These laundresses, including African American women, and some white enlisted men and their families, lived in primitive conditions. In a military system based upon hierarchy and rank, this was the lowest social rung.

Each company of the 38th Infantry, was allowed four laundresses. As Cathy had done during the Civil War, they received compensation in the form of rations and pay. One veteran described the laundresses, which included soldiers' wives, as "good, honest, industrious wives, usually well on in years, minutely familiar with their rights . . . which they dared to maintain with acrimonious volubility[, and as a result] were ever ready for a fight." Other laundresses, however, were considerably less virtuous in moral terms.

The problem of prostitution among laundresses, who consisted of an odd mixture of both virtuous working women as well as working girls, had long plagued armies. Indeed, this was a long-established military tradition.

In Napoléon's day, many of these "women had brats [to whom] they might be seen giving birth under a tree [and later] catching-up with their regiment." Faithful solders' wives, harlots, laundresses, cooks, and vivandières all followed Napoléon's armies across Europe, and in the process they created "a fantastic feminine saga which no learned study has ever chronicled and which will never be recorded apart from passing references."

Many soldiers found wives among the laundresses, indicating that a number at least were of marriageable age. During the early part of his career, for example, at least one of Napoléon's marshals took his wife from among the laundresses. The tradition of enlisted men marrying laundresses was a common feature among the Buffalo Soldiers of the 24th Infantry when they were stationed in Texas.

To Cathy Williams, now wearing the blue uniform, it must have not seemed that long ago when she was a lowly laundress with no prospects except to labor endlessly and to be ordered about by any white person. Those deep, if not painful, scars of a slave's life and "contraband" past no doubt still remained to haunt her soul like a ghost from another world. Cathy might well have deliberately stayed clear of "Laundresses' Row" and other black laundresses so as not to arouse suspicion of any kind.

By this time, every fort on the Western frontier employed laundresses who were primarily either African American, Irish, or Hispanic females. For instance, at Fort Phil Kearny in northeast Wyoming, one black laundress was known as "Colored Susan." Susan was a most enterprising and resourceful woman. She baked pies with stolen government flour and then made profits by selling the pies to hungry soldiers, who had long tired of the bland rations of salt pork, beans, and hardtack.

In addition, Susan also sold liquor, raking in more money from the meager soldiers' pay of $13.00 per month. Less enterprising laundresses made money by selling their bodies. Many unique brands of capitalism thrived on the frontier among former slaves who had been exploited by this same capitalist spirit.

Much like Cathy Williams's role with the 8th Indiana, the more trustworthy laundresses became almost part of the vibrant black community that was a Buffalo Soldier regiment. For example, when Gen. William Hoffman,

Fort Leavenworth's commander, denied permission for one laundress, evidently black, to accompany the 10th Cavalry, a white captain, apparently at the urging of his African American soldiers, instructed the woman to depart the fort and then rejoin the regiment on the ride west. The black soldiers then concealed the woman in a regimental wagon.

Private Williams's Company A, 38th Infantry, was not destined to linger at Fort Harker long because of the spread of the cholera epidemic to other Western outposts.

No doubt, Pvt. William Cathay probably saw Lieutenant Colonel Custer when his wife, Libbie, was staying at Fort Harker. Not surprisingly, Custer would be arrested in late July and court-martialed for his unauthorized leave of absence from his 7th Cavalry and departure from Fort Wallace to ensure his wife's safety at Fort Riley. Custer would be suspended for one year without pay.

Luckily, Cathy Williams was not stricken with cholera at Fort Harker. Many others, both men and women, were not so fortunate. After working both at a nearby community and Fort Harker, a Catholic priest would die along with two Catholic Sisters of Mercy, while attempting to comfort the disease's unfortunate victims. All the while, more graves filled the overflowing post cemetery. Fort Harker became a place of death, misery, and suffering.

During the early summer heat of 1867 and near the end of June, the companies of the 38th were issued new orders to report to Fort Union, New Mexico. Major Merriam formed his 1st Battalion, which now included Captain Clarke's Company A and Pvt. William Cathay.

During this lengthy march towards the mountains of northeast New Mexico, Private Cathay would come to better know another fine soldier, Major Merriam. He had been the first officer of the 38th Cathy had met upon enlistment. Merriam was present on November 15, 1866, when Cathy Williams first walked into the recruiter's office at Jefferson Barracks and signed up for three years.

In terms of military achievements, Major Merriam was the most distinguished officer of the regiment. As a lieutenant colonel he had won the Medal of Honor while commanding the 73rd U.S. Colored Troops during the assault on Fort Blakeley, Alabama, on April 9, 1865: the day General Lee surrendered to General Grant at Appomattox Court House. He was one of only thirteen white officers of colored troops so honored.

The 73rd USCT—formerly the 1st Louisiana Native Guards, which had been formed by Gen. Benjamin Butler in the fall of 1862—consisted of blacks from the New Orleans area. From beginning to end, Merriam had led his African American soldiers with skill and distinction during the Civil War years.

On the east bank of the Tensaw River just northeast of Mobile, Alabama, and at the northeastern edge of Mobile Bay, Fort Blakeley posed a formidable objective to Union forces. On April 9, Lieutenant Colonel Merriam led his black troops, who "were burning with an impulse to do honor to their race," forward against a powerful array of fortifications. He won his medal for "voluntarily and successfully leading his regiment over the works in advance of orders, permission having been given at his own request." Leading the way, Merriam's example inspired his men to overrun the imposing redoubts held by veteran Mississippi Rebels to turn the left flank of the fort.

By 1867, Major Merriam's future was bright and full of promise. The major's relationship with his soldiers of the 38th Infantry was good, continuing his legacy of Civil War service. By this time, Major Merriam was a rising star among the officer corps of the postwar army. He would eventually retire with the lofty rank of major general: no small accomplishment in the lean postwar years.[38]

Private Cathay no doubt rejoiced at the news to move out. Besides the good news of departing disease-ridden Fort Harker, service on the march made it much easier for her to maintain her disguise. First, unlike conditions in the confined quarters of the fort and especially her first duty station at Jefferson Barracks, campaigning in the open countryside allowed for an added measure of privacy, freedom of movement, and the guarantee of a greater physical distance from comrades to attend to various aspects of hygiene, especially bathing, toiletry, menstrual cycles, and sanitation. But most important, life on the march and in camp meant that Private Cathay would not have to change clothes on a regular basis, ensuring that neither her body nor her secret would be uncovered.[39]

Like other women who successfully served in the disguise as men in the Civil War, Cathy Williams probably drank as little water from her canteen as possible on the march in order to avoid the necessity of having to urinate, which would risk exposing her true identity. This was no easy task during the scorching hot weather of summer on the Great Plains. Clouds of choking dust kicked up by marching feet would only have added to her thirst. But Private Cathay would do anything and make any sacrifice.[40]

Most of all, Cathy Williams's disguise worked to perfection because she looked ever inch the soldier on the march. Mile after weary mile, she was determined to do as well as the men during the lengthy march across rough country, never straggling or falling behind. The weight of the heavy uniform gear and accoutrements would have to be borne without complaint day after day. Tall and athletic, Private Cathay not only looked like the model soldier but also acted like one as well.[41]

In addition, the fact that her cousin and "particular friend" probably still served in the ranks assisted her immeasurably in maintaining her disguise. These three probably would have slept together, eaten together, and marched together during the campaigning. In this way, these two males helped to protect Cathy's great secret.[42]

With Major Merriam leading the way, the troops of the 38th Infantry continued to march through the intense heat and swirling dust of the prairie, heading for the Santa Fe Trail. The column of black infantrymen now trudged toward the faraway outpost—Fort Union, New Mexico—to escape the cholera epidemic. The Buffalo Soldiers and Private Cathay were about to accept a new challenge in a picturesque and wild southwestern land.[43]

During the lengthy march to New Mexico, Company A remained part of Major Merriam's battalion. The new assignment called for the 1st Battalion to report to Fort Union in northeast New Mexico, and to face the Apache menace. With the spread of cholera finally coming under control at Fort Harker, Major Merriam felt that his battalion at this time was "apparently in good health."

In total, more than half of the eleven companies of the 38th Infantry— Companies A, C, D, E, F, H, and K—would be ordered to New Mexico between July to December 1867. These companies of the 1st Battalion remained under Major Merriam's able command. For logistical reasons and safety from possible Indian ambush, the battalion would march to New Mexico in separate columns, after beginning their movements to New Mexico on June 20. Meanwhile, the remainder of the regiment, Companies B, G, I, and J, remained on duty on the plains of Kansas.

Upon reaching Fort Union, Private Cathay and her comrades would not be the first African American troops in northeast New Mexico. The Buffalo Soldiers of the 38th were ordered to Fort Union, in part to replace the troops of the 125th Infantry. This black regiment had been organized in Louisville, Kentucky, during the spring of 1865. Most of the 125th had been transferred west to New Mexico throughout August 1866.

The majority of the 125th had garrisoned Fort Union before marching east to Fort Riley. Here, in east central Kansas and unlike the far-roaming 38th, the 125th Infantry would be disbanded in December 1867; though not before members of the regiment, who had served at Fort Harker, succumbed to cholera the same month.

Discrimination raised its ugly head during Major Merriam's long march toward New Mexico. First, a separate detachment of the 38th, consisting of Companies D and E, moved out from Fort Harker with inadequate medical supplies.

This lack of sufficient medical supplies would prove disastrous. Ten soldiers of these two ill-fated companies, would die of cholera during the lengthy trek through the rolling hills and prairies of western Kansas. Indeed, "inadequate medical supplies caused part of the loss of life among the members of the 38th infantry under [Major] Merriam as it traveled west from Fort Harker to Fort Union, N.M."

Meanwhile, in a separate column, Companies A and K and the headquarters company continued to be led forward by Major Merriam. This detachment consisted of a dozen officers, two hundred and twenty soldiers, nearly forty women, children, and servants, and another forty-four quartermaster employees. Through the sprawling prairies, the column pushed southward for Fort Zarah and then crossed the Smokey Hill River.

Throughout the journey toward the mountains of northeast New Mexico, the troops of Major Merriam's column remained vigilant toward health concerns, taking precautions with sanitation. Under strict orders, the men took steps to prevent the spread of disease. At this time, Merriam's command, including Private Cathay, was fortunate, remaining "comparatively free from the disease," wrote Surgeon Ely McClellan.

Unlike some regimental medical personnel, Major Merriam correctly ascertained the source of the cholera's spread by this time: the thousands of civilian settlers moving westward. This experienced officer, therefore, carefully avoided the long-established campsites now contaminated by cholera-infected migrants.

Private Cathay and her hard-marching comrades passed at a safe distance from the established rest areas and campsites. In addition, great care was taken by Major Merriam in securing fresh, spring-fed drinking water for his men. Merriam's concern for his troops' welfare benefited the soldiers in the ranks, perhaps even saving lives.

Despite these prudent precautions, however, cholera struck down one soldier of Captain Clarke's Company A. Fortunately, Private Cathay was not a victim. Certainly, Cathy Williams knew this young black soldier, who was no doubt an ex-slave like herself. The unlucky soldier had served as a nurse in the Fort Harker cholera infirmary, where he caught the dreaded cholera while assisting his stricken comrades. If she had herself attended to the sick at this infirmary, the news of the soldier's demise would have only increased Cathy's own fears. Because Company A was a small unit, this victim might even have been Cathy Williams's cousin or "particular friend."

Then, five other Buffalo Soldiers fell sick with the disease. The first death came on June 23, when Major Merriam's and Captain Clarke's soldiers marched past Fort Zarah, southwest of Fort Harker on the Arkansas River, after the detachment gained the Santa Fe Trail.

The sudden appearance of the disease caused considerable concern among the ranks. Meanwhile, to counter the outbreak, Major Merriam continued to establish and then shift the nightly camp sites to more healthy locations. By doing so, he continued his strategy of setting up campsites away from those usually utilized by the migrants from the wagon trains.

Such precautions, however, slowed Major Merriam's march to Fort Union, New Mexico, to a crawl. Far from forts and hospitals and isolated in an open country, the Buffalo Soldiers, including Cathy Williams and Company A, grew fearful with cholera's spread; and for good reason. A seasoned physician who knew about the disease and how it spread was Surgeon McClellan. Without exaggeration, he simply called the near panic among the troops as "choleraphobia."

As Surgeon McClellan reasoned, during this leisurely march, "the effect of remaining in camp was evidently so pernicious to the morale of the command, that it was decided to move camp each day, if enabled to make only a few miles." Fortunately, however, Major Merriam's careful precautions in marching along the Santa Fe Trail began to pay dividends. The threat of cholera ended as suddenly as it had begun.

The scourge of cholera finally ended on June 30 as the detachment of Buffalo Soldiers continued to march southwest through the flowing grasslands and rolling hills of the Great Plains, while moving up and parallel to the Arkansas River.

Spirits among the resilient Buffalo Soldiers began to rise as the imminent prospect of death by disease passed at last. Once again, Cathy Williams had given death the slip during the epidemic that had struck down comrades who marched beside her. By this time, ironically, she had already endured many close calls despite having yet to engage the Native Americans in battle.

With "choleraphobia" spreading across the Great Plains among both the military and civilian population, the panic was far from over, however. As the headquarters company and Companies A and K, approached Fort Larned, on the Santa Fe Trail, around forty miles southwest of Fort Zarah, the scare reached new heights.

Fort Larned's acting assistant surgeon was overwhelmed with panic, especially fearing the worst in regard to his own safety. He now worried that the fast-approaching Buffalo Soldiers of Major Merriam's 1st Battalion were bringing the scourge of cholera with them. He therefore requested the fort's commander to immediately issue orders to ban the soldiers of the 38th from entering the post.

Becoming unduly alarmed by a perceived threat that was in fact now nonexistent, Fort Larned's commander heeded the advice of his panicky surgeon. He issued a directive that forbade Major Merriam's soldiers from entering the fort. Denied entry into the post at the last moment, the worn Buffalo Soldiers were instructed instead to encamp within only a few hundred yards of Fort Larned on July 2.

Unfortunately, no reactions by the men in the ranks to this unfair order have been recorded. No doubt Private Cathay and her comrades were incensed by the order. At the encampment outside Fort Larned, Cathy Williams and Company A's soldiers rested for two days. Here, they allowed sore feet and legs to recover. Then, the weary soldiers drew supplies before the resumption of their lengthy march to the mountains of northeast New Mexico.

Shortly after departing Fort Larned, Major Merriam's detachment continued its march up the course of the Arkansas River. Traveling through the broad grasslands and rolling hills looming on all sides, the Buffalo Soldiers now trudged southwest, pushing west along the dusty Santa Fe Trail to reach Fort Dodge on July 7.

Here, on the north bank of the Arkansas, yet another wave of cholera panic struck. On July 31, Fort Dodge's commander, Bvt. Maj. C. S. DeGraw, and his assistant surgeon became convinced that cholera had reached the fort by way of "a detachment of 38th U.S. Colored troops, en route to New Mexico, under [Major] Merriam."

As before, however, this biased rush to judgment—the first cholera fatality in the fort's vicinity, a civilian, was in fact two days after the Buffalo Soldiers left the area and the epidemic would not become serious until July's end and weeks after Major Merriam's departure—was due more to racism than a real threat to life.

After two days of rest among the cool breezes and the cottonwood trees along the Arkansas River, in the vicinity of Fort Dodge, Major Merriam's detachment again shouldered muskets to continue the march. With disciplined step, Cathy Williams and her comrades departed the vicinity of Fort Dodge on July 9. They now continued their long journey to northeast New Mexico. Thankfully by this time, the cholera epidemic had run its course along the Santa Fe Trail, diminishing by the end of July.

The Buffalo Soldiers of the 38th Infantry stationed in Kansas, however, were not as fortunate as Private Cathay and the remainder of Major Merriam's detachment. The cholera epidemic struck Fort Hays, after having been transmitted to the Kansas River outpost by civilian wagon trains. The first soldier of this detachment of the 38th died on July 12. Twenty-three deaths would occur at Fort Hays throughout that summer, with the majority of fatalities occurring in Companies C, E, G, and I.

Also stationed with the Fort Hays garrison at this time was a company of the 10th Cavalry. As a cruel fate would have it, all cholera deaths at Fort Hays were among the African Americans. Ironically, some deaths resulted because the black soldiers, many of whom were superstitious ex-slaves and distrustful of the white man's medical treatments or even his advice, were hesitant to enter the post's cholera infirmary. Because of this, they failed to receive the medical care they desperately needed and thus accelerated the death rate.

Meanwhile, Captain Clarke's Company A suffered from no comparable lack of medical treatment. The Buffalo Soldiers of Company A lost no men to cholera at Fort Harker, despite having served there for nearly three weeks. By merely having served at Fort Harker during the height of the cholera epidemic Cathy Williams had had another close brush with death and survived. Her faith in God and good fortune continued to protect her from harm.

During the march, Private Cathay no doubt was impressed by the sight of huge herds of buffalo that roamed across the grasslands of the Great Plains. These vast herds covered the prairies and rolling hills for dozens of square miles, providing the Native Americans with the staples of life. Josiah Gregg, a Missourian and Jackson County resident during the antebellum period, described that the vast prairies along the Santa Fe Trail were covered by "innumerable buffalo paths, with which these plains are furrowed [and which] in a great many places . . . have all the appearance of immense highways, over which entire armies would seem to have frequently passed."

These buffalo herds were probably first seen by the Buffalo Soldiers of the 38th on the plains of western Kansas, while marching down much of the length of the Santa Fe Trail. Even at this time, the region around the Trail was still considered by the Indians as their sacred hunting grounds. And it was through these sacred hunting grounds that the great buffalo herds had migrated for centuries.

A ruthless master at modern warfare, General Sheridan would wage war on this seemingly inexhaustible food source of the Native Americans. Most of all, he realized that the decimation of the buffalo herds would lead to the destruction of the way of life of these nomadic people.

Indeed, the way of life of the Great Plains Indians depended almost entirely upon the centuries-old support system of the great buffalo herds. But the buffalo was much more than simply a food source to the Native Americans. The animal was revered and worshipped by the Indians who instinctively understood that their own fate was tied directly to the buffalo's existence. The eventual slaughter of the buffalo herds would doom the Plains Indians to destruction, striking at the heart of their spiritual, cultural, and economic system. Kiowa Chief Satanta complained bitterly that "a long time ago this land belonged to our fathers [but now the white] soldiers cut down my timber [and] they kill my buffalo; and when I see that, my heart feels like bursting [and] I feel sorry."

General Sheridan was no doubt awed by sight of the immense buffalo herds that roamed at will across the Great Plains. He wrote in 1868 that "the Plains were covered with vast herds of buffalo—the number has been estimated at 3,000,000 head—and with such means of subsistence as this everywhere at hand, the 6,000 hostiles were wholly unhampered by any problem of food-supply." One partial indication of the immense size of the Kansas herds was the killing of a rare white buffalo by white hunters on the Kansas grasslands as late as 1871.

By the late 1860s, many Great Plains Indians already understood the grim realities for their future, sensing the tragedy not only for the buffalo but also for themselves. Uttering a prophetic vision that promised the inevitable end of the Great Plains Indians' world, Lone Wolf, a Kiowa Chief, declared that "the sun is our father [and] all the buffalo are all his. Our father, the sun, told us that the white men would kill all of them."

While marching along the Santa Fe Trail and through an expansive country, Pvt. William Cathay and the other Company A soldiers saw the vast buffalo herds covering miles of open prairie and grassy valleys. Fortunately, for the hard-marching Buffalo Soldiers, the Indians were not as numerous as the buffalo. Before long, however, both the buffalo and the Great Plains Indians were destined to suffer an identical fate at the hands of the whites: virtual extinction. It was now only a matter of time before the end came for both.

For now, the Great Plains Indians remained a threat to the West's settlement. Against 6,000 warriors of the Great Plains, General Sheridan would lament during this period that "I had in all, east of New Mexico, a force of Regulars numbering about 2,600 men—1,200 mounted and 1,400 foot troops . . . the infantry [was composed] of the 3rd and 5th regiments and four companies of the 38th. With these few troops all the posts along the Smoky Hill and Arkansas had to be garrisoned, emigrant trains escorted, and the settlements and routes of travel and the construction parties on the Kansas-Pacific railway protected."

Quite unlike the more steadfast Buffalo Soldiers, many soldiers on the frontier were of an inferior and unreliable quality. At this time, the frontier army, including the famed 7th Cavalry, contained a high percentage of drunkards, malcontents, deserters, and recent immigrants unable to speak English, who possessed no military experience. Such men often deserted at the first opportunity.

One New York journalist complained that the "Regular Army is composed of bummers, loafers, and foreign paupers." A large percentage of these frontier soldiers—especially the Irish—consisted of urban poor from the ghettos of the major cities of the North and Northeast, such as New York, Boston, and Philadelphia.

Such was not the case, however, with the high-spirited Buffalo Soldiers, who were mostly from rural and agricultural environments. Not only in terms of overall hardiness and physical conditioning, these black troops remained superior quality in terms of motivation, *esprit de corps,* and morale compared with white soldiers. In contrast to white troops, a much larger percentage of black soldiers hailed from rural areas of the Deep and Upper South. In such an environment, like Cathy Williams herself, they had become acclimated both to an arduous and outdoor life as slaves, who led lives of physical activity and hard work. Combined with their previous harsh existence under slavery, this fact also made these black soldiers a more durable and reliable soldiery. The rates of desertion, suicide, and alcoholism were lower among the Buffalo Soldiers than white soldiers on the Western frontier.

During the summer of 1867, the 38th Infantry was part of Sheridan's trouble-plagued military district. This district, in the general's words, included "the States of Missouri and Kansas, the Indian Territory, and New Mexico. Part of this section of country—western Kansas particularly—had been frequently disturbed and harassed during two or three years past, the savages every now and then massacring an isolated family, boldly attacking the surveying and construction parties of the Kansas-Pacific railroad, sweeping down on emigrant trains, plundering and burning stage-stations and the like along the Smoky Hill route to Denver [Colorado] and the Arkansas route to New Mexico."

Meanwhile, Major Merriam's bluecoat troops continued to march along the Santa Fe Trail, pushing toward Fort Union, New Mexico. The dusty march down much of the length of the Santa Fe Trail from Kansas to New Mexico was anything but easy. All the while, Captain Clarke's soldiers were exposed to rains, searing sun, and winds that made life miserable for infantrymen marching down the Trail.

In journeying down the Santa Fe Trail, Josiah Gregg, of Jackson County, Missouri, never forgot the intensity with which violent weather often swept through the prairies or the "bleakest rains and the hottest suns of these bare plains." From Fort Dodge, Major Merriam's detachment of Buffalo Soldiers continued to push west for around fifty miles before crossing the wide Arkansas River.

Then, continuing their march without much time to rest, the black soldiers trudged onward southwestward and deeper into the vastness of the rolling plains of Kansas. The Santa Fe Trail seemed to flow endlessly southwest through the northwest corner of the Indian Territory, now Oklahoma, before finally leading into the mountains of northeast New Mexico. By this time, every soldier in Merriam's command looked forward to the prospect of reaching Fort Union.

Finally and after much effort, the Buffalo Soldiers of Major Merriam's 1st Battalion reached the heavily forested mountains of northeast New Mexico. This was a beautiful land of dense woodlands, spring-fed streams, and crystal-clear lakes swarming with trout. These were the most majestic and highest mountains that Private Cathay had ever seen in her life. Nothing in her home state of Missouri or the South through which she passed during the Civil War could compare.

Marching near and just south of the Raton Pass, where the Raton Mountains peaked, a toll road rose through the mountains. This was an obstacle avoided by Major Merriam because it was in private hands. To avoid the toll, however, was an arduous experience, even for these young and physically fit Buffalo Soldiers.

As the mountain slopes grew steeper, the pack on her back and the Springfield musket on Cathy Williams's shoulder must have felt like lead, growing heavier as the elevation up the mountain increased. In addition, the straps of her canteen, haversack, cartridge box, and other accoutrements cut into Cathy's shoulders: a tangle of gear when combined with a baggy and oversized uniform. Despite the heavy load, Private Cathay managed to gamely keep up with the men of Major Merriam's battalion.

After trekking more than 500 miles southwestward through the prairies of central and southwest Kansas and down more than half the Santa Fe Trail's extensive length, the southeastern corner of Colorado, the northwest corner of the Indian Territory, and the mountains of northeast New Mexico and across the Arkansas and Canadian Rivers, the weary black soldiers of Major Merriam's detachment finally neared Fort Union.

For hundreds of miles all along the trek from Fort Harker to Fort Union, Private Williams kept up with the fast-moving ranks of Company A. After much effort and determination to keep up on such an exhausting march that surpassed even her Civil War experiences, Cathy must have been proud of the fact that she never straggled or fell behind in the ranks. Here, was one factor that made Private Cathay such "a good soldier," in her own words.

Besides the Buffalo Soldiers of Major Merriam's 1st Battalion, five other companies of the 38th Infantry would march into New Mexico from July to October 1867.

After descending the timbered slopes of the Sierra Madre Mountains in late July 1867, Captain Clarke's Company A neared Fort Union, where so much early frontier history had taken place. Built in 1851 in the form of a square with buildings and quarters surrounding the parade ground, Fort Union guarded the Santa Fe Trail and northeast New Mexico. With a large U.S. flag waving over the installation, Fort Union was known as "the key bastion of the Southwest."

Providing protection against Indian attack, the log, timber, and adobe outpost served as the vital "life line of all the other forts strung throughout the breadth and length of Colorado, New Mexico and Arizona; the goal of every caravan going westward across the plains; the fear of the Utes and Apaches." Located in the sprawling valley of the Mora River northeast of Santa Fe, Fort Union was the largest and most important military installation in the entire Southwest and along the Santa Fe Trail in this region.

During the Civil War, earthworks were built around the fort to counter the threat from the nearby Texas Rebels to the east. At this time, Fort Union's commander was Bvt. Maj. William B. Lane. He was a Mexican War veteran who had sided with the Union at the outbreak of war.

Here, near the Mora River, both the Mountain and Cimarron branches of the Santa Fe Trail met on the main road leading from the fabled commercial city of Santa Fe. Cathy Williams's military career and personal destiny continued to take her farther westward along the Santa Fe Trail during the summer of 1867. This was a strange odyssey because her birthplace of Independence was the starting point for the Trail.

Near Fort Union, the mountain branch of the Santa Fe Trail that passed through Raton Pass and the Cimarron branch of the Santa Fe Trail met once again after splitting 250 miles northeast of Fort Union near Fort Dodge, Kansas, uniting for the remaining 90-mile trek southwestward to Santa Fe. At this time, the primary mission of Fort Union's garrison was to protect the settlers, migrants, and caravans of the Santa Fe Trail from rampaging bands of Ute, Kiowa, Jicarilla Apache, and Comanche of northern and eastern New Mexico.[44]

On July 20, 1867, and when finally near their objective after so much toil, the Buffalo Soldiers of Major Merriam's detachment were suddenly thwarted from marching into Fort Union by the unexpected arrival of a Dr. DuBois from the post. Once again, the rumors that the blacks of the 38th Infantry were the cholera carriers had surfaced. And as usual, this occurred at the worst time for the long-suffering soldiers in the ranks.

The physician galloped to the head of the battalion's column, where Company A and Cathy were located, to present Colonel Merriam with new orders. Dr. DuBois now acted on the intelligence recently received from the post surgeon of Fort Lyon, who wrote an urgent letter to Fort Union's commander to inform him "of the prevalence of Cholera in two companies of the 38th Infty en route" to his garrison.

Responding to this news, Fort Union's commander, Colonel Lane, and the post's chief surgeon decided to establish a quarantine camp for the fagged soldiers of the 38th outside the fort. These officers believed that it was absolutely necessary to stop the Buffalo Soldiers from reaching Fort Union for fear of spreading cholera to the garrison. No doubt to their dismay but probably not surprised by the sudden development, Cathy Williams and her comrades were now directed to resume their march to a preestablished location on Ocate Creek and await additional orders.

For troops who were dirty, tired, and hungry after having marched more than 500 miles from Fort Harker in central Kansas, the unexpected order that suddenly denied their entry into Fort Union when practically within sight of it was an outrage.[45]

Without a choice and no doubt angry by the injustice that was turning into an all-too familiar pattern, the thwarted Buffalo Soldiers were forced to resume marching. At last, Private Cathay and her comrades reached the quarantine camp on Ocate Creek nine miles from a ranch owned by a Mr. Calhoun, without ever having set foot in Fort Union. Not even the column's teamsters or the six laundresses were allowed to enter Fort Union.

After an exhausting 530-mile march that was no small accomplishment in the broiling heat of summertime, more than 223 Buffalo Soldiers of Major Merriam's detachment began to realize that the unexpected new orders now translated into an extra measure of recuperation rather than the usual routine of Fort Union's menial duties. Such assigned work at the fort would have normally included collecting firewood, cooking, kitchen, and cleaning details, and routine patrols of the surrounding countryside.

Clearly, some advantages were gained by the weary Buffalo Soldiers with this respite in quarantine. At long last, paradoxically, they had finally benefited indirectly from the lingering stereotype that blacks spread disease. The infantrymen of Major Merriam's command now enjoyed a relatively relaxed existence in the quarantine camp, resting sore feet and legs after the lengthy trek to New Mexico.

Fortunately, this campsite, located on picturesque Ocate Creek, was ideally situated. The new encampment was described as "one of the most beautiful and healthful . . . [situated] in a pine grove[, which was] more like a park [with] wood, fine grass, and pure mountain water in abundance."[46]

Here, Cathy Williams and the Buffalo Soldiers of the 38th recuperated from their long march into New Mexico. Finally, on August 12, 1867, the quarantine of Major Merriam's soldiers ended after more than three weeks of general inactivity. As in the past, the rumors that the Buffalo Soldiers were the carriers of the cholera epidemic proved false. A measure of ever-present racism was again responsible for playing a large part in labeling the black soldiers of Major Merriam's 1st Battalion as the epidemic's promulgators.

Now, Cathy Williams, along with the other infantrymen of the 38th, once again put on her gear and shouldered her musket. With Major Merriam leading the way, the battalion marched proudly into Fort Union with banners flying.[47]

Long before the arrival of Private Cathay and her comrades, Fort Union had encountered a host of other disease problems besides the cholera epidemic. The ravages of scurvy had spread through the garrison during the winter of 1867. In addition, Fort Union recently experienced another type of trouble that developed in December 1866. This was the nagging problem of women who knew how to make money on the side in other ways: prostitution was a common nocturnal occupation at remote frontier outposts. Like other frontier forts, Fort Union possessed its own "laundress quarters." Some Fort Union laundresses were as active in their lucrative extracurricular activities as in washing soldiers' dirty uniforms.

For example, one African American woman named Cielia was banished from Fort Union for "immoral conduct." However, she would return to the fort by the time that Private Cathay served there. Likewise, Annie McGee, an Irish woman, and a Hispanic woman named Coruz were also banished from Fort Union for immoral conduct with the men of the garrison.[48]

Here, amid the mountains of northeast New Mexico, Cathy Williams now found a place and a land that she would grow to love. She was no doubt overwhelmed by the majestic beauty and serenity of the wide valleys, grassy meadows, aspen-covered slopes, and snow-capped mountains, more than any other place that she had seen before. Additionally, the local Hispanic culture was more open and tolerant toward African Americans to a degree unimaginable in Missouri and especially farther south.

New Mexico was far more multicultural, with its unique blend of rich Hispanic and Indian heritage, traditions, and cultures. Unlike her native Missouri, Hispanic and Indian peoples in general looked upon blacks with a measure of greater equality and fairness than whites. For example, in a vote of confidence that demonstrated considerable respect, the black chaplain of the 24th Infantry, John N. Shultz, would in the future be selected by the people of New Mexico as the manager and director of New Mexico's educational affairs in the National Education Association.[49]

Most women, including officers' wives, in the frontier West, generally tended to be more open-minded, tolerant, and less prejudiced toward Hispanic peoples than army officers. Rejecting the prejudiced stereotype of an inferior culture, many white women became enchanted with Hispanic culture. Many officers' wives found special meaning in the traditional values and strong bonds of the Hispanic family that were fortified by the Catholic church and strong religious faith.

Cathy Williams, no doubt, also viewed Hispanics and their more open and tolerant culture with sympathy if not admiration. In general, the Buffalo Soldiers blended in more easily with the multicultural communities of the frontier West than the white soldiers who usually maintained strong beliefs in their own racial and cultural superiority. This was one factor that explained why the Buffalo Soldiers, both infantry and cavalry, were generally less dissatisfied with Western frontier duty than white troops.[50]

But perhaps the most significant factor bolstering the moral strength of the Buffalo Soldiers was their solidarity to succeed in their frontier roles despite the odds. In addition, they possessed a unifying experience rooted in both slavery and Civil War service along with unity of color, a shared ancestral heritage, and pride in a distinctive culture that also supported high morale. Throughout their distinguished history, the Buffalo Soldiers possessed "a strong desire among the men to prove to the army, to society, and to themselves that they could soldier as well as white troops."[51]

Duty for young Private Cathay and Company A's soldiers during their stay at Fort Union was brief. Major Merriam's battalion, including Captain Clarke's company, received another assignment in late summer. The battalion, along with Company A, was now ordered to Fort Cummings, New Mexico, to relieve the men of Company D, 155th Infantry. This infantry company was reassigned to Fort Union and was soon destined to be mustered out of service with the rest of its regiment.

With the blast of a bugle, Private Cathay and her comrades assembled. Captain Clarke formed Company A on the wide parade ground of Fort Union. Here, in a neat formation that included the remainder of Major Merriam's battalion, the Buffalo Soldiers of Company A stood at attention in full gear and prepared to march again.

Eager for the new assignment at Fort Cummings, 101 soldiers of the 1st Battalion, including Private Cathay and Company A, marched out of Fort Union on September 7. In the cool of early morning, the Buffalo Soldiers now pushed toward Fort Cummings in southwest New Mexico, less than 100 miles north of the U.S.-Mexico border. Even though the nights had grown chilly by this time, the troops of the 38th Infantry felt little concern for the approach of fall because their trek would take them into an arid region of southern New Mexico.

To Private Cathay and the other Buffalo Soldiers who had been on the move almost continually since departing central Kansas, and after having already trudged more than 500 miles down the Santa Fe Trail, this latest trek had them feeling that they were marching to the end of the earth. No doubt, some of the soldiers would have now wondered just how far their military service would take them or where the march would finally end.

On the march to southwestern New Mexico, the other officers of Company A, 1st Lt. William E. Sweet and 2nd Lt. Henry F. Leggett, made sure Company A's ranks were neat, closed-up, and in order. Straggling would slow down the column. And these officers were determined to prevent this vice as much as possible.

Evidently some discontent had begun to simmer and then fester among the Buffalo Soldiers by this time. The first signs of unrest surfaced during the lengthy march through the heart of New Mexico from Fort Union to Fort Cummings. Departing Fort Union caused some dissatisfaction among the Buffalo Soldiers because "Fort Union was the most beloved military post in New Mexico and . . . every soldier ever stationed there cherished and loved it as a college student loves his Alma-Mater."

An unknown number of Buffalo Soldiers of Cathy's Company A were also evidently upset by the never-ending orders that kept them on the move. While they marched endlessly across the Western frontier, most white soldiers remained billeted at comfortable forts, eating better food, and drawing the same pay for inactivity. In contrast, the men of the 38th were seemingly always ordered to keep moving on to the next fort, almost as if each post commander wanted to rid himself of the black soldiers. Some of Company A's soldiers, and no doubt Private Cathay as well, probably suspected racism as one explanation for their gypsy existence and the inexplicable orders from white officers that kept them marching for hundreds of miles by themselves.

In overall terms, however, the Buffalo Soldiers' reassignment to Fort Cummings indicated the changed situation in General Sheridan's military district, which now "was comparatively quiet," wrote the general, after "active military operations [were] . . . suspended in the attempt to conclude a permanent peace with the Cheyennes, Arapahoes, Kiowas, and Comanches, in compliance with the act of Congress creating what was known as the Indian Peace Commission of 1867." The order to reassign the Buffalo Soldiers of Company A from Fort Union to Fort Cummings was, however, apparently also due to the continuing rumor that they carried cholera.

As General Sherman's report noted, Indian troubles had eased by this time. A peace treaty would be signed at Medicine Lodge in the autumn of 1867 and during Pvt. William Cathay's term of service: an event for which she could have given thanks. This long-sought treaty eased the tensions in Indian country, offering a faint glimmer of hope for a brighter future and a peaceful frontier. Warfare on the Central Great Plains ceased for the most part. However, this was an uneasy and nervous peace, however, offering a grim foreboding of events to come as each side hoped for the best but expected the worst.

Many military men now believed that the Medicine Lodge Treaty—which resulted in the issuance of arms, ammunition, and other gifts, including old Civil War uniforms, to the Indians to demonstrate the government's good faith—was little more than a clever ploy by the Native Americans to rearm themselves before opening the next round of hostilities. For good reason and from bitter experience learned from past dealings with whites, the Great Plains Indians realized that this fragile peace would not stop the whites' hunger for land.

Consequently, the Native Americans acted accordingly, taking advantage of the opportunity to prepare for a renewal of hostilities. An Arikara chief named White Shield summarized the Plains Indians' feeling about this treaty, stating that the whites "are afraid of us [and] they ask for peace . . . Did we believe their words? No. Were we tempted by their promises? No. Did we act according to their advice? No."

During the last days of a balmy September 1867, meanwhile, Private Cathay and the troops of Company A and Major Merriam's battalion continued to trudge southeastward towards Fort Cummings. Along the way, the land gradually became more parched and arid, as they pushed toward the Mexican border. At some point along the march southward down the east bank of the Rio Grande, the Buffalo Soldiers forded the river, crossing from the east to the west side. Private Cathay and her comrades had no choice but to swim through the cold waters of the Rio Grande, as it descended from the mountains of northeast New Mexico and plunged through the lower desert lands and toward Mexico.

Evidently the Buffalo Soldiers were forced to swim the Rio Grande because they were unable to find a suitable fording point. Or perhaps they could not cross because the river was rain-swollen.

Along with extreme physical exertion, living and sleeping out in the open, eating scanty and poor quality rations, and marching day after day through heat, rain, and cold, Cathy Williams's ill-advised swim across the Rio Grande River contributed to the long-term deterioration of her health. After swimming across the river, she then slept on the cold ground with the rest of her comrades at the evening's campsite.

On October 1, 1867, and after much effort in trudging across the deserts of southern New Mexico, Cathy Williams and her comrades of Company A and Major Merriam's 1st Battalion finally reached the adobe and wooden compound known as Fort Cummings without incident. At no point in marching through Apache country had they encountered the elusive Apache. No doubt, Private Cathay, still a novice in regard to fighting Indians and frontier warfare, was relieved by reaching Fort Cummings without encountering hostile tribes.

Here, between the Mimbres Mountains to the north and the Florida Mountains to the south, Captain Clarke led his Company A through the gates of Fort Cummings. Relatively new, the fort had been established during the Civil War in 1863. At long last, the seemingly endless marching of Private Williams and her comrades finally came to an end.

The arrival of Company A and Major Merriam's 1st Battalion resulted in the relief of Company D, 155th Infantry, which was to now march back to Fort Union. Here, at the eastern entrance of Cooke's Canyon, near Cooke's Peak of Cooke's Range of mountains just west of Fort Cummings, the new assignment would prove to be beneficial for Captain Clarke, though not for the Buffalo Soldiers.

Clarke would soon take command of Fort Cummings, having received recognition for his leadership skills during both Civil War and postwar service. The captain's advancement no doubt initially delighted the men under his command. From the beginning, this fair-minded officer was admired by his troops. As they had learned from past experiences, however, the soldiers of Company A also probably realized that a good chance existed that their next commander could not possibly be as enlightened and fair-minded as Captain Clarke.

Just east of the Mimbres River and the imposing Continental Divide, Fort Cummings was one of the few protected and walled forts on the Western frontier. Located in the heart of the deserts of southwest New Mexico, Fort Cummings was built of adobe, with ten-foot walls that offered good protection for the diminutive garrison. Fort Cummings's structural strength indicated what was needed for defensive purposes and the extent of the fort's isolation deep in Apache country.

The first Buffalo Soldier to be killed in the Territory of New Mexico was Pvt. Samuel Taylor, 155th Infantry, who was slain in October 1866 by Apache.

Taylor was part of Fort Cummings's garrison and his death came only a month before Cathy Williams joined the 38th Infantry at Jefferson Barracks.

Private Cathay now found herself in the heart of Apache country. This was the most forbidding land in which the Buffalo Soldiers of the 38th Infantry had been stationed to date. This dangerous service in a barren desert did nothing to lift Company A's spirits. The land was bleak and parched, and in sharp contrast to the beauty of the mountains of northeast New Mexico.

Duties at Fort Cummings were focused on countering the ever-elusive Apache. On occasion, the Apache even approached the walls of the fort to steal horses and cattle. Consequently, the troops of the 155th Infantry were mounted on horses to fight the Apache more effectively. But no tactical adjustments or innovations by the frustrated post commander could match the combat prowess and skill of the wide-ranging Apache. In the words of the vexed commander of Fort Cummings, the hard-hitting Apache "could run faster and hide quicker than we could."

Named in honor of Maj. Joseph Cummings who was killed by the Navaho in 1863, Fort Cummings, surrounded by rough terrain, was nestled in Cooke's Canyon. Here, the isolated fort protected the main road leading from Mesilla, New Mexico, to Tucson, Arizona, along the southern route that led westward to southern California and Los Angeles.

For the remainder of 1867, Private Cathay faithfully performed her assigned duties at this isolated frontier outpost. Clearly, this remote assignment in the desert was essentially an exile in a parched, strange land, and this realization began to affect the soldiers' morale.

By far, the most dangerous duty for the Buffalo Soldiers at Fort Cummings were the daily wood details. The members of these details were forced to travel long distances across the desert in search of wood for fuel. These wood details were vulnerable not only because they went well beyond the safe confines of the fort, but also because they consisted of only small parties of soldiers.

The wood details were required to find wood in the barren landscape a good distance from Fort Cummings but initially no farther than fifteen miles away. This duty involved many hours of hard and thankless work with axes. Soldiers cut down trees, chopped up the wood, and then with wagons pulled by mules hauled the heavy loads back through the desert to the relative safety of Fort Cummings.

Worst of all, these isolated groups of woodcutters were especially vulnerable to Apache ambush or attack. The danger increased as wood sources became rapidly depleted and alternate sources in the immediate vicinity of the fort could not be found. The only solution was for the wood details to travel even greater distances from the safety of Fort Cummings and possible rein-forcements: a serious situation if a fight erupted. By the fall of 1867 the wood details were traveling as far as twenty-five miles west of Fort Cummings to cut trees along the Mimbres River.

During the winter of 1867–68, Cpl. Fredrick Wormley of Company A was in charge of the wood details and guards. Like other noncommissioned officers in the regiment, Corporal Wormley was an African American with leadership ability recognized by his white officers. The appointment of a cor-poral from Cathy's own Company A indicated that she was certainly a mem-ber of these wood details on occasion.

This is even more likely given the fact that the post commander was forced to employ every available soldier to cut and haul wood to meet the fort's ever-increasing needs. Wood was almost as scarce in this section of the New Mexico desert as water, especially after so much wood had already been cut by previous garrison troops.

Private Cathay remained a good soldier during the last eight months of her service, which saw her continuing to successfully meet the demands of her duty. Throughout her term of service, Cathy Williams's personal service record and own words indicate that she was not a disciplinary problem to her officers. When in good health, she continued to perform her duties as well and competently as any of her male counterparts of Company A. Neither Captain Clarke or any other white officer found reason to punish her for any offense. From beginning to end, she managed to stay out of trouble. All the while, she accomplished all assigned tasks and duties, including traversing more than a thousand miles on the march in a relatively short period.

During her term of service, Cathy Williams possessed an uncanny ability to steer clear of any kind of trouble, partly to avoid having her sex discovered, but most of all to demonstrate her equality, to prove that she was a "good sol-dier." Cathy did anything and everything by the rules and regulations, per-forming as well, if not better, than the other soldiers of Company A. Throughout her period of service, Private Cathay continued to demonstrate that she was a soldier who could be depended upon for any duty or assign-ment.

At Fort Cummings, typical duties for Private Cathay included guard duty, work details, and an occasional scout or patrol in the surrounding country-side. The soldiers of the 38th were now truly on active service, and in conse-quence discipline at Fort Cummings became more harsh, and punishment by white officers for infractions of the rules was swiftly delivered. At this time, typical field punishments included bucking and gagging, spread-eagling, marching in heavy gear, and suspension from thumbs or arms.[52]

Equally discouraging for the African Americans was the fact that menial labor was performed by the soldiers of the 38th more often than military duties. In general, the black soldiers of the Western frontier were handed more menial chores than white troops. This was another source of a simmering discontent among the proud Buffalo Soldiers at Fort Cummings, reminding them of the mindless labor they had performed as slaves not so long ago.

Typical manual labor consisted of chopping and hauling wood, building quarters or roads, erecting telegraph lines or bridges, painting, blacksmithing, carpentry, cooking, bricklaying, plastering, and driving wagons. In addition, much repair work was needed at Fort Cummings. Consequently, the post commander requested 5,000 feet of lumber and lime for the completion of two sets of officers' quarters.[53]

As time passed in the bleak deserts of southwest New Mexico, the mundane tasks and menial labor continued to sap the Buffalo Soldiers' morale, especially at such an isolated, cheerless outpost as Fort Cummings. After all, these African Americans had enlisted to fight Indians, make the West safe for settlement, and to facilitate westward expansion. As explained one disgruntled officer on the Western frontier: "[T]his 'labor of the troops' was a great thing [but] it made the poor wretch who enlisted under the vague notion that his admiring country needed his services to quell hostile Indians, suddenly find himself a brevet architect, carrying a hod and doing odd jobs."[54]

Despite the boring menial duties performed at Fort Cummings, which reminded these former slaves of their labor in the not-so-distant past, the Buffalo Soldiers continued to find solace by taking pride in their nickname, which had been bestowed upon them by their enemies. Perhaps the most fierce Indians of the Great Plains, the Cheyenne, gave the black warriors the sobriquet Buffalo Soldiers "because their heads are so much like the matted cushion that is between the horns of the buffalo," penned one officer's wife of the tribute.

But more significant, the proud name of Buffalo Soldier reflected the fighting spirit of these courageous black cavalrymen and infantry. The sobriquet was appropriate because these African Americans in blue uniforms were named in honor of the Indians' most revered creature. These Indians worshipped the buffalo more than any other animal, believing that it possessed special wisdom, strength, and courage. At first, the Indians called the African Americans "the black whitemen," but that name was quickly abandoned after the Native Americans learned the hard way of the fighting prowess of the black soldiers.

Indicating an even greater degree of respect for the fighting abilities and tenacity of the African American soldiers, the Plains Indians preferred to face white troops rather than African Americans in combat. The hard-fighting

"Buffalo soldier[s were] no good," explained one Indian of the Native Americans' fear of encountering black soldiers in combat.[55]

In time, however, that level of fear of the African American troops would evolve into an even greater measure of respect until an affinity developed between the Native Americans and the Buffalo Soldiers. Based upon a number of well-known incidents, it became a common belief among the troops on the Western frontier that "the Indians never shot a colored man unless it was necessary [and] they always wanted to win the friendship of the Negro race, and obtain their aid in campaigns against the white man."

Ironically, such an affinity between the African Americans and the Native Americans was sometimes stronger than between the Buffalo Soldiers and the native Hispanics of New Mexico. For instance, the black soldiers and Hispanics clashed in violent altercations, such as the confrontations between Fort Union's African Americans and local New Mexican residents in June 1869.[56]

CHAPTER SEVEN

Racial Clash at Fort Cummings

BY THE ADVENT OF THE COLD AND OCCASIONALLY RAINY DAYS OF DECEMBER 1867, all was not well in Captain Clarke's Company A. Perhaps having been ordered from beloved Fort Union and the beautiful mountains of northeast New Mexico to the remote desert outpost was sufficient reason to cause some discontent among the Buffalo Soldiers.

In addition, Fort Cummings was congested and uncomfortable. The fort's walls kept the garrison enclosed and confined in a relatively small area. Worst of all and unlike service at the picturesque Fort Union, the never-ending wood details and work at Fort Cummings involved a daily risk to life in the desert wilds.

In many ways, therefore, Fort Cummings seemed more like a prison than a fort. Hard work in making never-ending improvements, the ever-present dangers of Apache country, the harshness of the desert, the outpost's remoteness, and the overwhelming isolation of the place all combined to affect the Buffalo Soldiers's morale. This discontent was greater in Private Cathay's Company A than in any other company.

In this unforgiving desert environment and under harsh conditions that taxed even the most steadfast Buffalo Soldier, the ugly specter of racism now raised its head among the ranks of the 38th Infantry. A legacy of tensions from the Civil War, a considerable racial gulf existed between the white officers and their black troops, especially in the heavily politicized and cutthroat postwar army. Besides obvious racial factors, the socioeconomic, cultural, and class differences between black and white also served to widen the gap, which could not be bridged by military service and seemed to be acerbated by close association.

Such lack of communication and understanding between the races was not unusual despite the fact that these men were now battling for the same cause. This gulf was wider in regard to officers—the best educated and most aristocratic men of the regiment—and the common solders in the ranks—mostly former slaves—who could neither read nor write. To an ex-slave, an overbearing autocratic officer seemed little different than the slaveowner or overseer on the Southern plantation of old. Such a memory naturally made these former slaves highly sensitive in defending their newly won rights, especially if officers became abusive out of racism.

For instance, even the idolized Col. Robert Gould Shaw, an aristocratic blue blood from Boston, Massachusetts, who was killed during the Civil War while leading his 54th Massachusetts during the bloody assault on Fort Wagner, was never quite able to fully understand or closely identify with his own black troops.

As during the Civil War, a considerable gap existed between black and white soldiers on the Western frontier. Differences between blacks and whites in the army were highlighted by the inferior quality of the army's officer corps. Men unable to succeed in civilian society or who were frustrated by the lack of advancement opportunities in white regiments often served as officers of the Buffalo Soldiers.[1]

By this time, the world of Private Cathay entailed facing a variety of threats. The nonending hostility and prejudice from whites, both civilian and military, often forced the average Buffalo Soldier to arm himself with unauthorized weapons for self-protection against both abusive officers and hostile civilians. In addition and if such was the case, Cathy Williams possessed another good reason to arm herself for protection: her sex, especially if her true identity was discovered.

In the words of a Nebraska journalist during the postwar period, "colored men [in service] have a great hobby for carrying about revolvers and jackknives." Indeed, many Buffalo Soldiers had good reason to arm themselves for protection. While Cathy Williams was serving in 1867, for example, three black infantrymen were lynched by a mob at Fort Hays in west central Kansas, just west of Fort Harker where Private Cathay and Captain Clarke's Company A had been stationed. Unfortunately, during this period, "civilian animosity posed danger for African American soldiers nearly comparable to their confrontations with Native Americans or desperadoes."[2]

At remote Fort Cummings, omnipresent racism and ever-widening differences between blacks and their white officers finally erupted to cause turmoil. This volatile situation would force the black soldiers of Company A to take bold action in defense of their rights.

One of the most potentially serious racial clashes in the history of African American regiments first began from a racial incident caused by two autocratic white officers of Company A, especially Second Lieutenant Leggett. More a case of standing up for their hard-won rights rather than the army's official version of a "mutiny" or the long-accepted version of a black plot to kill the white officers in order to run off with the fort's white women to secure wives for themselves, the Buffalo Soldiers of Company A rose up in righteous indignation on Sunday, December 1, 1867.

The eruption of racial passions occurred exactly two months to the day that the companies of the 38th Infantry first marched into the gates of Fort Cummings. By this time the Buffalo Soldiers were even more frustrated with life at Fort Cummings. In general, hardened black veterans of the Civil War were often the quickest to resent insults and discrimination, standing up defiantly against unfair and abusive treatment from white officers. It was these veterans who often organized united protest against discriminatory treatment and punishment from racist officers.

Resentment among the Buffalo Soldiers against unfair or harsh treatment was explained in the words of a private of the 38th, George Douglas, who swore that "no white son of a bitch can tie a man up [a standard army punishment] here" at Fort Cummings. Clearly, these proud men were highly sensitive and vigilant of their personal rights and any unfair treatment stemming from racism.

Partly justifying their resistance to white authority, these Buffalo Soldiers of Company A now believed that open defiance was necessary because they were handed more severe punishments than white soldiers. In general, these newly freed African Americans felt that their freedom from arbitrary and discriminatory treatment had been ensured with slavery's death in 1865. After all, the Thirteenth Amendment transformed these ex-slaves into U.S. citizens with rights equal to any white citizen in the nation.

Unfortunately for the Buffalo Soldiers of the 38th, however, what had not died in the postwar army was racism, discrimination, and bigotry. Many white soldiers still resented the fact that African Americans were allowed the privilege of wearing the blue uniform and serving their country. To Company A's soldiers it must have seemed that the racism, the kind that had allowed slavery to flourish in America for generations, still thrived under the U.S. flag that flew over Fort Cummings.

In the postwar military, regulations, no matter how despotic, stupid, or unfair, had to be obeyed, and any purely democratic action of individuals, especially African Americans, standing up for fair treatment and against abusive conduct—resistance that was perfectly acceptable, if not admired, in civilian life—was interpreted as "mutiny" by the military. Such a natural protest and reaction against abusive authority, especially from the enlisted ranks and by black soldiers, was seen by white military authorities as a revolt.

Here, at forlorn Fort Cummings, the most serious trouble in the history of the 38th Infantry first developed from an incident involving a woman named Mattie Merritt, sparking the clash between black and white. Attached to Cathy's own Company A, Mattie evidently was a black female servant of Second Lieutenant Leggett.

Mattie was a longtime favorite of the soldiers of Company A, perhaps even a relative of some men. For whatever reason, Mattie Merritt was considered one of their own. In contrast, the dictatorial Lieutenant Leggett was the most unpopular and autocratic officer of Company A and perhaps of the entire regiment.

The difficulty first began when Lieutenant Leggett discovered money missing from his quarters on Sunday morning, December 1, 1867. Without investigating the matter in detail, he immediately blamed Mattie, his servant, for the theft despite having no proof. Instead he automatically assumed that she had taken his money.

It is not known if another white officer, or a Buffalo Soldier stole Lieutenant Leggett's money. In fact, trouble in Company A had been brewing for some time. An unbending martinet and disciplinarian, Lieutenant Leggett treated the black soldiers more like slaves than U.S. soldiers.

The acting officer of the day, First Lieutenant Sweet, ordered Mattie searched upon discovering that the money was missing. But none of Lieutenant Leggett's money was found on her. Evidently, the search was anything but gentle. Mattie, especially if innocent, certainly denied the charge, or might have either protested or even offered some resistance.

Either way, Lieutenant Sweet simply ordered the arbitrary search of Mattie without any evidence to do so. Apparently, the search was conducted not by a woman or a Buffalo Soldier but by white males, which only further aggravated the already simmering racial tensions. Perhaps the search of Mattie was more personal and thorough than was necessary.

Without discovering Lieutenant Leggett's missing money on Mattie or any evidence that she stole the money, Lieutenant Sweet now decided to order Mattie banished from Fort Cummings. Worst of all, an exiled and unarmed woman—or even a solitary soldier for that matter—banished from the safety of the fort into the harsh desert in the middle of nowhere, deep in the heart of Apache country, faced a virtual death sentence. The soldiers of Company A realized as much and decided to do something about it. They fully understood not only the injustice of Lieutenant Sweet's order but also its almost certain fatal implications for Mattie Merritt.

The soldiers of Company A were incensed by Mattie's banishment order by the time they formed in a neat line for Sunday morning inspection. In a surly mood, the Buffalo Soldiers were "sullen and insolent" because of the unfair treatment dealt out to Mattie. Lieutenants Leggett and Sweet quickly recognized the open discontent in Company A.

The two officers, now concerned, decided to intimidate their dissatisfied black soldiers by instilling harsher discipline in an attempt to keep the men in their places. In this way, they hoped to defuse the situation and demonstrate their authority. As events would prove, however, this strategy was a mistake because Company A's soldiers would no longer be cowed by injustice.

The two white lieutenants attempted to flex their authority during the Sunday morning parade ground inspection. While inspecting, Lieutenant Sweet discovered what he considered to be dirty Springfield muskets, uniforms, and accoutrements among Company A's soldiers.

Punishments, more severe than usual, were immediately issued for those soldiers who allegedly had dirty gear and weapons, which may or may not have been soiled. As usual, however, Private Cathay was not singled out for any infraction.

Taking advantage of the opportunity to apply the full weight of his authority to intimidate his troops, Lieutenant Sweet became more overbearing than usual. The severity of these punishments was unwarranted under the circumstances. He ordered several offenders to stand tightly bound atop water barrels in the center of the parade ground for a lengthy period. Such a public humiliation was not only an unusually harsh punishment but was especially degrading to a proud Buffalo Soldier.

Again, such infractions for dirty gear and weapons during the Sunday morning inspection were usually not serious offenses, especially for white soldiers. These African Americans, however, were now not being severely punished primarily because of the state of their kit; they were being punished in part because they were black, in sympathy with Mattie's plight, and disgruntled over her harsh treatment.

Given this volatile situation and the severity of the punishments combined with Mattie's ordered banishment, Company A was suddenly transformed into a powder keg of resentment. The angry men of Private Cathay's company, perhaps including Cathy herself, decided to resist and rise up in protest. They would now defy their officers and the U.S. Army for what they believed was right. These soldiers of Company A were now determined to stand up against what they felt was wrong.

Concerning Mattie's ordered banishment, Lieutenant Sweet's actions might be understood if in fact he had been drinking or harbored a personal grudge against Mattie. Perhaps she had earlier resisted an advance by him. But most likely, racial tensions had escalated during the fatiguing march from Fort Union until they erupted with Mattie's ordered banishment. The Mattie Merritt incident merely brought simmering racial animosities to a boiling point, acting as a catalyst that led to an eruption of emotions.

This situation had escalated partly because Lieutenants Leggett and Sweet evidently began to fear for their own safety. These two veteran officers had therefore decided that only harsh discipline could stop developments from spiraling out of control. Clearly, Lieutenant Sweet had overreacted, compounding previous mistakes by adding fuel to the increasingly volatile situation, stacking one bad decision upon the other.

To confront the crisis and to save their beloved Mattie, the soldiers of Company A assembled on their own and without orders around 2:00 P.M. during the tense Sunday afternoon after inspection. Given her past experiences and independent nature, Cathy Williams was most likely present beside her comrades.

The disgruntled Buffalo Soldiers gathered around the post's flagstaff in the parade ground to discuss their options in the emotion-charged situation. They wanted to do all in their power to keep Mattie safely within the fort's walls and out of harm's way. Symbolically standing up for their rights under the inspiring sight of "Old Glory" waving over the parade ground, this was an unauthorized gathering of black enlisted men and noncommissioned officers who met to confront the emergency situation.

At the time, this ad hoc assembly was unknown to the white officers. Clearly, the disgruntled African Americans had decided to take matters into their own hands. Consequently, they were now acting independently and taking defiant action that they believed was necessary under the circumstances.

The central figure and leading spirit of Company A's resistance was the highly respected sergeant of the guard, Thorton Reeves. Instead of ordering the Buffalo Soldiers back to their quarters as was his duty, he instead rallied additional support among his increasingly defiant men. Returning from Lieutenant Sweet's quarters, 1st Sgt. William Yeatman arrived to ascertain the purpose of the unauthorized gathering around the post's flagpole.

Sensing serious trouble in the air, an incredulous Yeatman, who feared the wrath of white authority and retribution, immediately went up to Sergeant Reeves and asked if he were drunk to allow such an illegal assembly of enlisted troops without officers' knowledge or consent. As if standing up to defy a harsh master or overseer, Sergeant Reeves angrily responded: "No, By God, I isn't drunk, the best thing you can do is go to your quarters!"

Demonstrating that he was the leading spirit of resistance, Sergeant Reeves then roared that "he had hell in him." He also warned First Sergeant

Yeatman that "I have read you through, and God damn you I'll kill you if you are the last God damned nigger that lives!" With this none too subtle warning, Sergeant Yeatman was understandably concerned about his own welfare.

Finally learning from Sergeant Yeatman of the unauthorized assembly on the fort's parade ground, and after the Buffalo Soldiers had ignored the black sergeant's order for them to return to quarters, Captain Clarke took action. He stalked to the parade ground. Captain Clarke immediately ordered his men back to their quarters. Only then did the Company A soldiers "reluctantly obey" the orders from their respected commanding officer. Only the high amount of esteem that the Buffalo Soldiers held for Captain Clarke broke up the gathering.

Captain Clarke, however, failed to inquire about either the source or the nature of the problem or the severity of the situation. He therefore underestimated the seriousness of the problem and never fully understood either why his men were upset or the degree of their anger. Evidently, the captain believed that it had been not much more than an unauthorized social gathering.

Captain Clarke was perhaps unaware of Mattie Merritt's ordered banishment and saw no cause for open defiance among his men, and suspected none. By this time, a rift existed not only between the black soldiers and their white officers, but also between Captain Clarke—who was viewed by Lieutenants Leggett and Sweet as too sympathetic to the African Americans—and his junior officers. The situation within the company was not helped by the personal animosity between the two Buffalo Soldiers, Sergeants Reeves and Yeatman. So the intensifying conflict within Company A went beyond purely racial lines, also embracing personal divisions based on rank, political cliques, and social status.

First Sergeant Yeatman failed to inform Captain Clarke of the situation's seriousness because of Sergeant Reeves's threat and the punishments that would surely follow for such open defiance. Consequently, the heated emotions within Company A continued to simmer throughout December 1. The situation was now escalating. The harsh discipline of Lieutenants Leggett and Sweet had failed after misplaced optimism allowed them to believe that the Buffalo Soldiers could be easily cowed by their authority.

More discontent developed within Company A from the actions of Pvt. John Holt. He continued to encourage the men to stand up for the rights of all African Americans. The soldiers of Company A continued to gather in small groups without orders, grumbling quietly among themselves in their discontent, while steaming over the injustice to Mattie. The sight, however, of Sergeant Yeatman, whom the blacks did not trust as they considered him an "Uncle Tom," caused the Buffalo Soldiers to disperse once again.

Finally, the sun set over the deserts of New Mexico. The darkness that descended over Fort Cummings did nothing to smother the anger still smoldering among the soldiers of Company A. Private Cathay probably shared her comrades' grievances and acted defiantly. If not, however, that was understandable given her unique situation. Unlike the men in the ranks, Cathy Williams had more at stake and more to lose if arrested and confined: an immediate discharge if her sex was discovered.

On the following morning, Monday, December 2, the African Americans were even more angry with Lieutenant Sweet because of Mattie's impending banishment. The leader of the protest continued to be the defiant Sergeant Reeves. A natural leader, Sergeant Reeves was a tough Civil War veteran of the 16th U.S. Colored Infantry, which consisted of ex-slaves mostly from Tennessee.

At some point, Lieutenant Sweet and Sergeant Reeves confronted each other on the night of December 1. Sergeant Reeves swore that Lieutenant Sweet, who was attempting to intimidate Company A's leader, threatened to kill him. The African American sergeant then began carrying a loaded revolver at all times for protection. Sergeant Reeves declared that he would "kill him [Sweet] before tomorrow night," before the lieutenant could make good on his own promise to murder Sergeant Reeves's.

Deciding that the best defense was an aggressive offensive, Sergeant Reeves soon moved across the fort's parade ground with revolver in hand in broad daylight. He now searched for Lieutenant Sweet to eliminate the threat to his life. Sergeant Reeves was determined to immediately confront Lieutenant Sweet, for he feared that the white officers would shoot him in the night. Sergeant Yeatman ordered Sergeant Reeves to report to his office, but he refused to obey Yeatman's orders, assuming that Sergeant Yeatman was in league with the white officers.

As so often in the past, hardened Civil War veterans of African heritage and former slaves were the most vocal and quickest to react to unfair treatment from whites. While Captain Clarke remained unaware of the situation's seriousness, the two white lieutenants of Company A and the black soldiers loaded weapons for the expected confrontation.

All the while, racial tensions between black enlisted men and noncommissioned officers and white officers continued to escalate. At some point during the night at the house of a Pvt. Henry Tally whose wife was a post laundress, two revolvers were suddenly thrust through a window and into Sgt. Samuel Allen's face. The two white officers, Lieutenants Leggett and Sweet, made this threat to deter any future black retaliation. But this attempt was a serious miscalculation that immediately backfired. Sergeant Reeves was no longer the only one who felt personally threatened by these white officers.

When Sergeant Yeatman was informed of the incident at Tally's house, he ordered a detail of six Buffalo Soldiers to search the area for signs of any mysterious individuals who had threatened Sergeant Allen, or their weapons. Of course, no individuals or any weapons were found. Meanwhile, Sergeant Allen took action to protect himself. He shouted that it was time to "get's Little Johnnie's shot gun and began to load it."

Sergeant Allen loaded both barrels of the shotgun because he knew exactly who had threatened him. Sergeant Allen yelled, "[I]t was them two damned sons of bitches, Legget and Sweet!" Clearly, events in trouble-plagued Company A were quickly spinning out of control in a racially charged atmosphere. It seemed as if nothing could stop the escalating tensions and a seemingly inevitable violent clash between black and white at Fort Cummings.

The Buffalo Soldiers now rose up as one to defend themselves against any retaliation. Sergeant Reeves declared, "God damn it, we'll find them [as] [w]e've got to do this thing and we may as well do it at once." Then, Sergeant Reeves, Sergeant Allen, and Cpl. Robert Davis assembled in defiance. They boldly stood before their quarters that evening armed and ready. Meanwhile, the remainder of Company A's soldiers rallied around their fiery leaders to deal with Lieutenants Sweet and Leggett. As their actions indicated, these ex-slaves took the recent threat of violence from the white officers seriously.

Remaining defiant despite the potential cost to themselves, the soldiers of Company A stood side-by-side in solidarity and with muskets ready, while Sergeant Reeves and Corporal Davis were armed with six-shot revolvers. Sergeant Allen's fully loaded double-barrel shotgun was loaded and ready. It is not known if Cathy Williams grabbed a musket, but perhaps so.

The situation became increasingly serious as all orders and warnings for Company A to disperse were ignored. By this time, the soldiers were determined to stand their ground for what they believed was right.

Meanwhile, two black noncommissioned officers, First Sergeant Yeatman and Corporal Davis, who accompanied Yeatman so that he would not warn the two white lieutenants, set off to locate Captain Clarke. They knew Clarke was more fair-minded than either white lieutenant. Captain Clarke, however, was not found at his quarters. Then, Yeatman and Davis departed, going to Lieutenant Sweet's quarters.

Both Lieutenants Leggett and Sweet were also absent from their quarters. These two white officers feared for their lives by this time, and made sure that the African Americans would not find them. Perhaps to avoid a confrontation, both white officers, along with Captain Clarke, were socializing and drinking at the sutler's store just outside Fort Cummings.

Failing to confront either lieutenant eased the tension for the moment and the likelihood of a violent clash between the races. The absence of these three white officers, however, was viewed by the Buffalo Soldiers as another case of discrimination. Indeed, unlike these whites, the African Americans were barred by orders from leaving the post at night.

By this time, Captain Clarke was departing the sutler's establishment when he was informed of the increasingly volatile situation by First Sergeant Yeatman. Nearby, Corporal Davis ensured that Yeatman gave no indication of the full extent of the unrest for fear of serious repercussions for actions that would be seen officially as "mutiny."

Not realizing, however, that Company A's soldiers were so incensed, because First Sergeant Yeatman understated the situation with the presence of Sergeant Allen, Captain Clarke merely directed First Sergeant Yeatman to order the men back to their quarters. Meanwhile, not yet knowing how serious the situation had become by this time, Captain Clarke went to Tally's house to investigate the latest incident involving Sergeant Allen.

In the meantime, the Buffalo Soldiers became even more threatening. Once again, they ignored First Sergeant Yeatman's orders to disperse and return to their quarters. This accommodating sergeant, who was a good soldier, carried little respect among the African Americans in the ranks. Instead of dispersing as instructed, the Buffalo Soldiers now loaded their muskets, ignoring Yeatman's orders and preparing for resistance if necessary.

Taking an even more threatening stance, the Buffalo Soldiers then brought weapons to their shoulders as if to open fire. In addition, other infantrymen of Company A began to load their weapons as well, as events continued to swirl out of control. If Cathy Williams held a musket and stood beside her comrades of Company A, which was most likely the case, then she was now involved in what the military would view as a "mutiny." Additional orders from First Sergeant Yeatman to return to quarters were ignored by the angry troops of Captain Clarke's company.

The uncompromising spirit of Company A's resistance remained in the embodiment of Sergeant Reeves. An angry Reeves yelled out to First Sergeant Yeatman that the men of Company A should for all practical purposes now shoot him down and they would then "go up and kill every damned thing in the garrison that wore shoulder straps"—white officers. Once again, First Sergeant Yeatman ordered the men to disperse and return to quarters, but now he was told by Private George Stratton that "his orders want worth a damn."

This remote frontier outpost seemingly was about to erupt in a racial war. These ex-slaves seemed prepared to turn on white officers who ironically had served in the Civil War and fought white Southerners to end the curse of slavery only a short time before. Clearly, discriminatory treatment at Fort Cummings had led to the reopening of the old wounds for these ex-slaves, who were once brutalized and now must have been reminded of years of bad treatment by slave owners and other whites.

As time passed and tempers cooled a little, most African Americans of Company A and their white officers returned to their respective quarters. Meanwhile, First Sergeant Yeatman went out again, this time alone, to inform Captain Clarke of the crisis. At this point, the last thing that the soldiers wanted was to involve Captain Clarke in this racial confrontation, because as a good officer bound by regulations he would be forced to side with the other officers despite having some sympathy with his men's plight.

The Buffalo Soldiers, therefore, wanted to settle the matter between themselves and Lieutenants Leggett and Sweet without the knowledge of the captain. Thankfully, a lull settled over the heated emotions consuming Fort Cummings. At last, the racial tension and animosity eased but for only about a quarter of an hour.

Now, the "mutiny" leaders, Sergeants Reeves and Allen and Corporal Davis, departed Fort Cummings. Without orders, they boldly passed through the north gate in search of Company A's lieutenants. After the threat to his life, Sergeant Allen was eager to confront Lieutenant Sweet, strutting to Tally's house in person. But when frustrated upon not finding the lieutenant at Tally's house, an angry Sergeant Allen could not resist venting his contempt by yelling, "[T]hat damned son of a bitch Leggett has gone to the rear."

First Sergeant Yeatman, meanwhile, feared for his own life, if it was discovered by Sergeant Reeves and the other Company A soldiers that he had given Captain Clarke an accurate assessment of the extent of the revolt. Finally, the "mutiny" lost momentum. Tensions eased in the night. No confrontations developed in the tense darkness. Here, in the remote deserts of New Mexico, racial issues had finally come to a head for Cathy Williams and her comrades of Company A.

The consequence of the Buffalo Soldiers' defiance would be swift retaliation, once the extent of their so-called "mutiny" was ascertained by the white officers. Later, the two black sergeants, Reeves and Allen, and seven other Company A soldiers were arrested for their actions on December 1 and 2. The African American prisoners, sullen yet defiant, were then escorted southeastward by rail by Captain Clarke and Lieutenants Leggett and Sweet, to Fort Selden. At this time, Fort Selden was a remote outpost located just north of Las Cruces, New Mexico. It was on the Rio Grande River and the Texas border, fifty-five miles east of Fort Cummings.

Here, the Buffalo Soldiers would be tried by general court-martial. A number of witnesses to the revolt were also among the parties to testify at the court-martial. Such a small party traveling from Fort Cummings to Fort Selden even by rail was not without risk in Apache country. Fort Selden was occasionally raided by the Apache, as in November 1867, when the garrison's horses and mules were stolen in lightning raids.

With the court-martial about to begin at Fort Selden, another outburst of racial animosity was about to erupt at Fort Cummings, partly because the hated Lieutenant Leggett now commanded Company A in Captain Clarke's absence, after Leggett returned from Fort Selden. On December 7, tension at Fort Cummings continued to escalate because Lieutenant Leggett, learning nothing from the past mistakes and flaunting his victory over the enlisted ranks, once again ordered Mattie's banishment from the post. It seemed as if Leggett had won in the end, reestablishing his authority at Mattie's expense. Leggett now exercised the full limits of his authority in Captain Clarke's absence.

Despite his men's anger, the uncompromising Lieutenant Leggett refused to budge an inch in regard to Mattie's expulsion from the fort. At last, Mattie was escorted out of Fort Cummings by three members of the post guard. No doubt, Lieutenant Leggett reveled at the thought that he had demonstrated this power and had the full weight of military authority behind his inhumane decision.

Leggett had proved his point, or so it seemed. Orders were orders and Leggett, as usual, was adhering to the most strict interpretation of the regulations. The lieutenant was determined to prove that he was right, even if it meant Mattie's death in the desert. He would not be dictated to by a bunch of ex-slaves who hardly knew how to read and write. Nevertheless, the Buffalo Soldiers would not be denied, regardless of the consequences.

To save a friend and defenseless woman from almost certain death and in defiance of the hated lieutenant, twenty to forty men of Company A grabbed muskets. They now took action before it was too late to save Mattie. The black soldiers overwhelmed the post guard of a corporal and two privates, and then rushed forward, while yelling "Halt!" at Mattie's escort.

With moral authority on their side, this handful of Buffalo Soldiers took Mattie from the escorts' custody. Then these African Americans declared to the guard that Mattie would not be banished from Fort Cummings under any circumstances. According to their carefully laid plan, Merritt was then rushed by her friends to a safe location outside the fort beyond Lieutenant Leggett's reach.

In Captain Clarke's absence and before his return from Fort Selden on December 7, post commander Lt. James N. Morgan was understandably upset by the Buffalo Soldiers' continued defiance. He ordered the African Americans to lay down their arms and return to the quarters, but they defiantly refused to obey the post commander. Lieutenant Morgan's directives were repeated and backed up by Lieutenant Leggett's orders to immediately desist—or else. Eventually, the Buffalo Soldiers acquiesced, retiring to their quarters. Mattie Merritt, however, was now safe. In the end, it was the Buffalo Soldiers who had won the game in the test of wills with their leaders.

Not every member of Company A now laid down arms and returned to quarters. The three most spirited and determined privates of Company A, George Newton, Henry Watkins, and George Stratton, still stood defiantly, seething in anger. At last, the trio dispersed but only grudgingly, muttering angry words while departing to their quarters as ordered.

When the officers later learned that Privates Stratton and Watkins had used threatening language, both soldiers were immediately arrested and thrown into the guardhouse. These two additional Company A prisoners were soon on their way to Fort Selden to join the court-martial proceedings that began in January 1868. In total, thirteen soldiers of Cathy's Company A were charged with "mutiny" but only seven of these were tried. In keeping with her perfect record, Private Cathay was not charged with any offense.

The court-martial was later relocated from Fort Selden to Fort Bayard, New Mexico, where the leader of the uprising, Sergeant Reeves, was acquitted. Sergeant Reeves was fortunate. He had been acquitted of the serious charges of "mutiny," as well as threatening to kill First Sergeant Yeatman, releasing himself from arrest, and unholstering a revolver to resist military authority. A guilty verdict would have probably resulted in his execution.

Despite compounding his problems at Fort Selden by cursing at a white captain when he roughly threw Sergeant Reeves in the guardhouse, Sergeant Allen was also acquitted of "mutiny." Despite their predicament, Company A's soldiers continued to maintain solidarity even in the face of possible execution. No doubt, these Buffalo Soldiers felt they were taking on the entire white military establishment of West Point officers and aristocratic Easterners, who it seemed were almost as racist as their former slave owners and overseers.

How could these soldiers have escaped the death penalty for mutiny? Fortunately for the men of Company A, a competent young attorney from Missouri, Thomas Benton Catron, had played a key role in saving the day. He performed brilliantly, sparing these Buffalo Soldiers from serious penalties, including death.

Considering the seriousness of the charges, someone in a high place, probably Captain Clarke, evidently played a role in granting Sergeant Reeves a reprieve. Destined to become a fine soldier as Captain Clarke realized, the feisty Sergeant Reeves would reenlist five more times in a long and distinguished career. Finally, when the "mutiny" at Fort Cummings had become only fading memory, he would retire in 1892 after nearly thirty years of service.

Sergeant Reeves's distinguished service record both before and after the "mutiny" at Fort Cummings gave credence to his declaration during the court-martial proceedings that the real source of Company A's unrest was in fact Lieutenant Leggett's autocratic rule and unfair and harsh punishments. Speaking freely, Sergeant Reeves stated that "before that damned son of a bitch, we were getting on like soldiers ought to."

In fact, only Corporal Davis was found guilty of "mutiny" and all other charges during the court-martial proceedings. He was dishonorably discharged, and would serve the remainder of his period of service in punishment. After the sentence's approval by General Sheridan, Corporal Davis would be sent to the Missouri state penitentiary at Jefferson City to serve a sentence of ten years. Despite the harsh sentence, Corporal Davis had at least escaped the death penalty.[3]

Unlike the esteemed Sergeant Reeves, Captain Clarke would not escape unscathed the political fallout of the racial incident at Fort Cummings. Because his Company A rose up in defiance and evidently because of his strong sympathy for his men, Captain Clarke, perhaps the most popular white officer in the regiment, would suffer long-term consequences that adversely affected his career. It would not, however, be detrimental in the short term; indeed, Captain Clarke would shortly become Fort Cummings's commander.

When the 38th Infantry consolidated with the 41st Infantry, Clarke became a convenient scapegoat for his men and their actions. In November 1869, the men of these two regiments would be consolidated into the better-known Buffalo Soldier regiments, the 24th and 25th Infantry. In January 1870 and upon the advice of Brevet Major General Grover, Captain Clarke would be deemed "unfit for service," unlike Lieutenants Leggett and Sweet who were assigned to the 25th Infantry. Captain Clarke would then be reassigned to the 17th Infantry in April 1870.[4]

In regard to the fate of the chief catalyst of the December 1867 "mutiny" at Fort Cummings, Mattie Merritt was eventually banished from the fort by Captain Clarke, who was forced to obey orders. Although he helped to save Sergeant Reeves from execution, he had no choice but to support Lieutenants Sweet and Leggett. Some fear continued to exist among the white officers that the spirit of defiance might still spread from Company A to the other companies of the 38th. Therefore, Mattie had to be expelled to maintain overall discipline and to demonstrate that open defiance of white officers brought no positive results.

Because Fort Cummings, however, was located deep in Apache country and nearly twenty miles from the nearest settlement on the Mimbres River to the west, Captain Clarke made Mattie's banishment as benign as possible. He arranged decent shelter for her at the stage ranch just outside Fort Cummings. Then, the captain secured a cart to pick her up and take her safely beyond the post.

He probably had Mattie sent to the Mimbres River settlement, a small agricultural community around twenty miles northeast of Silver City, New Mexico. Clearly, if such humane treatment had been accorded to Mattie in the first place, then the Buffalo Soldiers of Company A would never have been forced to take matters in their own hands to ensure justice.[5]

CHAPTER EIGHT

Winter Campaign
against the Apache

As if the excitement of the "mutiny" was not enough, a new offensive campaign was on the horizon for the African Americans of Company A, 38th Infantry. Here, in the parched lands of southwest New Mexico, these former slaves were about to be hurled into the midst of a centuries old conflict that had raged between the Hispanic peoples and the much feared Chiricahua Apache.

For centuries, both peoples had struggled for possession of the land that they loved, but the Apache were by far its most fearless antagonists. The great Chiricahua Apache chief Cochise perhaps best summarized the primary bone of contention that led to the seemingly endless conflict between whites, both Hispanic and Anglos, and the Apache: "[W]hen I was young I walked all over this country . . . and saw no other people than the Apaches [but now] another race of people had come to take it." Fiercely independent, the Apache were determined to force the whites off their ancestral homeland and drive them back to wherever they had come from.

The 6,000 Native American peoples of Apache homeland, which included southeast Arizona, southwest New Mexico, and northern Mexico, were most formidable in the art of war. In part, their tenacity in warfare stemmed from the fact that the wide-ranging Apache "were a product of their habitat, harsh, cruel, and pitiless," which had transformed these warriors into "the most implacable savages on the American continent."

History revealed that the Apache were resilient and tough. Throughout the past they had repeatedly caused a depopulation of two states of northern Mexico, Sonora and Chihuahua, by their raids. But the small towns and rancheros of New Mexico were the favorite targets of these relentless Apache attacks, which struck suddenly out of the remote mountains, deserts, and canyons.

Among the most aggressive of the Apache were the Chiricahua. Their raids often penetrated deeply into the lands south of the Rio Grande. These were lightning strikes that could not be stopped. With a tribal structure based upon "family clusters," the Apache were prepared to fight to the death to remain in possession of the remote mountains and deserts of southeast New Mexico that they called home. Not surprisingly the most demanding service of the Buffalo Soldiers in the frontier West was in the wild lands of Apacheria, where Cathy Williams and her Company A comrades were stationed.

From beginning to end, the reputation of the Apache warriors for unmatched ferocity was known far and wide. For centuries, they had successfully resisted all efforts by the Spanish, Mexicans, other Indian tribes, and Americans to suppress them. The legendary combat prowess of the Apache was based upon a combination of hit-and-run tactics, lightning-quick raids, and masterful ambushes that were deadly and effective. Tenacity and success in warfare belied their small numbers. Early Apache attacks caused a Spanish priest to describe in the earliest days of Spanish settlement that these nomadic Apache were "very spirited and belligerent."

This Apache spirit of resistance stretched back for centuries. In 1630, a Spaniard described the Apache as "a people very fiery and bellicose, and very crafty in war." Not surprisingly, a Spanish padre in the 1700s marveled at the supreme dominance of the hard-riding Apache, writing that "the savages play the master in Sonora." During the next century, a Mexican described in 1831 that the Apache was the "most malignant and cruel" of all the Native American tribes in North America.

Ceaseless raids by these fierce warriors caused such widespread destruction that "all of northern Mexico was becoming a wilderness" by the 1850s. Then, when U.S. forces were occupied in battling Confederates, the Apache took the offensive and nearly drove all of the Anglos and Hispanics from Apacheria.

Despite the best efforts of the Spanish, Mexicans, and Americans to subdue the wide-ranging Apache, the Chiricahua continued to rule the region around Fort Cummings and all of southern New Mexico, especially in the Dragoon and Chiricahua Mountains. Because they refused to become farmers or herders and did not rely upon a single supply source like the Plains Indians' dependence upon the buffalo, the Chiricahua lived off the spoils of their hard-hitting raids, which struck terror into the Hispanic settlers and the domesticated Pueblo, leading to endless warfare.[1]

Embodying the spirit of perhaps the most independent and warlike Native American peoples, the Chiricahua Apache chief, Cochise, explained the harsh reality for the Apache in relation to the white interlopers who coveted Apacheria as their own land: "God made us not as you; we were born like the animals, in the dry grass, not on beds like you. This is why we do as the animals, go about of a night and rob and steal. If I had such things as you have, I would not do as I do, for then I would not need to do so. [God] said the world was for us all; how was it? When I was young I walked all over this country, east and west, and saw no other people than the Apaches. After many summers I walked again and found another race of people had come to take it."[2]

By 1867, the Apache were determined that the whites and Buffalo Soldiers would not be allowed to "come and take" their ancestral homeland. Among those fearless warriors who resisted the white interlopers were Apache women. These warriors rode and fought beside their men in raids that covered a hundred miles in some cases.[3]

For the Buffalo Soldiers posted at Fort Cummings and elsewhere in the Southwest, another factor explained the desperation of Apache resistance by this time: a brutal policy of paying bounties for Apache scalps and a war of extermination. Hispanics of the Mexican states of Sonora and Chihuahua offered a good many pesos for not only scalps of Apache warriors but also for those of women and children.

Even greedy Anglos from the United States got in the act, turning scalping into a money-making venture. Making a business out of killing and taking scalps of every Apache that they could find regardless of either age or sex, these American scalp hunters showed no mercy, collecting as many scalps and as much money as possible in their barbaric but lucrative trade.[4]

Another largely forgotten reason, but certainly one of the most important, explained why the Apache so vehemently hated the Spanish, Mexicans, Hispanics, and whites. The Apache tenacity in warfare stemmed from resistance to the institution of slavery because thousands of Apache had been enslaved only a few decades before.

Slavery began at an early date when the Spanish seized Apache and sent them south to labor and die in the Mexican mines. In 1772, official Spanish policy called for the transportation of captured Apache to Mexico City to labor for the rest of their lives as household slaves for wealthy Hispanic families. Soon, capturing Apache—men, women, and children—and selling them into slavery became a lucrative business venture endorsed by the Spanish governors, who profited from this trade in human beings.

As late as 1810, some Apache captives were transported as far as Havana, Cuba. And when Confederate troops occupied Apacheria during the Civil

War, one Rebel general wanted to sell the Apache as slaves. So profitable was the Apache slave trade that the New Mexicans opposed the idea of settling the Apache on reservations as a means of ending the bitter warfare because of the loss of revenue from slave trading.

Finally, in a much belated attempt to end the curse of slavery in the New Mexico Territory in June 1865, Pres. Andrew Johnson issued orders to the area's officials to halt the Apache slave trade. In 1867 an outraged U.S. Congress passed a new law to deal with the issue of involuntary servitude: "An Act to Abolish and Forever Prohibit the System of Peonage in the Territory of New Mexico and Elsewhere."

Apache slavery, nevertheless, continued to thrive in New Mexico, long after the American republic abolished African slavery. Ironically, perhaps as many as 2,000 Indian slaves toiled in New Mexico by the time Private Cathay, the ex-slave from Missouri, and other Buffalo Soldiers, who were also mostly former slaves, served at Fort Cummings.

Unlike the Great Plains Indians, the Apache fought not only against the theft of their ancestral homeland but also to destroy the slavery that continued to flourish in New Mexico and Mexico. The fact that these ex-slaves in blue uniforms were now dispatched by a nation in which slavery had thrived, to subjugate a native people who had likewise been brutalized by slavery was cruelly ironic.[5]

Kit Carson described the Apache with a measure of compassion because by the mid-1850s, those Apache "that are now committing depredations are those who have lost their families during the war [and] they consider they have nothing further to live for than revenge for the death of those of their families that were killed by the whites . . . they have become desperate." By the time of Private Cathay's service at Fort Cummings, the Apache were even more fierce.[6]

In January 1868, the black troops of the 38th Infantry prepared to play a leading role in a winter offensive operation against the Apache. This offensive thrust was planned to eliminate an Apache village from which raids had long been launched throughout southwest New Mexico. African American infantrymen marching deep into the Apache homeland hardly represented the romantic images in which heroic white cavalrymen in tidy blue uniforms rode into the pages of history while conquering the West.

Displaying their audacity as recently as May 1867, the Apache raided the post herd immediately outside Fort Bayard. They stole horses, mules, and cattle in one strike, catching the garrison by surprise. But this was only business as usual for the Apache. They always took from the enemy what they needed to survive in a harsh land: the way of life of a resilient people. Military authorities believed that the Mexicans encouraged such hard-hitting raids into southwest New Mexico to profit from the booty that was then carried across the U.S.-Mexico border and the Rio Grande.

Top American military commanders in Santa Fe decided that now was the time to launch a retaliatory strike to teach a lesson. The offensive operation called for complex maneuvers by three separate columns, which would converge on the Apache village as one. More than half of the troop strength of three converging columns would consist of African Americans of the 38th Infantry. At long last, here was an opportunity for the black infantrymen including Private Cathay and her Company A to demonstrate their mettle in combat by meeting the most resourceful and cunning opponent ever faced by U.S. troops in the West, the elusive Apache.

The strategic plan spelled out the details for the three columns dispatched from Forts Cummings, Bayard, and Craig to launch a deep thrust into Apacheria and to converge on the Apache village, or "go-tah." This Chiricahua village was situated on the southeast edge of the rugged Black Range Mountains.

Here, in their mountain sanctuaries, the Apache lived in "wickiups," consisting of circular dwellings, which looked somewhat like tepees. These Apache "wickiups" were made of branches and covered with animal hides. Orders from the headquarters of the New Mexico Military District in Santa Fe were not to simply eliminate the Apache village but also to destroy it, along with all adult male inhabitants who refused to surrender.

For the first time, the soldiers of the 38th Infantry earned a leading role in demonstrating the doctrine of total warfare by striking deep into the Chiricahua Apache homeland. Because this mission called for the Apache village's destruction in the dead of winter, the white man's war in southwest New Mexico was now being waged not only upon the warriors but also upon their women and children.

What made this offensive operation unique in the West's military history was a combination of four distinct factors: first, the launching of an offensive campaign in winter; second, the majority of the strike force would not be composed of U.S. cavalry but of infantrymen; third, most of the soldiers employed in this operation would be African Americans; and, fourth, one of the members of this offensive operation was a young, ex-slave woman from Missouri, Pvt. William Cathay. Cathy Williams was about to become the first and only female in the Regular U.S. Army to engage in active offensive operations against the Apache or any other Native American tribe.

Contrary to the stereotypes that romanticized the image of U.S. Cavalry troopers riding grandly to victory under the colorful banners and the clear skies of Monument Valley, the truth of this harsh campaign was quite the opposite. Because of logistical limitations and the unsuitability of horses to traverse rough terrain in arid regions with little forage or water, mounted operations against the Native Americans generally proved ineffective. Black Elk, the Ogalala Holy Man, merely concluded that "the cavalry of the Wasichus did not know how to fight."

The harsh desert environment of southwest New Mexico made the use of cavalry all but obsolete compared to the employment of infantryman for extended periods far from supply depots, communication lines, and forts. With water in canteens and rations in haversacks, the hard-marching infantrymen could conduct active campaigning for extended periods unlike mounted troopers. Cavalry horses in an arid region proved ineffective without regular and plentiful amounts of forage or water.

Col. William B. Hazen, the commander of the 38th Infantry, explained the wisdom of employing infantry rather than cavalry in Indian operations: "[A]fter the fourth day's march of a mixed command, the horse does not march faster than the foot soldier, and after the seventh day, the foot soldier begins to outmarch the horse, and from that time on the foot soldier has to end his march earlier and earlier each day, to enable the cavalry to reach the camp the same day at all."

As late as the 1870s, much debate within military circles would continue to center upon whether the infantry or cavalry was more suitable for offensive operations against the Indians. By early January 1868, however, an offensive operation employing the Buffalo Soldiers of the 38th Infantry made good tactical and logistical sense, or so it seemed.[7]

The demands about to be placed upon the Buffalo Soldiers would be extreme in this campaign. Now part of an offensive operation during the height of winter, Cathy Williams and the African American infantrymen, who were accustomed to the warm climate of the South, would have to deal with colder temperatures and harsher winter conditions than they had ever experienced before. At this time, duty—and especially offensive operations—for U.S. Cavalry in Apacheria during winter was understood to be more demanding than any other type of service. And this case was doubly challenging because the black infantrymen now prepared to accomplish what cavalry could not achieve.

To compensate for the lack of infantry mobility in the absence of cavalry and to gain the element of surprise, the tactical plan of this operation called for a lengthy march across rough country in the dead of winter. At least on paper, this plan seemed sound. Winter was the only time of the year that the Apache were stationary and even remotely vulnerable.

Indeed, in winter the Chiricahua Apache finally ceased their lightning-quick raids and lived a peaceful existence; it was also when they eased their legendary vigilance. In tactical terms, this offensive winter operation would bestow upon the "Long Knives" and Buffalo Soldiers the element of surprise by launching a strike when the Apache were most vulnerable and least expecting an attack. Descending upon the Apache village from more than one direction by employing three converging columns was a wise strategy to ensure both surprise and entrapment.

By pushing deep into the Apache homeland in winter, the frontier regulars planned to snatch the initiative from the Apache warriors, whose mode of warfare depended upon striking only when it was to their advantage to do so or when they were least expected. And because the Buffalo Soldiers would be unleashed to attack the Chiricahua village, the Apache warriors would be encumbered by concern for their wives and children enhancing the chances for the attackers' success.

If they caught the Chiricahua by surprise and defeated them, then the infantrymen of the 38th would fulfill their mission of destroying the village's winter supplies and provisions. By this means, the attackers would eliminate the Apache resources and means of waging war for some time to come. A surprise strike in winter, however, might not only kill the warriors but also the women and children because they would be dispersed and become vulnerable to the ravages of winter, after the Apache winter provisions had been destroyed.[8]

This aggressive policy of striking deep into the Apache homeland was a good example of the total war policies of Generals Grant, Sherman, and Sheridan. The official government policy now echoed the harsh words of an Indian agent in 1857 who recommended a grim solution to the Apache "problem" in the Southwest: "[T]here is only one way to wage war against the Apaches: a steady, persistent campaign must be made, following them to their haunts [where] they must be surrounded, starved into coming in, supervised, or put to death."[9]

This, nevertheless, was a risky winter operation for the 238 soldiers, black, white, and Hispanic, assigned to participate in the expedition. But at least in the minds of military leaders at headquarters in Santa Fe, the potential gains for wiping out a hostile Apache village were worth the risk, ensuring peace in the months ahead if successful. The odds, however, of widely scattered converging columns of infantry from three different forts advancing undetected across rugged country to strike in unison deep into the Apache homeland were slim at best. By any measure, this was a daunting task and a formidable tactical challenge.

Perhaps the relatively low probability of success was the reason why the difficult mission was handed primarily to the men of the 38th Infantry, and especially to the soldiers of Company A. Because of the recent arrests the already small Fort Cummings garrison was further depleted by the absence of both Company A's officers and those enlisted men who were now involved in the court-martial proceedings at Fort Selden fifty-five miles to the east.

The Fort Cummings garrison was so stripped of manpower that the acting commander, Lt. James N. Morgan, initially balked at the order to dispatch troops. In fact, the district commander in Santa Fe was forced to repeatedly order him to send his soldiers forward to participate in the risky winter operation against the Apache. When he finally decided to comply, Lieutenant Morgan ordered what was in essence a token force from Fort Cummings to undertake the expedition: only twenty-five African Americans of Company A, including Cathy Williams.

Clearly, the acting post commander decided that it was more prudent to risk the lives of twenty-five Company A soldiers rather than to make Fort Cummings less secure by significantly reducing the already diminutive garrison.

In addition, Lieutenant Morgan might well have found a convenient excuse for eliminating his troublesome Company A by dispatching many of them in an isolated column on an undermanned expedition. Against the cunning Apache, sending such a small force out alone in an attempt to catch the Apache by surprise was nearly a suicidal mission. As usual, Private Cathay and the handful of her remaining comrades of Company A had no idea of what political maneuvering, leadership decisions, and cynical considerations lay behind the sudden orders that they had received and were sworn to obey.

On the frigid morning of January 1, 1868, a bugler sounded the call for the Buffalo Soldiers of Company A, 38th Infantry, to assemble on the parade ground of Fort Cummings. Feeling the sharp bite of the winter cold, the African American soldiers bundled up in warm clothes as best they could. Then, they hurriedly strapped on cartridge boxes and gear in preparation for their first offensive campaign.

On the double, the Buffalo Soldiers of Company A spilled out of the wooden barracks and assembled on the parade ground. With Captain Clarke involved in the court-martial proceedings at Fort Selden, none other than the infamous Lieutenant Leggett formed the black troops of his under-strength Company A into line.

This handful of Buffalo Soldiers were the only troops from Fort Cummings's garrison selected for the assignment of eliminating the Apache rancheria, or village. Far away in the haunts of Apacheria, this targeted Apache village was located about forty miles southwest of Fort McRae. Fort McRae was situated up the Rio Grande and north of Fort Selden and northeast of Fort Cummings.

The mission to strike deep into the Apache homeland would now present Company A with an opportunity to redeem itself after the recent "mutiny." Consequently, while their friends and comrades were being tried at Fort Selden, the African Americans of Company A were determined to prove that they were good soldiers and not disgraced "mutineers."

With Lieutenant Leggett now leading the column, there is little doubt that Company A's soldiers remained disgruntled but were determined to serve as best they could in fulfilling their mission. Nagging these soldiers, and probably Private Cathay, was the fact that the Buffalo Soldiers feared that their comrades in custody would be executed for mutiny. But worst of all, the Buffalo Soldiers would have to serve under the detested Lieutenant Leggett during an active campaign. It would require a large measure of self-control to once again take orders from a despised officer.

In terms of overall command experience Lieutenant Leggett was a fine officer to lead Company A's mission. After enlisting at Camp Keyton, Kentucky, in October 1861, Leggett had served as captain of Company A, 9th Kentucky Volunteer Infantry. He was mustered out of service in November 1864 as a captain of Company A, 49th Ohio Volunteer Infantry. Leggett's three years of service in leading Civil War troops would now prove a boon to Company A's soldiers during their Apache campaign.

This distant Chiricahua village might have included some captured whites or even blacks, who lived among the Apache. One such captive African American woman was named Biddy Johnson Arnold. In addition, the Apache possessed a tradition of female warriors. For instance, the Apache chief Victorio often rode into battle with his sister, Lozen, who was the second highest ranking warrior among the Warm Springs Apache.

The possibility existed, therefore, that Cathy Williams might confront other females and even African Americans, if Company A succeeded in catching the Chiricahua village by surprise. Despite the opportunity to feign sickness—not an uncommon practice—to escape risky duty in the harsh winter weather, Private Cathay was present in Company A's ranks. As in the past, she was ready for whatever duty was required of her.[10]

The Fort Cummings's column, one-third of the total strike force consisting of three columns, was the smallest, composed of only Company A. In contrast, the largest column, led by a German captain, marched from Fort

Craig, north of Fort McRae located farther up the Rio Grande. This column consisted of nearly forty troopers of Company B, 3rd Cavalry, and thirty-three African Americans of Company C, 38th Infantry, under the command of a black sergeant.

To additionally dwarf Fort Cummings's diminutive force, the Fort Craig column would be augmented by sixty-seven New Mexico volunteers of a Hispanic militia company. This unified command represented the close harmony between whites and Hispanics in the multicultural society of the Territory of New Mexico.

Meanwhile, the third and final column ordered to converge on the Apache village was dispatched from Fort Bayard. Led by an Irish immigrant and hero of Gettysburg, this column consisted of seventy-two Buffalo Soldiers from Companies D and F, 38th Infantry. In terms of numbers, this was the second weakest column.

Despite being the weakest of the three columns, Company A was a key player in the overall offensive strategy. The column of Buffalo Soldiers from Fort Cummings was about to be led north not only by Lieutenant Leggett but also by a Hispanic citizen from the town of Mimbres. He was among those individuals who first ascertained the exact location of the Chiricahua village on November 20, 1867.

Confidence, if not naïveté, was high among the soldiers of Company A, as Lieutenant Leggett led his troops through the gates of Fort Cummings. The tiny column then pushed northward through the frigid desert on a course roughly parallel to the Rio Grande to the east. Amid the clear weather of southwest New Mexico in the grip of winter, the barren landscape that the Buffalo Soldiers now marched through was picturesque in the wintry frosts of early January.

High mountains loomed on each side of Lieutenant Leggett's command, which seemed lost amid the expansiveness of the surrounding countryside and snow-capped mountains. Cooke's Range rose up to the west and the Good Sight Mountains could be seen to the northeast, while to the northwest loomed the towering Mimbres Mountains. Farther to the northeast about twenty miles, and beyond the Good Sight Mountains, stood the Caballo Mountains on the east side of the Rio Grande.

Hour after hour, the small band of Company A soldiers marched northwest of and parallel to the Rio Grande, toward the first creek north of Fort Cummings called Tierra Blanca. After getting their feet wet in crossing the small stream, the Buffalo Soldiers continued northward to cross Perche Creek. Then, Lieutenant Leggett and his bluecoats waded through the waters of Las Animas Creek, which ran southeastward into the Rio Grande.

All three creeks flowed eastward from the Mimbres Mountains to enter the Rio Grande to the east. Neither Private Cathay or her comrades had time to dry their feet. They continued onward with wet feet, and soaking shoes and socks.

By this time, neither Lieutenant Leggett nor his Buffalo Soldiers understood the full extent of the Apache cunning or elusiveness. Novices at Apache warfare, the Company A soldiers had never fought the Apache. Like many inexperienced troops, they underestimated their opponent while overestimating their own capabilities. Gen. George F. Crook declared without exaggeration that in battling the Apache in their home territory, "regular troops are as helpless as a whale attacked by a school of swordfish."[11]

For hours, the Buffalo Soldiers continued moving northward into the vastness of the wintry landscape, which was brownish-hued and seemingly sterile. Everything was strangely quiet. All the while, the small column of black troops pushed farther from the safe and warm confines of Fort Cummings.

As a cruel fate would have it, the African Americans of Company A were improperly clothed for the harsh weather and demands of a winter campaign. When the district commander from his warm Santa Fe headquarters issued the orders to launch an offensive operation in the dead of winter, however, he was unaware of the unsuitability of the Buffalo Soldiers's uniforms.

Unlike white troops serving on the Western frontier like General Custer's 7th Cavalry, Company A's soldiers possessed no warm Buffalo coats, robes, trousers, and overcoats. Such winter clothing was the only effective protection against the harsh winter winds and cold of the Western frontier. Unfortunately for the soldiers of Company A, not until the 1870s would the War Department finally issue suitable uniforms and clothing for winter campaigning to the frontier's defenders.[12]

In overall tactical terms, the column from Fort Cummings was especially vulnerable not only because of its small size but also because it was without cavalry to scout and reconnoiter the advance. Consequently, any Apache ambush could not possibly be detected by the foot soldiers until it was too late. As a result there must have been a feeling of apprehension within the column.

Perhaps the New Mexico guide became unnerved by the lack of strength of the small Fort Cummings column. He became especially worried when the black infantrymen reached a vast canyon. The Apache had earlier slipped through this rocky canyon to reach their village, indicating their close proximity. A new tension filled the air among the guide and the rookie Buffalo Soldiers.

To the soldiers this deep canyon must have looked especially eerie and foreboding. Such an imposing natural formation could seemingly swallow up

Company A. Clearly, Lieutenant Leggett's isolated company now confronted a formidable natural obstacle. Lieutenant Leggett wisely hesitated before ordering the advance of his small unit into the canyon's depths. He knew better than to lead his handful of troops into the deep canyon, especially without knowledge of the area or cavalry to scout the terrain. Leggett now sensed the possibility of an Apache ambush so near to their village.

In addition, this experienced officer reasoned that the rugged canyon posed an impassible obstacle to Company A's advance. Most of all, the canyon was a potential death trap. At last, the officer so recently the object of the Buffalo Soldiers' hatred was now an asset and source of sound leadership.

Relying on natural instinct and past experience, Lieutenant Leggett decided that entering the canyon was far too risky. He immediately ordered the Buffalo Soldiers to take up defensive positions. Here, before the canyon, Leggett decided to await the arrival of the Fort Bayard column. With only twenty-five soldiers and far from support, Lieutenant Leggett made a sound tactical decision under the circumstances. He simply refused to risk his diminutive task force against the warriors of an entire Apache village who might be waiting in ambush in the canyon.

Despite the coldness of the days and especially the bitter and windy nights, Lieutenant Leggett probably ordered his soldiers not to light fires so as not to betray their exact locations to the Apache. If so, then the Buffalo Soldiers, already insufficiently clothed, additionally suffered in the harsh winter conditions of early January.[13]

But nothing stirred in the canyon. No indications of the Apache were detected. The land around Company A remained strangely quiet. As a hardened veteran of numerous Civil War campaigns, Lieutenant Leggett understood that the longer his men waited in a stationary position for the arrival of Fort Bayard's column, the more vulnerable they then became to Apache attack.

More time passed without incident, yet no column of soldiers could be spied on the horizon from the direction of Fort Bayard. What had happened to the Fort Bayard column? Had the Fort Bayard garrison even received orders to march out and link with the company from Fort Cummings? If ordered out, had the Fort Bayard column been dispatched in a timely manner or was it lagging far behind schedule? Or had the Fort Bayard column been ambushed or become lost in this vast and uncharted land? In tactical terms, was a timely linkage between three widely divergent columns even possible in the first place?

As more time passed, Lieutenant Leggett began to sense the greater vulnerability of his command. Most of all, he knew only too well that Fort Cummings's commander had ordered him out with little more than a mere token force simply to comply with headquarters directives rather than to ensure success. In fact, Lieutenant Leggett's command would not even be able to adequately defend itself if the Apache now struck.

Because the hard-nosed Lieutenant Leggett had been a primary cause of the recent racial disturbances, had Fort Cummings's commander sent his controversial lieutenant out with insufficient force for a reason not specified in orders? Was he in fact hoping that Lieutenant Leggett would be killed by Apache, and Company A wiped out to eliminate the commander's most vexing problem?

If so, then this also might explain why Company A was chosen for the dangerous assignment. In this sense the possibility existed that Company A might have been set up as a sacrificial lamb to be martyred on the altar of Fort Cummings's politically minded commander and the Santa Fe headquarters. At this time and unknown to her, perhaps Private Cathay was caught up in what was in reality a political drama that had now placed her far from the protective walls of Fort Cummings and in a potentially life-threatening situation.

Or had Fort Cummings's commander hoped that the Buffalo Soldiers would once again rise up in revolt and eliminate Lieutenant Leggett on their own? Like "fragging" during the Vietnam War, angry enlisted men shooting unpopular officers was not uncommon during the Civil War. The answer may never be known but it hardly seems like a coincidence that Lieutenant Leggett and a mere handful of black infantrymen of Company A—the only Buffalo Soldier company to "mutiny" at Fort Cummings—were chosen for this dangerous assignment so soon after the racial incidents.

After nearly a week since marching out of Fort Cummings, Lieutenant Leggett finally decided that the risks outweighed his orders of linking with the Fort Bayard column. By this time, he simply refused to risk his command any longer. Leggett evidently feared—incorrectly—that the Fort Bayard column had not been dispatched. If so, then this would have sabotaged the overly ambitious tactical plan of three columns uniting in a remote wilderness to attack the Apache village in a closely coordinated joint offensive operation. Or perhaps, fearing the worst, he began to see a setup by his superiors for both him and Company A.

Whatever the reason, Lieutenant Leggett now ordered his company to prepare to march back to Fort Cummings. Certainly, Private Cathay and her comrades were relieved with the order to return to the fort. Eager to escape the many dangers of Apache country as soon as possible, Lieutenant Leggett prepared to return Company A the way it had come—away from the Apache village they had never seen.

For Private Cathay, her first and last campaign against the Apache seemingly came to an abrupt and inglorious conclusion. Nevertheless, this campaign was far from over. Danger remained for Company A, which was still on its own, and Lieutenant Leggett possessed no idea of the location of Apache war parties. Were the Chiricahua preparing to strike his diminutive command on its return march?

Even worse, the lieutenant now no doubt worried that the Apache might have slipped into his rear to set up an ambush along the route that his command would have to take to return to Fort Cummings. Therefore, the tension and apprehension continued to run high for the Buffalo Soldiers of Company A.

Elsewhere the ambitious offensive operation was doomed to failure, with the other two converging columns meeting with no success. This ill-fated winter campaign to catch the Apache by surprise—a virtual impossibility deep in Apacheria at this time of year—had turned into a fiasco. As if verifying the wisdom of Lieutenant Leggett's decision to abort the operation, the onset of harsher winter weather, including a heavy snowfall and strong winds, swept the Fort Bayard column as it ascended into the Black Range Mountains.

The bitter sting of winter turned this campaign into a march of misery for the black and white soldiers. The leather shoes of the marching troops of the Fort Bayard column quickly wore out and fell apart, while the men struggled through two-foot snow and rough terrain. Then, rations ran low in the wilderness of the Mimbres Mountains, and the suffering soldiers went hungry in a wintry hell.

Understandably, the black troops, many of whom were from the Deep South, proved extremely vulnerable to the harsh winter weather of the New Mexico mountains during their seventeen-day expedition. The mission, nevertheless, went on for the unfortunate Fort Bayard troops. They continued to attempt to locate the Apache village, even after the campaign ended for Cathy Williams and Company A.

Mocking the winter campaign's futility, the half-frozen "Long Knives" finally discovered that the targeted Apache village was abandoned. Other Chiricahua villages were also found deserted during this ill-conceived operation. Some cattle were retrieved by the bluecoats but no Apache were encountered. The winter campaign had been a failure.

The two blue columns returned to their respective forts, following Lieutenant Leggett's example. Not surprisingly, the ever-elusive Apache had apparently simply vanished into the Apacheria wilderness. The Chiricahua possessed a legendary reputation for slipping away before an enemy could strike, fleeing as much as a hundred miles before stopping.

Despite the campaign's lack of positive results, what proved successful was the deployment of African American infantry in the war against the elusive Apache. These black infantrymen served well under trying circumstances and harsh winter conditions. In this sense, the Apache expedition was a successful experiment for the employment of infantry.

Unlike the African American cavalry regiment, the black infantry had not been used before in offensive operations against Indians, especially during winter. In overall terms, this first deployment of African American infantry in offensive operations proved successful in demonstrating the fortitude, durability, and resiliency, of the black soldiery. And in her first Indian campaign, Cathy Williams likewise rose to the challenge, exhibiting the same sterling characteristics as her comrades. During this brutal winter campaign, the Buffalo Soldiers of the 38th Infantry continued the legacy of the black troops who fought with distinction during the Civil War.[14]

CHAPTER NINE

Final Service in the Southwest

At long last and with much relief, the weary Buffalo Soldiers of Company A trudged into the protective walls of Fort Cummings, reaching safety without incident. Lieutenant Leggett made a correct decision by aborting the ill-planned mission. Like everyone else, Private Cathay was worn, half-frozen, and exhausted after the arduous campaign.

The detrimental aftereffects of this demanding campaign would linger for months with Company A's soldiers. Aggravated by the harsh conditions in the field, the health of the troops continued to suffer during the winter of 1867–68.

Disease had always been a problem on the Western frontier. Its ceaseless ravages struck year around, with usually the worst period in summer, until the recent winter campaign. The poor rations and water, primitive living conditions, hard work, active campaigning in extreme weather, and poor sanitation led to a wide variety of diseases, including malaria, dysentery, and pneumonia.

But cholera was always the most deadly disease on the Western frontier. Besides the 38th Infantry, even the Buffalo Soldiers of the famed 9th Cavalry were ravished by cholera as early as the fall of 1866, even before the famous horse regiment completed its organization for active service. Then, in the summer of 1867, the 10th Cavalry was ravaged by the disease. As in other cases, the culprit for cholera's spread was migrants, including recent immigrants from Europe, who traveled in the wagon trains along the Santa Fe Trail and stopped at U.S. forts.

Some disease among the black troopers was not so accidental in origin and may have resulted from prejudice and racism. On one occasion, the Buffalo Soldiers of the 10th Cavalry at Fort Leavenworth were ordered by the post's commander to encamp on low, swampy ground, which might have also served as the post's latrine. Often latrines and water sources were located in close proximity, becoming essentially one in the same—endangering the soldiers' health. These unhealthy practices served as a deadly breeding ground for the spread of disease. Such discriminatory treatment was experienced by the soldiers of the 38th Infantry at a number of Western outposts.

Their bodies weakened to make them more vulnerable to illness, the Buffalo Soldiers also received inferior rations more frequently than white troops. In addition, logistical and transportation problems and government corruption and fraud often resulted in meager rations being sent to frontier outposts. The diet often consisted of the detested substitute for baked bread, hardtack. This hardtack was sometimes a leftover from the Civil War years and its texture was well deserving of its name. Occasionally, weevil-infested, greenish-colored, and moldy hardtack was issued to the black troops defending the West.

From beginning to end, a bland diet of beans and rice was also standard fare of the Buffalo Soldiers. Beans were the same basic staple for both cavalrymen and infantrymen on the frontier. Almost as bad were rations of stringy bacon, beef, and salt pork. These also were often issued spoiled and rancid.

During their tour of duty, Private Cathay and the Buffalo Soldiers of Company A certainly suffered from the lack of decent rations. Such scant and inferior fare sent a steady stream of these soldiers to the infirmaries, where far more men continued to die from illness than Indians bullets and arrows. In fact, the inferior quality and low supply of rations forced Fort Cummings's commander to dispatch hunting details out into the countryside in search of game during the fall of 1867.

The Buffalo Soldiers of Company A assigned cooks to each mess for ten-day periods. Private Cathay would have acted in this role whenever assigned the task. With her Civil War experience with the 8th Indiana and for General Sheridan's headquarters in the Shenandoah Valley, she was probably the best cook of Captain Clarke's Company A.

The Buffalo Soldiers were the last priority for almost anything and everything issued by the government—except hard and dangerous duty. Such discriminatory treatment combined with poor rations affected the Buffalo Soldiers' morale on occasion but did not dull their fighting spirit. Indeed, the black soldiers not only persevered but also continued to rise to the challenge of the most arduous duty in the West.

Even General Custer, who ate like a king compared with his ill-nourished 7th Cavalry troopers, complained in 1867 that "bad provisions were a fruitful cause of bad health [and] scurvy made its appearance, and cholera attacked neighboring stations." An angry army surgeon at Fort Wallace would blame the ravages of scurvy on the many "hardships and privations of arduous winter scouts which were frequent with often little time intervening for purposes of recuperation . . . and a monotonous pork diet." Occasionally, the warm weather spoiled the beef ration at Fort Cummings, causing the Buffalo Soldiers to go without meat for long periods.

To escape the hardships of enduring the thankless task of serving on the Western frontier, thousands of white soldiers quit in widespread epidemics of desertion, which could not be stopped: unlike the vast majority of Buffalo Soldiers, who faithfully remained in service. For instance, in 1867, while thousands of white soldiers—one-fourth of the entire U.S. Army—deserted to seek a better life in the civilian world, fewer than 575 African Americans deserted. Pvt. William Cathay often had the opportunity to desert but refused to leave her comrades, despite serving under the unpopular Lieutenant Leggett.

Like the fate of other Buffalo Soldiers of Company A, the recent winter campaign against the Apache in January 1868 caused Private Cathay's health to rapidly deteriorate. Insufficient clothing, poor rations, and the long days and nights in the winter weather wreaked havoc on her already fragile system.

Shortly after the end of the winter campaign, she was admitted to Fort Cummings's infirmary on January 27, 1868, with a bad case of rheumatism. This ailment was perhaps a legacy of Cathy Williams's years of service during the Civil War, becoming worse when combined with the severe privations of the recent Apache campaign. Her condition must have been especially bad for her to risk hospitalization.

Only three days later, however, Private Cathay returned to active duty, evidently after treatment for cold and exposure. A good chance existed that the brief medical treatment that she received was inadequate. Evidence indicates that medical treatment at Fort Cummings was extremely poor. On one occasion, the fort's surgeon did not even possess the necessary medical instruments to adequately operate on an injured Hispanic who was carried to the post for treatment. This unfortunate New Mexican was later escorted to Fort Bayard for medical treatment by four soldiers of Company F.

By February 1868, the leadership skills of Capt. Charles Edward Clarke, the original commander of Company A, were officially recognized when he became the commanding officer of Fort Cummings. He took command from Lt. James N. Morgan. In part, Lieutenant Morgan was relieved because he had failed to win the confidence of the local people, who felt that they were not being adequately protected from the Apache after a mail carrier was killed near Fort Cummings in November 1867.

In addition, the local citizens also resented the presence of so many African American troops. In part, Lieutenant Morgan paid the price for commanding black soldiers, receiving the wrath of the locals who occasionally clashed with the African Americans. But the recent unrest by the members of Company A certainly sealed Lieutenant Morgan's fate.

Meanwhile, the Buffalo Soldiers of Company A, including a rejuvenated Cathy Williams, continued to perform their unglamorous duties at Fort Cummings. During the first week of March 1868, Cpl. Fredrick Wormley of Company A was placed in command of a detachment of eight or ten privates. They were required to quarry and carry stone for a stone wall to be built around the post cemetery and garden. It is not known if Private Cathay served on this detail but a strong possibility exists because she was healthy during this quiet period, and Company A was probably the smallest unit in the garrison. But Cathy's labor in these mundane work details was soon to come to an end.

With harsh weather lingering into early spring and her rheumatism acting up again, Private Cathay reentered the post infirmary for treatment of an unknown ailment on March 20. Once again, this illness was sufficiently serious to have risked a physical examination from the physicians who might have discovered her sex. As during the incident in January, she returned to active duty after only three days of medical treatment. Quite possibly, Private Cathay forced herself to return to duty without fully recovering simply to avoid the discovery of her sex.[1]

Meanwhile, Indian trouble once again surfaced during the spring of 1868, despite the recent Medicine Lodge Treaty of the previous October. General Hancock's previous aggression that resulted in "Hancock's war" had left a deep wound that eventually festered into a full-scale Indian war. As General Sheridan lamented: "Although the chiefs and head-men were well nigh unanimous in ratifying these [Medicine Lodge peace] concessions, it was discovered in the spring of 1868 that many of the young men [of the Great Plains tribes] were bitterly opposed to what had been done, and claimed that most of the signatures had been obtained by misrepresentation and through proffers of certain annuities, and promises of arms and ammunition to be issued in the spring of 1868. This grumbling was very general in extent."

In this situation the Buffalo Soldiers of the 38th Infantry at Fort Cummings remained on the alert because the treaty made with the southern Great Plains tribes, including the Comanche, Cheyenne, Arapaho, Kiowa-Apache, and Kiowa, was unravelling like so many others had done. This impractical agreement, like so many white promises, was simply "worthless" and the Indians quickly realized as much.

Fundamentally, no possible solution existed between whites and Indians that could possibly avoid open warfare. What the whites failed to understand was the simple fact that the Indians would not forsake everything that they loved and cherished just because of what was written or marked by Xs on worthless pieces of paper by unknown individuals.

In 1867, for instance, a Comanche chief, Ten Bears, summarized the Indians' disgust by declaring in disbelief in regard to the whites' desire to place nomadic tribes on reservations like so many domestic cattle or sheep: "So, why do you ask us to leave the rivers, and the sun, and the wind, and live in houses? Do not ask us to give up the buffalo for the sheep [because the whites] have taken away the places where the grass grew the thickest and the timber was the best. Had we kept that, we might have done the things you ask. But it is too late. The white man has the country which we loved, and we only wish to wander on the prairie until we die."[2]

Nevertheless, the first few months of 1868 were marked by "a decidedly uneasy quiet" on the Western frontier, including the area of southwest New Mexico. That uneasy peace, however, would be shattered by summer. Then, Cheyenne, Sioux, and Arapaho warriors struck in north central Kansas, attacking whites along the Solomon and Saline Rivers. By this time, the Western frontier remained a dangerous place with a fragile peace in place, regardless of the recent treaty. Quite simply, the Native Americans were not about to submit to white domination. They simply refused to forfeit their nomadic way of life, ancestral homelands, and sacred hunting grounds to squander their existence on sterile reservations just because government officials in Washington, D.C., wanted them to live like whites: a concept incomprehensible to any free people, especially Americans, red or white.

As war clouds gathered, another risk for Cathy Williams emerged from the thieves of Company F. These men would take anything that was not nailed down, including trousers and coats of their fellow soldiers. With new uniforms in short supply, articles of clothing became special targets of thieves. In addition, some soldiers of the 38th stole from the government, taking tobacco and clothing. Perhaps this was appropriate because of unfair treatment and discrimination, since these Buffalo Soldiers were forced to take what the government refused to provide them.

Additionally, a thriving clandestine trade was maintained between the men of Company A and the locals of this part of New Mexico. For example, a hungry Buffalo Soldier exchanged his light blue trousers for a dozen eggs from a

Hispanic vendor, while on a mission from Fort Cummings to Fort Selden. Then, the former "mutineer" of Fort Cummings, the hot-headed Sergeant Allen, stole two army greatcoats, which he then sold to a Hispanic woman.

Thievery by the underpaid soldiers, both black and white, was not uncommon among the poorly supplied garrisons on the Western frontier. Insufficient pay of only $13.00 per month led to an epidemic of thefts for the eventual purchase of extra food, entertainment, alcohol, laundry service, or prostitutes.[3]

It was well that Private Cathay returned to active duty, for another new assignment beckoned during the spring of 1868. On June 6, the Buffalo Soldiers of Company A swung out of Fort Cummings with flags and guidons flying. They were being ordered to report to yet another remote post in southwest New Mexico, Fort Bayard.

After traveling nearly fifty miles to the northwest and crossing to the west side of the Mimbres River, Private Cathay and Company A entered the Cameron Valley in the foothills of the Pinos Altos Mountains, approaching Fort Bayard. Certainly this march was difficult and demanding for Private Cathay. She was still suffering from the affects of the winter campaign against the Apache. No doubt the Buffalo Soldiers were eager for a new assignment at another post and under a new commander, after the racial incident at Fort Cummings.

Here, at the base of the Santa Rita Mountains, Fort Bayard was located in hostile Apache country. The fort had suffered a number of raids. In May 1867 the cattle, horses, and mules had been taken, while another Apache raid struck in the vicinity of the fort in mid-January 1868. This lightning-quick strike resulted in the mounting of infantrymen of the 38th to give chase, which of course proved useless. With Indian trouble on the rise from the summer to the winter of 1868, the mounted black soldiers from both Forts Cummings and Bayard would be dispatched in scouting and reconnaissance missions in futile efforts to eliminate the Apache threat in southwest New Mexico. Occasionally, the soldiers of the 38th Infantry were also mounted for escort duty, and to drive government horses and herds of cattle to other outposts in the southwest. Perhaps Private Cathay may have participated in some mounted assignments. Fort Bayard was dangerous duty for Pvt. William Cathay. Indeed, wrote one Buffalo Soldier officer "[T]he Indians would come down through the pine forests close to Ft. Bayard and fire into the post and the sentinels at the haystacks were often found killed with arrows[.] It was unsafe to leave the post without an escort."

Major Merriam, who had taken companies of the 38th from Kansas into the Southwest, would become the commander of Fort Bayard by 1869. Fort

Bayard was every bit, if not more, remote than Fort Cummings. Lt. Frederick E. Phelps described Fort Bayard as a dreary outpost on the isolated Southwestern frontier, though situated in a picturesque location near the mountains: "[T]he locality was all that could be desired; the Post [was] everything undesirable. Huts of log and round stones, with flat dirt roofs that in summer leaked and brought down rivulets of liquid mud: in winter the hiding place of the tarantula and the centipede, with ceilings of 'condemned' canvas; windows of four and six panes, swinging, door-like, on hinges (the walls were not high enough to allow them to slide upward): low, dark and uncomfortable [and] six hundred miles from the railroad . . . with nothing to eat but the government rations . . . Fort Bayard was the 'final jumping off place' sure enough."

This was a new fort. Fort Bayard had been built in 1866 to protect the region from Apache raids, including the nearby trade route that connected with the Santa Fe Trail, and the county seat of Central City, New Mexico. Nestled between the Gila River to the west and the Mimbres River to the east, Fort Bayard was named in honor of an ex–Indian fighter and Civil War hero killed at Fredericksburg, Capt. George D. Bayard. The fort was well-prepared defensively against Apache attack, consisting of log and adobe fortifications that ringed the installation. In fact, Fort Bayard was in the best condition of any fort in the Southwest.

Because Fort Bayard was located near the border of southeast Arizona, it endured searing heat during the summer of 1868. Duty at this outpost also ensured the usual poor and unsanitary living conditions, hard duty, and strict discipline. All of these factors severely affected the increasingly fragile health of Pvt. William Cathay. With her physical condition deteriorating from a steady decline that first began with contracting smallpox at Jefferson Barracks, worsened with her swimming across the Rio Grande during the march to Fort Union, and finally was aggravated during the winter campaign against the Apache, a seriously ailing Cathy was admitted to the Fort Bayard infirmary on July 13.

Here, at the sparsely provisioned post hospital, the army surgeons diagnosed her as having a case of neuralgia. But most important, the physicians failed to discover her sex: a feat that she was repeatedly able to perform by some unknown strategy and means. Her case was so severe that Cathy received medical treatment at Fort Bayard for nearly a month, recuperating at the post infirmary as best she could under the circumstances.

Fortunately, Private Cathay now benefited from the good drinking water that was so scarce at Fort Cummings. Throughout her period of hospitalization, Cathy Williams drank the cold and clear waters drawn from nearby Cameron Creek. This creek supplied Fort Bayard with good water from numerous springs flowing from the foothills of the Pinos Altos Mountains. Certainly, along with better medical treatment than had been available at Fort Cummings, the spring water assisted in Private Cathay's recovery at the Fort Bayard infirmary.[4]

Meanwhile, General Sheridan was about to unleash his brutal brand of total warfare upon the Plains Indians. It would be General Sherman who immortalized the frontier axiom that was embraced by white settlers and soldiers to promote genocide: "[T]he only good Indian is a dead Indian." Sheridan was about to give the Native Americans a harsh taste of what he had inflicted upon the Southern people of the Shenandoah Valley in 1864. In October 1868 and in response to Indian outrages against civilians, Sheridan received approval to unleash a ruthless type of warfare from his superior, General Sherman, who had made his own reputation for waging total war on the populations of Georgia and South Carolina.

General Sherman now informed Sheridan that they were to employ "all the powers confided in me to the end that these Indians, the enemies of our race and our civilization, shall not again be able to begin and carry out their barbarous warfare." Already, newspapers across the West were clamoring for harsher measures against the remaining tribes, and military men of all ranks had concluded that "they must be hunted like wolves." What would now be inflicted upon the Great Plains Indians was little more than "racial warfare" and genocide.[5]

An increasingly impatient General Sherman now prepared to launch an aggressive campaign during the winter of 1868 to end the Indian troubles once and for all. "Old Billy" believed that "these Indians require to be soundly whipped and the ringleaders in the present trouble hung, their ponies killed, and such destruction of their property as will make them very poor": this was to be total warfare of no mercy to bring decisive success to the American republic in the land of the free. In a repeat of his famous March to the Sea in which his army tore the heart out of Georgia, General Sherman laid plans to send out thousands of troops in offensive operations during the winter of 1868 to hit the enemy when they would be the most vulnerable.

On August 11, 1868, General Sherman reorganized his command into two new military districts to subdue the Indians with the aim of eventually placing them into two separate reservations. One district commander was Maj. General William Babcock Hazen, a West Pointer (Class of 1855) and a former West Point tactics instructor. In the past, he had served as the first commander of the 38th Infantry. Cathy Williams knew him from the time when he commanded the regiment as colonel.[6]

By the early fall of 1868 and only a short time after the hostilities resumed once again, the combined effect of Cathy Williams's years of servitude as a slave combined with the years of Union army service and arduous duty as a Buffalo Soldier, left her health devastated. At this time, even the daily demands of an average settler's life on the frontier was significant to wreck one's health. The price was far higher for a Buffalo Soldier who marched and served across a wide stretch of the West.

In regard to Cathy Williams's case, alleged female physical weakness was certainly not a factor that led to her health problems, instead it was an extremely hard life led over a lengthy period of time in service to her country. For every 1,000 Western soldiers, for example, surgeons on the frontier treated 1,800 medical cases on an annual basis. Some 1,550 cases were disease and illness-related, while only 250 cases consisted of battle wounds and other injuries.

Besides lingering illness, Cathy Williams's personal priorities had changed by this time. She was no longer interested in military life, growing tired of the endless rules and regulations that seldom made any sense or contributed to the greater good. Pvt. William Cathay's attitude changed in regard to her admiration for military service. As she stated in no uncertain terms, Cathy was now thoroughly "tired of army life."

By this time, a variety of factors had combined to sour her opinion of military life: the recent unfair treatment of Mattie Merritt and the racial tensions resulting in the so-called "mutiny" at Fort Cummings; the overbearing attitude of white officers like the martinet Lieutenant Leggett; the mindless regulations that had everything to do with outdated rules rather than common sense; the endless political maneuvering that may well have resulted in Company A being sent out during the Apache campaign without sufficient strength; the ever-present racism and prejudice throughout the army; the isolation of life on the bleak Southwest frontier; fellow soldiers who possessed a penchant for theft; the dangers of facing the ruthless Apache; the ill-fated winter campaign that helped to destroy her health; risking one's life for a thankless duty not even appreciated by the openly hostile civilians that the Buffalo Soldiers protected; no prospects for future advancement or higher rank; the poor quality of life, rations, living conditions, and medical treatment. It was a long list.

It is not known but perhaps Cathy Williams was also tired of living a lie month after month, having to go to such great lengths to conceal her sex and identity. This endless masquerade alone caused a measure of stress and anxiety, if not paranoia, as time passed. There was also the fact that she could not be truthful to her comrades whom she felt close to and perhaps considered as brothers.

All these were deciding factors that convinced Cathy Williams to leave behind the military and its festering problems forever. Clearly, Cathy had had enough of military life. What she now needed most of all was a new and fresh start. In her own words, she employed a common slave tactic that was often used to elude hard labor in the fields or to escape the clutches of abusive overseers: "[F]inally I got tired and wanted to get off [so] I played sick, complained of pains in my side, and rheumatism in my knees" to the post surgeon at Fort Bayard.

After nearly two years, during which Cathy had successfully "performed all the duties expected of a soldier . . . she secured her discharge after feigning illness." Indeed, she had marched about a thousand miles from the prairies of central Kansas to near the border of Mexico, while in full gear and shouldering a Springfield rifle.

Cathy Williams's career as a Buffalo Soldier came to an abrupt end when she once again entered the post infirmary. But this time—for the first time ever—Cathy did not attempt to conceal her sex from the surgeons as she had so often in the past. At long last and only when she had made the decision to do so, her sex was finally discovered. Because of her changed attitude about military life, Cathy allowed her true identity to be revealed to the post surgeon. As Private Cathay explained the situation that resulted in the sudden conclusion of her military career: "[T]he post surgeon found out I was a woman and I got my discharge."

Not unexpectedly, the stunning news of Private Cathay's true identity spread quickly through Company A and the rest of the 38th Infantry. All of Fort Bayard was alive with the unbelievable truth. Strangely, Cathy's fellow Buffalo Soldiers did not take kindly to being duped for so long, reacting in anger and perhaps even with threatening behavior. This hostile reaction partly sprang from the realization that they had indeed missed a good many opportunities to be with a real live woman. In contrast to the reactions of the rank and file, no evidence exists that the white officers, including Lieutenant Leggett, reacted with hostility to the revelation that Private Cathay was a woman.

In Cathy's own words, which told of the extent of the hostile reaction to the sudden discovery of her sex: "[T]he men all wanted to get rid of me after they found out I was a woman [and] some of them acted real bad to me." Indeed, "her former army companions treated her pretty meanly when her sex was known."

On a memorable October 14, 1868, Pvt. William Cathay received what she now coveted most of all and now needed to start a new life on her own: a certificate of disability from the assistant surgeon of Fort Bayard. In this document, the military surgeon stated that Pvt. William Cathay was of "feeble habit . . . he is continually on sick report without benefit [and] unable to do military duty[;] this condition dates prior to enlistment." This conclusion was inaccurate because it overlooked a host of documented illnesses suffered by Cathy Williams during her period of service spanning nearly two years.

For whatever reason, the surgeon made a hasty diagnosis without checking into Cathy's service record, which indicated her illnesses and periods of hospitalization. If Cathy Williams's medical disabilities had existed "prior to enlistment," then they would have been ascertained and she probably would not have been allowed to enlist in the first place. Or she would have been earlier discharged from service as unable to perform duty. But this was not the case.[7]

After serving her country for nearly two years, Cathy Williams finally took off the blue uniform: an abrupt end to a dream that she had once envisioned continuing for many years. At long last, Cathy ended her military service, and most importantly for her, on her own terms.[8]

The commanding officer of Company A, Captain Clarke, who had led the company since May 20, 1867, described that when he first encountered Private Cathay "at that time [she] was doing Garrison duty at Fort Harker, Kansas." The captain also stated that Private Cathay while under his command "has been since [that time] feeble both physically and mentally, and much of the time quite unfit for duty [and that] the origin of his infirmities is unknown to me."

Clearly, Cathy Williams took advantage of a common slave ruse of feigning feeblemindedness in order to assist her in concealing her true identity, intelligence, true thoughts and feelings, and most of all her sex to both black and white soldiers, especially the white officers and her immediate commander, Captain Clarke. This had long been a most successful trick that worked to perfection as she carefully planned. This was no small accomplishment because Cathy Williams was successful in serving in the ranks for nearly two years. And the ruse only ended when she wanted it to end.

As an intelligent and calculating woman, Cathy Williams successfully employed a clever mask: the slave stereotype of the African American "Sambo" of the antebellum South. The racist stereotype that she played up while in service to conceal her sex was what whites perceived was the typical slave mentality and psychology: an African American who was docile, childlike, dependent, feeble-minded, and humble. She was also uneducated and illiterate, traits probably perceived as feeblemindedness by those in authority.

This stereotype is of course a myth, but it helped slaves to conceal what they wanted to hide, such as intelligence and cunning; a form of defense against the hostility of white masters, in order to avoid punishment. In much the same way, Cathy Williams cleverly employed this time-honored slave tactic to conceal her sex.

For Private Cathay, slyly playing the "Sambo" role around white officers, especially the troublesome Captain Leggett, certainly kept her out of trouble and perhaps won for her some extra benefits, while ensuring that her disguise was maintained. In stark contrast to the role, her months of solid military service while successfully disguising her sex, indicated a high intellect, shrewdness, and cunning on her part.

If not for her deteriorating health or changed attitude in regard to military life, no doubt Private Cathay would have served as a Buffalo Soldier for longer. If she could successfully mask her true identity and sex for nearly two years, then Cathy Williams could have probably continued the ruse for many years to come.[9]

During the entire period of her military service and despite numerous physical exams and having been repeatedly hospitalized in four different infirmaries and under the care of numerous physicians and surgeons, Cathy Williams's sex was never discovered until at last she allowed it to be revealed to ensure that she would receive her discharge and release from military service.[10]

In demonstrating that she could perform duty as well and as competently as her male counterparts, Private Cathay's career as a Buffalo Soldier was a success. The undeniable fact that she had been a dependable and "good soldier" was certainly a source of pride to the young ex-slave from Missouri. As she proudly stated in regard to her military service, "I carried my musket and did guard duty and other duties while in the army."[11]

Departing the service, nevertheless, might now have brought a sense of regret to Cathy Williams that perhaps things could not have turned out better. Or she might have felt some remorse upon leaving the men, company, and regiment that she had served faithfully for so long. Such sentiment, however, was not reciprocated by her fellow Buffalo Soldiers. The hostile reactions of Cathy's comrades after they learned of her true sex demonstrated that there was no real love lost—perhaps because of a physical love lost—from the men in the ranks.[12] A good chance existed that Cathy Williams's feelings ran deeper than those of her comrades. As her own words indicated, she was hurt by the way that her former comrades reacted once her identity was revealed.[13]

Although the vast majority of white women on the frontier found the Western frontier experience anything but liberating, Cathy Williams in contrast became more self-reliant, independent, and stronger as a result of the Western experience. For Cathy the more egalitarian environment of the frontier played a key role in transforming her into a stronger person who could successfully overcome even greater challenges and obstacles in the future.

The liberating influence of the egalitarian West was for the most part a myth for white women, but Cathy Williams successfully turned that myth into reality by the strength of her own decisions, willpower, and determination to not only survive but also to succeed against the odds.[14]

Cathy Williams's life was already a success story because she had accomplished so much on her own. Cathy had not only accepted but also overcome almost insurmountable odds. As Pvt. William Cathay she had embraced the life of a Buffalo Soldier and triumphed with grace, competency, and pride, while faithfully serving for nearly two years as a "good soldier" on the Western frontier.[15]

CHAPTER TEN

On Her Own Again

DESPITE HAVING RECENTLY TAKEN OFF THE UNIFORM OF THE BUFFALO SOL-
dier and departed the 38th Infantry, Cathy Williams decided to remain close
to military life out of necessity. This is not surprising because it was the only
real life that she had known outside the institution of slavery. Although she
was more than willing to end her military service, Cathy was not ready to
completely sever her ties with military life.

By this time, Cathy Williams had been transformed by what she had accomplished, seen, and experienced in her life. Her years in military service
had in many ways turned her into a new woman. She was now more self-reliant, independent, and capable of surviving on her own than ever before. Finally freed of the shackles of military rules and regulations, Cathy Williams
would now do as she pleased, making a living on her own and without anyone's help or assistance.

Not surprisingly, therefore, Cathy Williams decided to stay on the fringes
of the Western frontier instead of returning to her home state of Missouri. For
her, the bitter memories of slavery still lingered in Missouri. In addition, the
life that she had once known in "Little Dixie" was no more. It was now time
to move forward as in so many other times in her life.

Cathy Williams's decision to remain in the West might have been based
on the fact that her cousin and friend still remained in service with the Buffalo Soldiers. Almost symbolically, therefore, Cathy Williams's decision to remain in the West closely tied her to the Santa Fe Trail where Buffalo Soldiers
continued to be stationed. Or it is possible that she might have had a lover in
a Buffalo Soldier command.[1]

For most of the remainder of her life, Cathy Williams was destined to remain in the area around Fort Union. One company of the 9th Cavalry would be stationed here, while the regiment's headquarters was located at Santa Fe by 1876.[2]

By the time this young African American woman took off the uniform of a Buffalo Soldier for the final time at Fort Bayard, some of the best years of her life had been devoted not to family life, marriage, or motherhood, but to military service. And these past decisions were made at considerable personal sacrifice in regard to her personal needs and the desire to fulfill her role as a mother.

After so many years on her own, she might have now viewed these natural maternal longings as confining to her sense of individuality and spirit of independence. Cathy's personal decisions in regard to forsaking married life and motherhood originally evolved more out of necessity than anything else. She could not possibly have started a family during the Civil War or as a Buffalo Soldier. Cathy knew that having a child would have ended her connection with the military life.

Determined to survive slavery's painful legacy, America's lingering racism, and perhaps the demons of her own slave past, Cathy Williams most of all continued to want to be her own woman. And this could best be accomplished by her remaining in the more egalitarian Western frontier.

For Cathy Williams, personal independence was by now a cherished way of life after her experiences in the harsh autocratic worlds of slavery and the military. Only the frontier West offered a greater measure of freedom and independence for people such as her. As James Weldon Johnson explained: "[The] West is giving the Negro a better deal than any other section of the country [for] there is more opportunity . . . and less prejudice . . . in this section of the country than anywhere else in the United States."

As for most ex-slaves attempting to start new lives of freedom in the West, economic issues were paramount to Cathy Williams. She no longer received the regular pay of $13.00 per month as a Buffalo Soldier. Because Cathy never married, no male—other than her white masters—had ever provided for her. She decided to now remain on her own and to make do as best she could, relying once again on her own abilities and intelligence to create a new life for herself. Cathy Williams would, therefore, remain close to military life for sound economic, if not personal and psychological, reasons.

Another reason why she chose to remain close to military life was because her early years as a slave had left Cathy Williams with nothing to show for a lifetime of labor and sacrifice except the ability to survive on her own.

As a black female, Cathy Williams's greatest challenge during her post–Buffalo Soldier period was simply to provide for herself. This was no easy task for former slaves, especially single women without families who were forced to start a new life from scratch after the Civil War. And survival would be more difficult for her because Cathy was now more on her own than ever before.

Upon successfully escaping slavery and fleeing to the North, Linda Brent faced comparable economic challenges as Cathy Williams after she left the Buffalo Soldiers. In Linda's words: "[M]y greatest anxiety now was to obtain employment." Much like racism and prejudice, this central economic dilemma dogged former slaves for the rest of their lives.

Fortunately for Cathy Williams, domestic work, including cook and laundress, drew better pay on the frontier than in the East. The better pay that an enterprising black woman could earn in the West partly explained why she decided to remain on the frontier, working on her own as an independent business woman.[3]

A new life in the West would bring not only new economic but also new personal opportunities and challenges for Cathy. For the last two years from 1866 to 1868, Cathy Williams had been caught in a dilemma. In order to serve as a Buffalo Soldier and live a better life than as an ex-slave in the South or in her native Missouri, she could not marry. Now that she was no longer a Buffalo Soldier, however, Cathy now possessed the chance to marry for the first time in her life—if she chose to do so.

It is not known but perhaps one reason why she left military service was because of a desire for marriage and a family. The Western frontier, however, contained relatively few African Americans or potential marriage partners for a black woman. In any case, the possibility of marriage for Cathy was remote because she preferred an independent lifestyle in which she answered to no man or woman. Free from military service, a top priority of this young ex-slave was to retain her personal freedom from those things that would restrict or infringe upon her independent nature. This ever-present need to be free of societal controls and artificial restrictions—a quality that would define her being and spirit for most of her life—might have stemmed partly from the psychologically damaging experience of slavery.

For Cathy Williams, it almost seemed as if true personal happiness could only be found far outside the confines of those man-made institutions, rules, and regulations, which made life so unbearable for women of color. With her $13.00 per month pay as a Buffalo Soldier having proved insufficient to provide her with even the smallest measure of financial security or a good chance to save enough money, she was now forced to survive amid a rapidly deteriorating economic situation. As so often in the past, she simply would have to make the best of it.

In addition, another factor no doubt played a role in shaping her decision to remain on the frontier West and not to return to her native Missouri. Probably still haunted by the bitter memory of slavery, Cathy Williams no doubt felt much like Linda Brent who described the psychological damage that she had suffered from slave life before the day of liberation: "It has been painful to me, in many ways, to recall the dreary years I passed in bondage [and] I would gladly forget them if I could." Cathy Williams also no doubt desired to escape its terrible memory by remaining far away from that land—the Upper South—that reminded her of racism, prejudice, and slave life. If there was a place where her slave past could be forgotten, it was on the Western frontier.[4]

To Cathy Williams and other African Americans, the West remained a symbol of hope. The Western frontier was described to eager black migrants as the "Promised land." Placards that beckoned African American migrants advertised "Ho! for the New El Dorado!" Besides economic opportunity, the West was also viewed as a place relatively free of prejudice and discrimination compared with the rest of the country.

As early as 1833, the Philadelphia convention for "the Improvement of the Free People of Color" recommended that African Americans migrate west, "where the ploughshares of prejudice have as yet been unable to penetrate the soil." Such promises and the undying faith of a better life in the more egalitarian West influenced Missouri free blacks, such as Missouri farmer George Washington Bush, to push toward the setting sun in search for a better life.

A black exodus of hopeful migrants continued to pour from the South, spurred by the realization that at least African Americans would "be free from the persecution, and cruelty, and the deviltry of the rebel wretches . . . it is better to starve in Kansas than be shot and killed in the South." But the migration of African Americans to the West during the 1800s was only a continuum of the earlier black Western settlement, which began with the first push from the Eastern seaboard in the 1700s.

The distinguished contribution of blacks in winning the West embodied a relentless march of hopeful, optimistic pioneers determined to be free at any cost or sacrifice. One historian maintained with ample justification that African Americans and other "minority peoples should be at the heart of historical claims for Western distinctness."[5]

With her decision to remain in her beloved West, Cathy Williams was also searching for what she had yet to find in her life: a free land without the curse of racism and prejudice. She was looking for a place where she would not be judged by skin color and her slave past. In conjunction with this life-long pursuit, Cathy was also probably searching for a measure of inner peace. Both these objectives were interrelated. And the best place for achieving these goals was on the Western frontier in the greatest democracy in the world.

An additional factor that certainly must have influenced her desire to remain in the West was her health. Cathy experienced failing health from her service as a Buffalo Soldier on the frontier. Despite being only twenty-four by this time, Cathy's years of faithful service for her country were beginning to take a toll on her body.

Another reason that might also partly explain why she now looked forward to a new start in the West was that Cathy Williams, despite her young age, might have been going through a premature midlife crisis of sorts. She now had nothing to show for all the hard work and sacrifices of her life—few friends, no children, no husband or immediate family, and ever-diminishing economic prospects in life—except for the vivid memories of her military service, which certainly served as a source of pride. Indeed, she carefully preserved her discharge papers and kept them with her, maintaining pride in her military service.

Without much chance for future success in a society hostile to both women and blacks, the ex-private of the U.S. Army remained hopeful for her future prospects. If Cathy could survive slavery, Civil War service, and life as a soldier on the frontier, then she knew that she could not only survive but also succeed in life on her own. With this faith in herself, Cathy traveled northeastward from Fort Bayard to Fort Union, New Mexico, in search of a new start.

Day after day, Cathy made her way through the heart of New Mexico, crossing the Rio Grande River once again—on her own. No doubt, the sight of this historic river of the Southwest brought anything but fond memories. She perhaps was once again forced to swim across the river in crossing from west to east.

With her military service now behind her, the former slave from Missouri now settled easily into the role of an independent African American female. She became Cathy Williams once again. She began living and acting as a woman. Cathy no longer had anything to hide. This in itself was a liberating experience. It also must have been a refreshing change from nearly two years of masquerade in the almost exclusive company of male soldiers.[6]

First, she began to search for an employer at Fort Union. In short order, Cathy Williams was able to secure employment as a cook for a colonel and his family at the post.

Fort Union was familiar territory because it was located on the Santa Fe Trail. Here, returning to the role she had known during the Civil War, Cathy cooked for the colonel and his family throughout 1869 and 1870. Such an employee for a high ranking officer and his family would indicate that she had become a good cook. Cathy benefited from the steady employment and economic security, regular shelter, and food. In the process, she successfully made the difficult transition from being a Buffalo Soldier fighting the Apache to doing house work for whites. This time, however, she was paid a regular wage unlike during slavery.[7]

For some unknown reason, Cathy Williams suddenly broke off her ties to the U.S. military at Fort Union. Always ambitious and looking for something better, perhaps she had learned of more ample opportunities elsewhere. Maybe the colonel became overbearing. Or the break may have resulted from the colonel's retirement or transfer to another fort. Or perhaps Cathy Williams simply tired of the menial job of cooking for a white family, which was probably not much different than when she served the Johnson family at their "big house" in Cole County, Missouri.

Evidently learning of greater opportunities in nearby Colorado, Cathy departed northeast New Mexico and headed northeastward for Pueblo in south central Colorado, south of Denver. In her own words: "[A]fter leaving the army I went to Pueblo, Colorado." By this time, she had earned and saved enough money to purchase a wagon and team of horses. Successfully acquiring some savings demonstrated thrift, financial savvy, and an ability to successfully manage her own affairs without assistance: no small task for a female ex-slave starting anew, making her way in life by herself and without family support.

South central Colorado was a beautiful, wide, and booming land. While Anglos continued to settle in Colorado, the older ways of Indian and Hispanic life persisted to create a multicultural blend on the frontier: an environment that Cathy Williams, as a woman of color, naturally found appealing and refreshing after the stuffy world of the white military establishment. Here, at Pueblo on the Arkansas River just east of the Rocky Mountains and just west of the western edge of the Great Plains, this fertile and well-watered piedmont, or heartland, of Colorado was a land of opportunity.

For a period of two years, Cathy Williams found employment at Pueblo working as a laundress for a Mr. Dunbar. Here, she continued to earn sufficient money, and worked to create a new life for herself.

Life as a laundress in the West offered an African American woman distinct financial possibilities. By this means, Cathy Williams now possessed a chance for a good life with a decent future. For instance, by way of her laundry business that earned her fifty cents for each flannel shirt she washed, Clara Brown eventually became a businesswoman and a leading citizen of Central City, Colorado. She was a former Virginia slave whose children had been taken from her and sold on the auction block. Clara had then served as a cook for gold prospectors, before migrating by wagon train to Colorado. With thrift, hard work, and industry, Clara had earned enough money to eventually became a woman of wealth and prestige in her Western community.

Like Cathy Williams, other black women across the West also prospered after starting their own businesses. One such successful African American woman was another former Missouri slave named Elvira Conley. She was tall, stately, and "black as ebony and proud of it." Elvira's success stemmed from her laundry business in Marshall, Kansas, in 1868.

Elsewhere, an ex-slave from Tennessee, Mary Fields, created a prosperous life for herself in Cascade, Montana, with a laundry business. She continued to operate her booming enterprise well into her seventies. Many black women in the West became successful and resourceful businesswomen to support their families. They established and managed restaurants, laundries, hair parlors, and boardinghouses across the frontier.

In working around Pueblo, within sight of the snow-capped top of Pike's Peak to the north, Cathy Williams enjoyed a successful life for herself. She earned enough money to save what was then a fairly substantial amount of money, especially for a female ex–slave. At some point, she also made income as a cook in addition to that as a laundress. In her own words: "I made money [at Pueblo] by cooking and washing."

With money in her pocket and a wagon and team of horses, she was ensured a measure of independence and freedom of movement. Cathy could come and go wherever she pleased in order to seek new opportunities to fulfill her dream of building a better life for herself. Such independence and personal mobility—which of course she was denied as a slave and was unattainable in the Civil War and during her months as a Buffalo Soldier—were important to her sense of freedom by this time. This must have been a liberating development in her life. She remained determined that she was not to be restricted or limited to any one location, occupation, or employer if they proved to be an obstacle to her ambitions.

During this successful period when she was finally doing so well that money was no longer a primary concern, a man suddenly came into Cathy Williams's life at Pueblo. And he was no ordinary man. She felt that he was special, someone who was different from the rest. It is not known but perhaps one reason why she departed Fort Union was because she had met this man whom she loved. If so, then perhaps they had left together to start a new life in Pueblo.

Suddenly free of constraints and longing for a home, family, and children now that the opportunity had finally come to her for the first time, Cathy's life suddenly changed when she married this man in Pueblo. At long last, it now seemed as if all of Cathy's dreams were coming true.

Because of the scarcity of women on the Western frontier, the chances of marriage were actually greater for women of color than for white females. In fact, an African American woman was more likely to marry on the frontier than in the East.

Unfortunately, little is known about Cathy Williams's husband except from her own brief words describing an event in her life that she wished to forget. But most likely, he was an African American and probably a miner who worked in the area. Mining was a readily available occupation to black men in the West. He could even have been a veteran of a Buffalo Soldier regiment, like herself.

The relationship, however, between the ex–Buffalo Soldier and miner was a mismatch. Trouble between the two arose almost from the beginning. Even though her free-spirited nature and independent mind were bound to clash with a husband who was evidently an equally strong-willed person and no doubt chauvinistic in the tradition of the day, Cathy was not the principal source of the problem. Still only in her mid-twenties and with relatively little experience in love, her years spent on a Missouri plantation and in military service combined to make her emotionally vulnerable in what was apparently her first serious relationship.

Cathy Williams was apparently a poor judge of character in regard to choosing a suitable mate, especially if she was in love for the first time in her life. Or perhaps she had little choice, as he might have been the only one to have ever asked for her hand in marriage. Although Cathy was smart, she was still naive and inexperienced as to the requirements of a successful relationship. What was worse, she married a man who was no good.

A Trinidad, Colorado, historian merely concluded that this was "an unfortunate marriage." In Cathy's own words about her life in Pueblo with her husband: "I got married while there, but my husband was no account [as] he stole my watch and chain, a hundred dollars in money and my team of horses and wagon." Quite possibly, her husband, evidently more worldly and experienced in the ways of both love and life, perhaps married her more for economic than romantic reasons.[8]

This disappointing episode, fortunately brief, also revealed much about Cathy's character and spirit. After discovering that her husband had stolen her prized watch and chain, money, and team of horses and wagon, which she had worked so hard to earn, Cathy immediately "had him arrested and put in jail," as she recalled in an interview with a St. Louis newspaperman in late 1875.

As this incident indicates, for anyone who caused her serious trouble by taking advantage, there would have to be a price to pay. Cathy Williams lived in the harsh world of the frontier West, where it was survival of the fittest. Most of all, Cathy was a survivor who knew how to persevere and endure by strength of character: legacies of a hard life lived in slavery and on the wild Western frontier. She survived the disillusionment of her first and only husband, learning a great deal in the process. She became wiser and a stronger person during what was certainly a difficult time.

Cathy learned from the experience, drawing positive lessons from yet another negative event in her life: a strength of will helping her survive and persevere through the many disappointments in her life. Her husband's betrayal was something that she would never forget. She apparently never again thought about marrying.[9]

After her Pueblo employment ended, and perhaps to escape the presence, if not wrath, of her jailed husband after his release, Cathy Williams struck out on her own once again, and began a new search for another place. Once again, she was on the move in search for a new start and a better life.[10]

Cathy now journeyed southeast in her wagon following the course of the Arkansas River. Symbolically, she was returning once again to the Santa Fe Trail.[11]

Skirting the eastern edge of the Rockies and the Arkansas River, Cathy must have marveled at the beauty of the snow-capped mountains dominating the western horizon. She passed the remains of Bent's old adobe fort where General Kearny's Army of the West and Colonel Doniphan's Missouri regiment had encamped on their march to Santa Fe during the summer of 1846.

Established more than ten years before the Mexican-American War, Bent's Fort was once a key trading post on the Santa Fe Trail. She was almost directly west of her native county, Jackson, Missouri, which was more than 500 miles to the east. The Santa Fe Trail led from her hometown of Independence to this historic fort on the Arkansas River.[12]

Cathy Williams's solitary sojourn across the High Plains southeastward along the Arkansas River and through the wide stretches of short grass prairie of southeastward Colorado finally ended near the small town of Las Animas. Situated in a picturesque location on the river, Las Animas was built near the site of Bent's Fort.[13]

She might have discovered a small African American community at Las Animas. If so, then this could explain in part why this point was her destination or why Cathy decided to stop here. Charles Bent, who founded Bent's Fort, owned slaves, such as Dick and Andrew Green. Dick's wife, Charlotte, was the cook at the Fort, and "her cooking became famous from St. Louis to Santa Fe." Like Cathy, and having been raised on the Mississippi, Charlotte probably had been a Missouri slave. These African Americans or their descendants might well have remained in the area after Bent's Fort was abandoned.[14]

During the 100-mile journey to Bent County, where the small community of Las Animas served as the county seat, and besides breathtaking scenery,

Cathy might have seen herds of deer, pronghorn antelope, prairie dogs, buffalo, wolves, and coyotes along the way. The natural beauty of the region might have beckoned for her to stay.

Here, on the rolling high plains southeast of Denver, Las Animas was located in Bent County, Colorado, near both Bent's Fort, a short distance to the west, and Fort Lyon, immediately to the east. This semiarid region of forests and grasslands at the confluence of the Arkansas and Purgatoire Rivers was both fertile and picturesque, causing other pioneers, like Kit Carson, to call Bent County home.

Clearly, Cathy Williams wished to remain close to military life. Fort Lyon was located nearby along the Santa Fe Trail. She settled close to the fort, which nestled among the green rolling hills and broad sweeping plains lining the Arkansas River. The fort was named after the liberator of Jefferson City, Missouri, Gen. Nathaniel Lyon, who was later killed at Wilson's Creek Missouri in August 1861.

Here, in Bent County, Cathy Williams gained employment and steady income as a laundress. Again, she found a means of survival with her own initiative and determination. Thanks to Hispanic influences, Colorado was more openly tolerant than Western states farther east. For three years in the mid-1870s, the town of Yankee Hill, Colorado, was kept safe by its black sheriff, a former Buffalo Soldier named Willie Kennard, while elsewhere in the territory Henry O. Wagoner, a former slave, served as the deputy sheriff of Arapaho County. The African American town of Dearfield, Colorado, was an all-black community on the high plains. Dearfield developed from a colonization effort from the migration of impoverished African Americans from urban areas to agricultural regions on the frontier. Here, they could thrive in the free lands of Colorado. In this way, the black migrants made an attempt "to get back to the land, where they naturally belong, and to work out their own salvation from the land up." The African American experiment at Dearfield, Colorado, proved successful, and was destined to boom as late as the First World War.[15]

After remaining about a year in the Las Animas area and probably working as a laundress for the soldiers at Fort Lyon, Cathy once more packed up and moved farther south. She again traveled along the historic Santa Fe Trail, journeying to the southwest.

During her journey across the bountiful countryside, Cathy Williams passed through Bent, Otero, and Las Animas Counties, traveling along the mountain route of the Santa Fe Trail. She was now retracing her earlier journeys, for this was the same trek that she had followed with the 38th Infantry during the long march from Kansas to Fort Union, New Mexico.

She finally settled in the small town of Trinidad, in southern Las Animas County. In her own words, "I came here" to Trinidad and decided to make a new start. Nestling in a valley dominated by towering mountains, Trinidad was located immediately north of the New Mexico state line.

Indicating the extent of the latest twist in Cathy's personal odyssey, Trinidad was nearly 500 miles northeast of Fort Bayard, New Mexico. Here, Private Cathay had seen "his" last duty as a Buffalo Soldier. Once again, Cathy Williams's strange destiny seemed intertwined with the route of the historic Santa Fe Trail.

Amid the sprawling prairies of western Kansas, the Santa Fe Trail split into the shorter Cimarron route and longer mountain route. Trinidad was located on the mountain route of the Santa Fe Trail. This route was preferred by Western migrants because it was better-watered and timbered, while passing through a beautiful countryside inhabited by less hostile Indians.

The small town of Trinidad had long served as a rest stop before the wagon trains continued south to labor through the Raton Pass, the mountainous gateway to New Mexico, before the final push southwest to Santa Fe and the Hispanic world.

By 1876 and two years before the railroad reached Raton Pass, the wagon caravans flowed, transporting an annual average of 15,000 tons of freight and products of New Mexico, such as wool and mineral ores, to the Colorado railheads for transport to Eastern markets. In addition, herds of Texas cattle were driven northward through Trinidad and toward the Western railheads that shipped beef to the cities and markets of the East.[16]

Just north of the Colorado–New Mexico border, Cathy Williams found much that she liked in this promised land. Trinidad was now her new home. At this time, "if one state has remained in people's imagination as symbolic of the Rocky Mountain West, it is surely Colorado. Prospering and growing with the gold and silver booms of the mid-nineteenth century, Colorado saw a wild mélange of railroaders, mountain men, cowboys, whores, ranchers, miners, hoteliers, lawmakers, soldiers, guides, hunters, entrepreneurs, philanthropists, teachers, newspaper editors, ministers, and more. And all of these were black."[17] Here, in Las Animas County, Cathy Williams worked and earned a living as a laundress and a seamstress.

The number of African Americans in southern Colorado helped to create a distinctive multiracial and multicultural community in Trinidad. Comparable demographics were found in the largest town in northeast New Mexico, Santa Fe. More so than in Missouri or the South and a legacy of America's conquest of this region in the Mexican-American War, this part of the West was in fact a melting pot. Here, African Americans, Asians, Hispanics, and Indians met and closely interacted with Anglos. Cathy had probably never experienced such ethnic diversity before, and no doubt she liked what she saw in this multicultural world.

In a small house on the north side of town, Cathy Williams now settled into the mainstream of life in the community of Trinidad. She boarded with a black family that consisted of a couple and two children. Here, she found a home, a pleasant domestic environment, and a surrogate family, before she made enough money to live on her own.

By 1870, more than 450 African Americans called the Colorado Territory home. In fact, a total of nearly 285,000 blacks, or 12 percent of the total population, lived in the Western states and territories in 1870.

Despite the relatively small number of blacks in Colorado, they were nevertheless politically astute, enterprising, and active in demanding equality. This egalitarian spirit might well have been a factor that prompted Cathy Williams to first migrate to the territory.

Both during and immediately following the years of the Civil War, Colorado's African Americans struggled to deny statehood to the Colorado Territory until black voting rights and citizenship were guaranteed. Consequently, these ambitious African Americans petitioned Congress to deny statehood until white politicians of Colorado lived up to the republic's principles and America's vision of equality for all. In the end, the determined efforts of the territory's African American community were successful.

In early 1867, Colorado's blacks finally won the right to vote before the official ratification of the Fifteenth Amendment, which guaranteed comparable suffrage rights in both the Northern and Western states. With the passage of the Fifteenth Amendment, blacks across the West celebrated the victory in their struggle to obtain suffrage equality. No doubt, Cathy Williams also celebrated this event. At Portland, Washington, the brass band of an African American regiment joined in the festivities to celebrate the passing of the amendment.

Besides earning money as a laundress and seamstress, Cathy Williams also occasionally served as a nurse in Colorado, to earn extra income. In early January 1876 when the town of Trinidad was officially incorporated and Colorado became the 38th state—a memorable numerical designation that certainly held special meaning to Cathy Williams—some eight years after leaving the Buffalo Soldiers, the story of Cathy Williams became public for the first time, when it was published in the St. Louis, Missouri, *Daily Times*.

During the lengthy interview that she gave in late 1875, a contented Cathy, who had found peace and stability at last in Trinidad, informed the St. Louis journalist concerning the community of Trinidad: "I like this town. I know all the good people here, and I expect to get rich yet. I have not got my land warrant. I thought I would wait till the railroad came and then take my land near the depot. [The government] Grant owns all this land around here, and it won't cost me anything. I shall never live in the states again. You see I've got a good sewing machine and I get washing to do and clothes to make. I want to get along and not be a burden to my friends and relatives."

What Cathy Williams hoped to obtain at this time was a land grant from the Homestead Act of 1862. In all fairness, Cathy's lengthy service in the Civil War and nearly two years in the 38th Infantry should have entitled her to such a land grant. Congress had already made 46 million acres of land in the Deep South available to ex-slaves after the Civil War, while other African Americans migrated to receive Western lands under the Homestead Act.[18]

For the first time, Cathy Williams had found what she hoped to be a permanent home amid an African American and Hispanic community instead of a military outpost or fort. In the process, she also carved out a life of her own. Here, at Trinidad, she was not an outcast but an accepted and respected member of not only the black and Hispanic community but also the white community as well. To both black and white and Hispanics, she was affectionately known as "Miss Kate" or "Kate."

Trinidad was a colorful and vibrant frontier community and included a wide variety of people. This multicultural town had a mixture of large ranchers, ex–Civil War and frontier soldiers, recent settlers, Apache and Navajo, both black and white prostitutes, Hispanics, aging mountain men and trappers, ex–slave owners and Confederate veterans from the Deep South, small farmers, European immigrants, black coal miners, Indian fighters, cowboys, buffalo hunters, fur traders, former Buffalo Soldiers, thieves, drunks, murderers, and worse in some cases.

Some cowboys of the area were African Americans who, like the Buffalo Soldiers, were usually given the most difficult duties during the trail drives of cattle, which passed from Texas through bustling Trinidad. In addition, some black Indians may also have spiced this colorful blend of diverse peoples.

Such a mixture of peoples did not occur without good reason. Here, on the Western frontier of southeast Colorado, a large measure of equality and opportunity existed like nowhere else in the country. Unlike in the East and especially the South, the races more easily mixed without the artificial constraints of society. Both black and white cowboys drank together in the saloons, ate the same food, and slept beside each other on the cattle drive. This open environment embodied the egalitarian spirit of the West, where people of all races and nationalities freely interacted together.

On occasion, even some Buffalo Soldiers, both on and off duty, from the forts along the Santa Fe Trail spent time in Trinidad. In late 1880, three 9th Cavalry deserters from Forts Cummings and Bayard were arrested in Trinidad by the sheriff.

In addition, another factor that perhaps helped Cathy Williams settle smoothly into the pace of life at Trinidad was that some permanent residents and leading citizens were Missourians, both white and black. One leading white citizen, George S. Simpson, was a Missourian. The towering sandstone bluff that overlooked Trinidad on the north side of town was named "Simpson's Rest" in his honor. In 1882, the marshal of this rowdy frontier community was the famous Bat Masterson. Masterson's job was a challenge because the Trinidad area by this time "became a safe haven for every badman in the West." Here, Masterson broke up the thriving prostitution rings of Trinidad, a town that contained far more men than women.

Discrimination would never again force Cathy Williams to pack up and move on. Here, on the north side of Trinidad, the black and Hispanic community provided a secure home and refuge for her. For generations, Trinidad served as a vibrant crossroads of Hispanic, Indian, and Anglo cultures, which came together because of the heavy traffic along the Santa Fe Trail. European immigrants, including Russians, Poles, and Swedes, worked the coal mines in the area, contributing to Trinidad's melting pot community.

Here, the restrictive Eastern standards of class, family lineage, and social status simply were unimportant. More than two dozen nationalities were represented in the small but colorful multicultural Trinidad community. Unlike anything that she had experienced before, a measure of racial equality became a dream fulfilled for Cathy Williams.[19]

In this more egalitarian and open environment, "Miss Kate's" sewing and laundress business prospered from the steady commerce and traffic passing along the Santa Fe Trail. The special qualities found in Trinidad gave her the opportunity to make and save more money than at any other time in her life. Not surprisingly, she preferred the Western frontier and Colorado Territory to any place she had ever been before in her life.[20]

The only glimpse of Cathy's life comes from her newspaper interview. But how and why was a story written about the life of Cathy Williams in late 1875? A curious white journalist from St. Louis had accidentally stumbled across the incredible story of Cathy Williams while visiting Trinidad. As he wrote in his article: "A character in Trinidad is a colored woman by the name of Cathy Williams. She is called by the residents "Kate." The [*Daily*] *Times* representative having heard that [this] woman served as a soldier during the late [Indian] war and was in other respects an interesting individual, recently called at her humble abode for the purpose of learning something of her history."[21]

As the St. Louis reporter continued: "She resides alone in an 'adobe' building of one room in the northern portion of the town. She received the *Times* man very politely, though with an [exaggerated] formality that had a slight touch of the ridiculous. Like her Mexican [and African American] neighbors, she had no chairs, but knowing that Americans preferred sitting to squatting on the floor, she requested her visitor to be seated on a [small table or bench] which occupied a corner of the room. The room was scantily furnished, but everything was neat and tidy": a sense of order and neatness that was clearly a legacy of her military service.[22]

The reporter was immediately impressed with this remarkable woman who still possessed a great deal of pride in her past accomplishments and military service. In the journalist's words that betrayed a sense of admiration: "Kate is tall and powerfully built, black as night, masculine looking and has a very independent air both in conversation and action. Dressed in male attire she would readily pass for a man . . . she appears hard and sinewy as if her life had been one of exposure."[23]

Besides her dignified bearing and presence and "very independent air," the reporter was impressed when Cathy presented her army discharge papers and surgeon's certificate from Fort Bayard. She had proudly kept these for years, and now offered them as evidence of her remarkable story of life as a Buffalo Soldier.[24]

In the journalist's words: "The *Times* man examined the [discharge] paper and found it to be a service document, a discharge from the army, dated Fort Bayard, New Mexico, October 14, 1868. The discharge was granted in the surgeon's certificate, and stated that the character of the discharged William Cathy [*sic*] was good." The St. Louis reporter was now convinced that he indeed had a great story that had to be told throughout the country.[25]

After learning first-hand of her life story, the journalist explained that "in detailing the above [story] the woman sometimes failed to recall dates and the names of places [to be expected from an uneducated woman with a slave past who knew nothing of geography], but otherwise her narrative was smooth and well connected. The *Times* representative returned his thanks for the information and retired with the promise to give a truthful account of what he had been told."[26]

Clearly, this insightful journalist, who knew a good story when he found one, was so impressed by the veracity of Cathy's exciting narrative that he had no reservations about having it published in one of the largest newspapers in St. Louis, the largest city west of the Mississippi River.

But most important in terms of ascertaining Cathy's success and happiness at this point in her life, she revealed to the reporter that she loved

Trinidad and its people and that this was her home. At long last, Cathy Williams finally found not only a permanent home but also a refuge in a friendly, tolerant Western town of small wooden structures, haciendas, and adobe buildings.

For Cathy Williams, the refreshing atmosphere of tolerance was only matched by the natural beauty and serenity of this land around Trinidad, nestling as it did in the fertile valley of the Purgatoire River. Here, the mountains around the small town rose to an elevation of more than 6,000 feet among slopes covered with dense stands of pinon and juniper. To the west loomed the snow-capped peaks of the majestic Sangre de Cristo Range of the Rockies, which in Spanish means the "Blood of Christ," as named by the early Spanish explorers.

This was a land of peaks, mesas, sparkling lakes, green meadows, rolling prairies, and deep canyons. From the mountains surrounding Trinidad, Cathy Williams could look southward and see bluish-hued Raton Peak in northeast New Mexico. And this beautiful land was blessed with a mild, semiarid climate of low humidity, a boon to Cathy's still fragile health. All in all, the town of Trinidad, its black and Hispanic community, and the surrounding countryside was a psychological, spiritual, and physical refuge for the former slave woman from "Little Dixie."

All in all, life was never better for Cathy Williams than at this time. Here, at Trinidad, she lived, earned a steady income, and made good and lasting friends. She was respected and well liked by many members of the community. She had finally found the peace that she had always searched for in life.

Life had improved for Cathy in no small part for having rid herself of a bad husband and less tolerant racial environments of former communities and the restrictive world of the military. She remained in Trinidad throughout the remainder of the 1870s and the early 1880s, living peacefully as an independent woman.

The story of her life was eventually published in the *Daily Times* of St. Louis on January 2, 1876. Appropriately, the article was entitled, "She Fought Nobly." A subtitle proclaimed: "The Story of a Colored Woman Who Served as an Enlisted Soldier during the Late War."

In Trinidad, after the story broke, Cathy Williams, now age thirty-three, became the focus of some local curiosity. The news that she had served in the ranks of the Buffalo Soldiers caused "some interest and amusement" among the local populace who suspected no such adventurous past life from this solitary, hard-working African American woman. Few knew of her military past, only that she lived quietly on her own and "got along as a laundress and dressmaker."

Cathy was not the type of person who bragged or boasted about her exploits. A positive and optimistic person, Cathy harbored no bitterness about the past. After the truth about her eventful life was revealed by the St. Louis reporter, a local Trinidad historian described Cathy Williams's life story as, "unusual and fascinating."

Impressed by both her no-nonsense demeanor and proud bearing, the journalist from St. Louis described Cathy Williams as she appeared in late 1875 when she gave the interview: "[H]er face is marked with small-pox." The scattered smallpox scars were permanent reminders of when she was stricken with the illness at Jefferson Barracks, not long after she had enlisted in the Buffalo Soldiers during the fall of 1866. Indeed, in this and other ways, the strain of those difficult years of physical labor, hardship, and exertion were now evident for all to see.

By the time of her interview with the *Daily Times* journalist, Cathy Williams was described as "about thirty to thirty-five years of age." This newspaper account was accurate in this regard, for she was now thirty-one years of age. In pants instead of a dress, she continued to wear her hair short as during her Buffalo Soldier service, which gave her a "masculine" appearance.

As evident from the final printed story in the *Daily Times,* Cathy Williams had opened up and presented the hidden details of her remarkable life. She had poured out some of the long-hidden feelings about her past, perhaps known to no others, while expressing her hopes for a brighter future. Despite the hard times of the past, a spirit of hope and optimism continued to burn deep within her. Cathy's resilient spirit and hopes for the future shined through the interview to appear in the printed final copy for all St. Louis and the nation to read.

Apparently, this was the first time in her life that Cathy Williams had ever told her story to anyone in such detail and length. With a surprising measure of candor and honesty, she had spoken quite freely of both the good and bad times. Cathy had articulated her thoughts so openly that it almost seemed like a cathartic experience for her. She had expressed and revealed some of her innermost emotions about herself. Because she was illiterate and never kept a diary, had she not given this in-depth interview to this Missouri journalist from the *Daily Times,* the story of Cathy Williams and Pvt. William Cathay would have simply faded away like so much African American history.

The story of Cathy Williams was in fact just one chapter of a distinguished chronicle that African Americans compiled in the winning of the West. Like the slave communities of the antebellum period, a vibrant black West not only existed but also thrived for generations, while providing some of the most dramatic chapters in the Western saga.

Life only got better for this independent businesswoman. At some point before her late 1875 interview, she made enough money to move into her own place. Fortunately, Cathy Williams's business ventures received a boost ten years after the end of the Civil War. As she had anticipated in late 1875, growth and new prosperity came to Trinidad, and then Santa Fe itself in 1880, when the iron tracks of the Atchison, Topeka, and Santa Fe Railroad finally reached the small Colorado town. Suddenly, the historic Santa Fe Trail, around which so much of Cathy's life and military service revolved, was made obsolete by the arrival of the train. Such a transformation changed the face of the West forever.[27]

By all indications, life at Trinidad continued to be good for Cathy Williams. In many ways, the independent life that she loved and made for herself was superior to that of many white women in the West. In the West, "the long-suffering white female pioneer seemed to be the closest thing to an authentic innocent victim. Torn from family and civilization, overworked and lonely, disoriented by an unfamiliar landscape, frontierswomen could seem to be tragic martyrs to their husbands' willful ambitions."[28]

But once again change was in the air for Cathy Williams. It was almost as if upheaval had marked so her life that she eagerly embraced change, if not actively seeking it out. She moved once again. Cathy departed Trinidad for some unknown reason. But apparently, as with her previous moves, she left in search of better opportunity. Optimistic and ambitious, Cathy Williams was still consumed by the promise of the West. Evidence exists that she left southeast Colorado and traveled to northeast New Mexico sometime in the mid-1880s. The 1885 census records for Las Animas County, Colorado—which included Trinidad—have no Cathy Williams listed.

By this time, she had saved enough money to set up home a short distance south—around twenty miles—just across the Colorado line and down the mountain route of the Santa Fe Trail in Raton, Colfax County, New Mexico. Some scant evidence exists that Cathy Williams became a businesswoman and ran her own boarding house in Raton, which would have been no small accomplishment.

If this was in fact true, then Cathy Williams might well have benefited from literacy skills and economic savvy developed in the schools established at Western outposts by the Army Reorganization Act of 1866. Many ex-slaves received their first education at these schools, which were operated by dedicated black chaplains. Private Cathay may have received an education from the first, and only, chaplain of the 38th Infantry in Kansas and New Mexico, Chaplain John N. Schultz. Fort Bayard also offered such a school of education for black troops.

After an amendment of the Congressional bill opened the doors to black enlistment in the Regular army for the first time in July 1866, provisions were made for black chaplains to provide "instruction of the enlisted men in the common branches of an English education." The need was great to educate these ex-slaves in preparation for the responsibilities of citizenship in American society.

In addition, African American women in the West made a determined effort to erase illiteracy by a vigorous educational effort. Cathy Williams may have received some education in the West by this means as well. Or she may have learned how to read and write as a slave, although this is unlikely.

In many ways, even before she ran a boardinghouse at Raton (if that is indeed the case) Cathy was already a successful businesswomen in her self-employment as laundress, cook, and seamstress, which required a degree of business sense and financial management. Her record of saving fairly large sums of money indicated a thrifty determination to amass capital to fulfill her dreams of a brighter future. In addition, this thrift also gave her more mobility to seek out new opportunities, lessen dependence on dead-end employment, and provide a greater guarantee of long-term survival.

In many ways, Cathy Williams was now simply following a historic pattern of African American women in the West. First, black women often migrated west alone, such as those African American women who went to Texas in the 1830s, including Harriet Newell Sands, and those who followed the California Gold Rush of 1849. Other black women, like Ester Moore, came west and eventually made it to New Mexico as a cook for a wagon train. In New Mexico, Moore operated a small tent restaurant for migrants traveling north from Mexico, and became successful.

African American women had other advantages in the West. The majority came from rural backgrounds in agrarian environments, and settled in small Western towns rather than in the countryside. In addition, African American women possessed a lower child-bearing rate than white women in the West. They were also more likely to be employed than white ladies on the Western frontier.

It is not known for certain, but some historians claim that Cathy's largest business venture was in fact the Raton boardinghouse, which "was a popular stop for General Phil Sheridan."

No primary documentation has substantiated the existence of this business, however. Most likely, she worked in Raton as a cook or laundress. But if General Sheridan visited the Raton boardinghouse, then he might well have remembered Cathy from her days as a cook and laundress for the general and his staff in the Shenandoah Valley. In the words of one historian, "General

Phil Sheridan liked to stop and eat [at Cathy's boardinghouse] when he was in the area."

Such may have been the case. It was not unusual for black women in the West to operate boardinghouses. In the development of the frontier, they met with considerable success in their independent business enterprises. A number of popular boardinghouses were owned by black women in California during the Gold Rush of 1849.[29]

At this time, other black women were doing well in northeast New Mexico, embracing economic opportunities that were denied to them elsewhere, especially the South. Another ex-slave from the "Little Dixie" region of Missouri, Mary Marshall, first came west to settle in Santa Fe. Here, she worked as a nurse during the Civil War and at the hospital of Fort Marcy, which protected the Santa Fe Trail. Her husband served as the hotel's head chef.[30]

Her decision to settle in northeast New Mexico was not without precedent. "Since the late 1800's, many truly outstanding Black women have resided in the State of New Mexico," one Western historian has concluded. These African American women were "brave, courageous and adventurous [and] they did not come in luxury, in honor, or in glory, but as slaves, as cooks on wagon trains, as laundresses for the military and other menial jobs." Despite encountering some prejudice and discrimination, these black women, like Cathy Williams, "persisted in laying the foundation for a *society* where all would be looked upon as equals," one day in the future.[31]

Cathy Williams either found decent employment in Raton or ran a boardinghouse business there because it was on the main road leading south from Denver and Pueblo, Colorado, to Santa Fe, New Mexico. Here, at the southern end of the Raton Pass that cut through the Raton Mountains, the wagon trains of the Santa Fe Trail had stopped before crossing the mountains. Like so many other communities, the town of Raton was born by way of the Santa Fe Trail. By this time, herds of cattle and sheep were also driven to Raton for shipment to the large Eastern markets.[32]

Like other black women in New Mexico, such as Ester Moore, Cathy Williams took advantage of the bountiful opportunities from the stream of traffic between the states and Mexico. Another black woman in the area also profited from the steady traffic along the Santa Fe Trail. A Creole, Choloe Martin, came west to marry a miner and establish roots in New Mexico. Here, Choloe and her husband became trappers, selling the furs to travelers along the Santa Fe Trail.

Even compared with Colorado, this area of northeast New Mexico was more egalitarian for African Americans and other people of color. When this land was owned by Spain before Mexico won its independence in 1821, Spanish-speaking blacks and mulattoes freely intermingled and intermarried with the Spanish, creating a multicultural society from as early as the 1500s.

The cross-cultural marriages and racial mixing between the Spanish and Indians, blacks, and Hispanics resulted in the formation of a large black-Spanish population and biracial community. Not unlike the African Americans who pushed west to escape slavery, these black Nuevo Mexicanos originally served as soldiers, militiamen, and settlers who migrated north to escape the discrimination of Mexico. African American slavery never became a regular feature of life and society in New Mexico because wealthy landowners exploited Hispanic peons and Indians instead. Given the multicultural and more tolerant environment that continued to exist after the Civil War, the all-black towns of Blackdom, El Vado, and Dora thrived in New Mexico.[33]

This intermixing between the races continued with the arrival of the Anglos. Hispanic women and Anglo men met and married, creating another unique cultural blend that in overall terms resulted in the Americanization of this land, which had once been part of the Mexican republic. This easy mixing of cultures created opportunities for Hispanic women in New Mexico such as Gertrudis Bardelo, who operated a gambling saloon in Santa Fe.[34]

Indeed, by the time Cathy Williams lived in Raton, more opportunities for people of color abounded in New Mexico than in any other portion of the West. For example, by 1890, more nonwhite stock raisers, herders, and drovers—a total of 333—could be found in the New Mexico Territory than any other state or territory in the Union, except Texas with its larger Hispanic population.[35]

In addition, northeast New Mexico was a land experiencing the democratic fulfillment of the Turner Thesis, and not just for whites. In relative terms, diverse groups of people for the most part mingled freely, especially when compared with the status-conscious and elitist East. In 1881 while Cathy Williams was still resident there, an Easterner from New England, C. M. Chase, declared "Raton as the town in New Mexico he liked best."[36]

One resident of Raton wrote with pride of the relatively easy melting-pot atmosphere of northeast New Mexico, which was hard to find elsewhere in America: "[T]here was little class distinction drawn [and] the breezy, frontier spirit of democracy made the community more [open-minded and tolerant, while] all classes mingled freely."

Hispanic culture—which dominated New Mexico—continued to place no restrictions on cross-cultural and mixed unions or marriages. In addition, Hispanic culture was much like African American culture, deeply rooted in a strong religious faith and the close-knit kinship and maternal systems that led to a vibrant community and social life.

In relative terms, a more open, easy, and informal integration between Hispanics, whites, and African Americans was a regular feature of life in northeast New Mexico. In such an environment, many open-minded whites became "hispanicized." For instance, the early white settlers of New Mexico, like Kit Carson and Charles Bent, married into the Hispanic elite of New Mexico. Other whites, especially the mountain men and trappers, lived, dressed, and looked more like Indians than whites, while often marrying Indian women.

In fact, the Territory of New Mexico was becoming gradually more black with each passing year. By 1880, New Mexico had more than 1,000 African Americans compared with only 172 blacks ten years before. This may have been a factor that caused Cathy Williams to call New Mexico home during this period. One modern historian described the black female migrants to the Trinidad, Raton, and other areas of the frontier West as consisting of all types, including "cooks, or prostitutes, or nurses, or nannies to white children."

Meanwhile, the country east of New Mexico offered much less equality for blacks primarily because it was chiefly occupied by whites, including many Southerners—ex-Rebels and former slave owners—who brought their own prejudices with them. This racism spread like a cancer in the West, where discrimination and prejudice lingered. In New Mexico, however, the predominance of Hispanic and Indian cultures and the long history of intermarriage and close interaction between diverse cultures created a more overall tolerant climate, where an African American women could enjoy a sense of freedom perhaps experienced nowhere else.

By the late 1870s as white Southerners gained ever-greater political, social, and economic control across the South after the end of Reconstruction, a mass exodus of blacks continued to flee west, migrating in the hope of fulfilling the promise of America. During this mass migration, African American women, like Harriett Tubman, led their families and bands of migrants out of Southern oppression to escape the legacy of slavery.

Many of these "Exodusters" migrated to Denver and Colorado Springs. Here, they helped to create a multicultural West where African Americans continued to pursue the American dream in a new land with less racism and discrimination than in other sections of the country. Esther Hall Mumford explained the mind-set among these black Western migrants: "Many women nursed their dreams that someday things would be better [and] they wanted to believe that this was still the land of opportunity . . . they were resilient, too." In this respect, Cathy Williams was no different, but had made the journey a decade earlier.

Cathy apparently liked Raton almost as much as Trindad. Much like Trinidad the community of Raton was a picturesque town nestled amid a beautiful countryside, especially during spring when wild flowers covered the slopes of the surrounding mountain sides. The town was situated in the mountains northeast of Taos, New Mexico, and Santa Fe.

Beginning as a ranch known as Willow Springs to officially become a town in 1880, Raton was one of the communities on the Santa Fe Trail, located in the high country and mountains of northeast New Mexico. Immediately west of town, Old Raton Pass ran through the nearby Raton Mountains of the Sangre de Cristo Range at nearly 8,000 feet above sea level. Because of the importance of the Raton Pass, the town of Raton early became known as "the Gate City."

This was a beautiful land dominated by crystal-clear lakes and dense evergreen forests of Ponderosa pines. Great flocks of ducks and geese filled the air in the spring and fall during their annual migrations. Herds of elk, deer, antelope, and flocks of turkey roamed the woodlands that covered the nearby snow-capped Sangre de Cristos Mountains. Turkey gobbled in the half-light of early morning and majestic Elk bulls bugled during the heat of rut, echoing over the tranquil peaks that seemed so inviting to both man and beast. And in the autumn, the days were cool and dry. Dense thickets of aspens lined the mountain slopes and choked the creek valleys, donned in radiant colors of bright yellow.

In many ways, Cathy Williams found life to her liking in northeast New Mexico, though some Missourians, perhaps former slave owners, were also now Raton residents.

In addition, a small African American community was growing and maturing in Raton. The size of the town's black community was perhaps also a factor that caused Cathy to relocate. No doubt, the African American communities of Trinidad and Raton were tied together by African American bonds of kinship, resulting in travel and communication between the two.

In time, the African American community of Raton became so large that another black woman was also named Cathy Williams. She would die in 1924, and would be buried in Raton. This Cathy Williams would often be confused by historians with the ex–Buffalo Soldier from Missouri. It is not known if this Cathy Williams of Raton was a distant cousin or relation to the former Pvt. William Cathay, but perhaps so.

In the history of the West's settlement, black churches often laid the foundation for vibrant African American communities. Continuing a spiritual tradition that endured through slavery, a strong religious faith continued to serve as a central foundation for African American communities. And in this respect, Raton was no different.

By the late 1800s, the Mount Pilgrim Baptist Church and its African American population of more than fifty people was part of a thriving spiritual refuge for Raton blacks. Some of the women may have been mail order brides from the East. Many African American women came west looking for a husband and, like Cathy Williams, opportunities to start a new life.

By 1889, the town of Raton consisted of 3,000 people, with Indians and Hispanics and the sounds of Spanish and Apache in the air. Stock-raising to meet the demands of the lucrative Eastern markets, coal mining, and the railroad brought in a steady income flow for residents, especially business people. These were the good times for Raton. Adobe structures in the Spanish and the Pueblo architectural style—plastered adobe, viga ceilings, and flat roofs—dominated Raton's architecture during this post–Civil War period.[37]

The business at Cathy Williams's boardinghouse, if that was the case, must have thrived with the military, stage, commercial, and railroad traffic that flowed through the town, along with the commerce that still moved along the Old Santa Fe Trail.

Typical boarders probably included the laborers and railroad workers as Raton developed and became prosperous. Also, saloons, hotels, and restaurants thrived during this boom period, when gunfighters, hard-drinking miners, and lawbreakers roamed the streets looking for a good time or a chance to enhance a reputation.

Indicative of the rich Hispanic heritage and influence of northeast New Mexico, this boom period became known as "Dias Felicidades," or Happy Days, by Raton's populace. Perhaps, Cathy Williams learned to speak some Spanish, if not becoming fluent in the language, in this rich multicultural community. No doubt if such was the case, the boardinghouse in Raton where Cathy Williams evidently stayed, worked, and perhaps even managed, was open to all, imposing no rules barring Hispanics or African Americans.[38]

As demonstrated by some historians, if Cathy Williams operated her own boardinghouse in Raton, then this was a personal success story that could only have developed for her in the frontier West. Opportunities continued to abound for black women here. Anna Graham ran a successful hairdressing business in Virginia City, Nevada, in 1874. Three other such black businesses thrived in this large African American section of town as well.

Cathy Williams, however, ended her association with the Raton boardinghouse after only a relatively short time. Perhaps a fire destroyed the business. Or perhaps the economic repercussions of the wild speculation in cattle ending in the commodities crash of the mid-1880s—which devastated the local cattle industry—were responsible. Whatever the reason, Cathy Williams left Raton.

As her time in Raton ended, Cathy Williams prepared to return to the other community she loved, Trinidad. If she owned a boardinghouse, Cathy may have liquidated her assets, making all the money that she could. Or she might have gone broke or gotten sick. For whatever reason, she crossed the Colorado line, returning the twenty miles to Trinidad probably in early 1886. As best can be ascertained, Cathy Williams's stay in Raton was relatively brief but not uneventful.[39]

Once more in the familiar setting of Trinidad, Cathy again settled in the black and Hispanic community on the north side of town. At long last, Cathy Williams's journey was over, coming to a permanent end at Trinidad. Here, Cathy Williams lived in peace for many years to come. Las Animas County, Colorado, once again became home for this remarkable woman who had been forced by circumstances to lead the existence of a gypsy for most of her life. Now the seemingly endless moving to one place after another across the West would stop for good.

She once again became laundress and seamstress, working as an independent businesswoman. Perhaps she even served as a midwife: a common occupation of black women in the West. However, some scant evidence exists that she may also have, "ran a farm" but no primary documentation has been found to verify that fact.

As in her previous time in Trinidad, Cathy had saved enough money to have her own place. She probably farmed a small plot of ground behind the house, growing vegetables and perhaps flowers. Like most migrants to the West and especially former slaves, she was realizing a lifelong dream by becoming a small landowner, if she purchased the property rather than renting.

As a former slave and like most Americans both black and white, she no doubt would have equated landownership with the fulfillment of the American dream and the promise of the West. Certainly, the great dream of an ex-slave—and white settlers—was to own their land and property. And now in southeast Colorado, Cathy might well have farmed her own land for the first time in her life.

If that was the case, then Cathy Williams's decision to become a landowner would have been a contradiction in many ways. In general, most African American women, especially former slaves and especially women, detested the menial farmwork of the fields, which reminded them of slave labor.

It soon, however, became increasingly difficult for Cathy Williams to perform manual labor of any kind. Her long-standing health problems again resurfaced in late 1889 or early 1890. Cathy's failing health resulted in a lengthy period of hospitalization—more than a year—in Trinidad.

Worst of all, she was apparently stricken with a chronic case of diabetes because all the toes on both her feet were amputated. Thereafter, for the remainder of her life, she would only be able to walk with difficulty with the aid of a crutch. Such a disability was certainly a considerable blow to a proud woman who had once marched more than a thousand miles as a soldier, and lived much of her life on the move.

With her physical condition and economic situation steadily deteriorating with her release from the Trinidad hospital after nearly a year and a half; with no job prospects in sight; and unable to continue doing backbreaking menial chores or farmwork, she had little choice but to ask for outside help. She was now only forty-seven years old.

Cathy's health continued to worsen until not even her pride could keep her from seeking relief by filing for an invalid pension with the government, which she did in June 1891. By this time, she could no longer work to support herself. Such action came as a blow to a woman who had long prided herself on independence and self-sufficiency.

Unfortunately, Cathy's claim would be based only upon her months of military service with the 38th Infantry because she could not claim her Civil War service despite serving with the 8th Indiana for more than three years. Officially and unofficially, she had served with the U.S. military almost continuously from late 1861 to nearly the end of 1868. By 1891, she was down but not out. Although her body was weak and broken, her spirits remained high during what was only the latest of a long list of personal crises.

Cathy Williams's period of arduous duty in Company A, 38th Infantry, directly contributed to the long-term process of destroying her health, which may well have begun in her days of slavery. From late 1861 to 1868, she had seen thousands of miles of the South, the Trans-Mississippi, and the Western frontier not from a train car, horseback, or wagon but by marching across a vast landscape on foot. But the clearest indication of ill health resulting from her duty in the West was the fact that she had been repeatedly hospitalized as a Buffalo Soldier and held an official disability discharge signed by Fort Bayard's surgeon on October 14, 1868.

Cathy's incapacity now made her unable to provide for herself and make a living, creating a critical situation. A host of ailments, including neuralgia, rheumatism, "itch," deafness, and diabetes combined to devastate her health.[40]

Cathy Williams, in a sworn statement, related the extent of her deteriorating condition at Trinidad to the county clerk of Las Animas County, Colorado, in June 1891. She explained the details of her failing health as the result of three ailments: deafness, neuralgia, and rheumatism. In an effort to gain an invalid pension because these illnesses were derived from her military service as a Buffalo Soldier, Cathy swore in an affidavit that she was hospitalized for nearly a year and a half in Trinidad until only two months before filing for the invalid pension.

Most revealing of all, Cathy now disclosed that she and Pvt. William Cathay were in fact the same person. This was a sworn statement by her to this effect. Cathy spoke freely of the facts before the doubtlessly astonished county clerk, who duly entered them in the application. For the first time, it was officially documented that Pvt. William Cathay was a female soldier who had faithfully served her country in the U.S. Regular army on the Western frontier: the first African American woman to accomplish this feat.

Without a doubt, the county clerk and other officials of Trinidad were shocked by the revelation that this black woman had served her country in the 38th Infantry. The response of the white officials to this surprising revelation of this hard-luck African American woman was not recorded.[41]

Cathy Williams then elaborated the basis of her application to the Las Animas County officials. Cathy continued to emphasize that she was suffering from the effects of her military service by being afflicted with rheumatism, neuralgia, and deafness. Two claim handlers, Attorneys William and Charles King of Washington, D.C., took her case.

But unfortunately, these two Eastern lawyers would provide relatively little valuable assistance in securing the entitled pension rights for a disabled black woman, at a time of such extreme need for Cathy Williams. After she had faithfully served her country, risked her life, and caught a variety of illnesses while in service, her chances of gaining a pension would now suffer from apathy, if not incompetence, among the attorneys who likely viewed this as an unprofitable case.[42]

To prove the extent of her failed health, Cathy went to a physician in Trinidad to verify her claim of disability. On September 9, 1891, a Trinidad physician, hired by the Pension Bureau, examined the ex–Buffalo Soldier to ascertain the basis for her claims with a physical exam.

At this time, the physician of Las Animas County described Cathy Williams as an African American of age forty-nine. Like so many other slaves she never knew the exact date of her birth, though she stated that she was twenty-two when she enlisted in November 1866, which would make her forty-seven.

In addition, Cathy was described as large, big-boned, and stout, weighing 160 pounds at five foot and seven inches in height. The physician conversed with her rather easily, as Cathy from all accounts was friendly and talkative. This caused him to hastily conclude that she was not deaf, but she might have been partially deaf.

The physician, however, did not take into account that Cathy may have been able to read lips, especially if her deafness had been long-lasting. He may also have possessed a vested interest in not acknowledging her infirmities in order to deny her pension for a number of reasons. Not the least of these may have been racism that clouded his judgment. He may have been directly influenced by the Pension Bureau. Perhaps the Trinidad physician found the idea of a woman masquerading as a man for nearly two years as repugnant, especially if he knew of her life story as revealed in the leading St. Louis newspaper.

Maybe the doctor simply resented the presence of the black community in Trinidad and its inhabitants. It is possible that he had not served in the Civil War or in any Indian War like Cathy Williams, and felt that he was less of a man upon meeting a female veteran of two wars. Whatever the reason, this physician would prove anything but receptive and open-minded to her years of hard service, the extent of her illnesses, and thus her claim.

The white physician seemed impressed by the fact that she was a "large[,] stout woman in good general health." This observation indicated that Cathy had probably gained some weight not only during her hospital recuperation period but also afterward because of her crippled condition. However, her overall physical state, "hard and sinewy," was evident throughout her life and indicative of an active, vigorous outdoor life.

The Trinidad physician, in attending mostly whites, was probably not familiar with the generally more sturdy physical characteristics of African American women who were often more sinewy and stronger than most white women because of difficult lives of physical labor. Unfortunately for Cathy Williams, her "stout" physical condition and perhaps her strong willed personality now helped to diminish her chances for gaining an invalid pension.[43]

During the physical exam, the Trinidad physician found no indications of either her rheumatism or neuralgia. His cursory exam of Cathy's joints, tendons, and muscles was, however, anything but thorough in ascertaining the full extent of her physical limitations and disabilities. Obviously, the doctor possessed little real interest or desire in providing a proper diagnosis for this black woman.

There was one physical disability that even the physician was forced to acknowledge and unable to dismiss. He discovered that all of the toes on both of Cathy Williams's feet had been amputated.[44]

Despite her disabled condition and the loss of all her toes, which required her to use a crutch, the doctor concluded that Cathy Williams's health was generally good. Incredibly, this caused him to declare a "nil" for her disability rating, thus excluding the possibility of an invalid pension for Cathy. The doctor emphasized that there was simply no clear indication that she was afflicted by the maladies she claimed, including rheumatism, neuralgia, and deafness. The physician's diagnoses were as quick and unprofessional as they were incorrect. For instance, Cathy Williams's case of rheumatism almost certainly resulted from many months of active duty that included swimming across the Rio Grande and the winter campaign of January 1868.

Consequently, the Trinidad physician denied the disability pension to a woman who was clearly disabled and in dire economic straits.[45]

Even laundresses who served in the Civil War and who had married soldiers, received Federal pensions. But of course these women were white. Not even the years that she had served in Union armies as a laundress and cook were of any assistance in helping her case because no official record existed of her Civil War service with the 8th Indiana.[46]

Despite her crippled condition and the evidence of her years of service, thanks to the Trinidad physician, the Pension Bureau rejected her claim for an invalid pension on February 1892. Besides the apparent apathy, if not racism, of the Trinidad physician or perhaps his duplicity with the bureau officials to deny her request for the invalid pension, the lack of detailed military records and paperwork regarding her medical condition and exact periods of military hospitalization also weakened Cathy Williams's case.

Even though military records existed of her cases of smallpox, the "itch," rheumatism, and neuraglia, this documentation was not referred to by the Trinidad physician either in conjunction with his examination or in his report of the physical exam.

The bad news of the rejection of her invalid pension claim must have come as a severe blow to Cathy Williams. Two months later in April 1892, her Eastern lawyers, Charles and William King, prepared to contest the decision. A slim ray of hope still remained for Cathy but not much, especially if they failed to find evidence of her illness in the military records housed in Washington, D.C. Certainly for Cathy Williams, the attempt to secure an invalid pension was an only too familiar struggle against injustice and discrimination fostered by a system that viewed her as a second-class citizen because of her race and sex.

Once again Cathy Williams was struggling against racism in a world dominated by whites who were unsympathetic, if not hostile, toward her sex and race and perhaps even toward her military service. Any woman, especially a strong African American female, who had performed as well as any soldier of Company A, 38th Infantry, and had the audacity to think of herself as equal and to act accordingly, was viewed by white men as a threat to their perceptions of traditional racial and gender roles.

In filing a new claim, Cathy's lawyers in Washington, D.C., who were too far removed to provide assistance in person, conceded that they discovered no proof of Cathy becoming deaf while serving in the army. Indeed, no evidence existed. If Cathy Williams became deaf while in service, however, then that would not have been documented, in part because she had wanted to avoid dealing with army physicians as much as possible.

Her attorneys, nevertheless, continued to argue from a weak position by maintaining that Cathy had lost her toes as the result of "frosted feet" during military service. However, this tactic overlooked the obvious fact that she would have received a medical discharge from the Army if so disabled.

In focusing her claim of deafness while the more serious infirmities of rheumatism, neuralgia, and the "itch" were ignored, her lawyers made a tactical error. But they were more on target when they emphasized that Cathy Williams's case of smallpox and a premature discharge from the military hospital in East St. Louis to join her regiment in Kansas combined with her arduous infantry service—especially the march from Kansas to the Mexico border and the winter campaign against the Apache—led to her poor health and crippling disabilities.

No corroborating evidence existed, however, in army records of either her frostbite or deafness. And, of course, the amputation of her toes was not stated in her discharge papers as a factor that led to her discharge at Fort Bayard. A slim possibility existed that she might have received frostbite during the January 1868 campaign against the Apache. Quite possibly, Cathy might have decided not to report this condition to the army surgeons for fear of having her sex discovered or that a case of frostbite would lead to amputation.

Even worse, for whatever reason, Cathy Williams's discharge papers were drawn up by the assistant surgeon at Fort Bayard in such a way as to indicate that her ailments predated her service in the 38th Infantry. As he stated, her poor, "[physical]condition dates prior to enlistment." Therefore, Cathy's lawyers probably should have emphasized that her health was good prior to enlistment or the army would not have accepted her into the 38th Infantry on November 15, 1866.[47]

Not surprisingly, her new claim, filed by her attorneys, failed to lead to the disability pension that Cathy Williams now so desperately needed. Again, the lack of detailed military documentation as to the extent of her illnesses while in service and either her lawyers' incompetence or apathy, or both, helped to sabotage her claim.

Despite having served her country for nearly six years during both the Civil War and as a Buffalo Soldier, the U.S. government now denied this crippled veteran her badly needed disability pension on the grounds that no serious illness was suffered by her in service. Clearly, as revealed by her time spent in four different military hospitals on five separate occasions in less than two years, Cathy Williams was disabled from her military service, a fact no doubt generally recognized by all except the Trinidad physician who examined her.[48]

In conclusion, the U.S. government successfully covered-up the military service record of Cathy Williams, or Pvt. William Cathay, by denying an invalid pension to this black woman who had faithfully served her country. It is possible that the Pension Bureau personnel and the Trinidad physician worked together to accomplish the same end: the denial of an invalid pension for a disabled African American women on the basis that it was technically illegal for her to serve as a soldier.

The most obvious reason why the U.S. government and the Pension Bureau denied the invalid pension claim to Cathy Williams was because of her sex. A woman serving in the 38th Infantry or any other military unit of the U.S. Army was an illegal act. This illegality, of course, would have provided sufficient grounds for the denial of the disability pension. The Pension Bureau, however, chose to ignore the controversial issue of her sex to avoid pointing the finger at the incompetence of military officials, surgeons, and officers for having failed to ascertain her true identity for nearly two years.

White women who served in the Civil War as men also met with comparable resistance from unsympathetic government officials, especially in the military, in regard to winning recognition for their military service. But Cathy Williams was not only a female but also an African American and ex-slave: a triple cause for official discrimination and denial. [49]

In relative terms, the full extent of the prejudice directed at Cathy's case because she was black came to be seen in the favorable treatment of white women who served as men in the Civil War. One woman's three-year service, including time spent in the Vicksburg campaign, was documented in the records of the 95th Illinois Volunteer Infantry. Her name was Jenny Hodgers, and like Cathy Williams, she successfully enlisted and served with her regiment under a male name—Albert Cashier.[50]

Unlike Cathy Williams, the Ireland-born Cashier continued to live as a male for more than a half century after the Civil War. Only when hit by a car was her true identity revealed. Even though she was a woman, her secret was closely guarded by sympathetic whites, including physicians and the former state senator of Illinois, Ira M. Lish, so that the aged veteran would be allowed to enter the Soldiers' and Sailors' Home at Quincy, Illinois. She spent her last years in good care at the home even though physicians knew that Albert Cashier was a woman.[51]

Cashier also applied for a government pension in 1890 but refused to take the medical examination, knowing that her "secret" would be discovered by the doctors. Later, she gained a disability pension that paid $12.00 per month: a sum that Cathy Williams desperately needed to survive but would never see in her lifetime. Ironically, counting both Civil War and frontier service, Cathy's term of duty for her country was nearly double that of Albert Cashier.[52]

Annie Etheridge, who served, disguised, in two Michigan infantry regiments in the Civil War, also benefitted from the political support of a senator. In 1886, less than five years before Cathy Williams attempted to secure an invalid pension, Sen. Thomas Palmer pushed through a bill that granted Annie a pension of $25.00 a month for her Civil War service. As a poor ex-slave Cathy Williams had no such support from people in high places.

In contrast, in 1884, the impoverished condition of Kady Brownell, who served with Rhode Island regiments during the Civil War as a man, was relieved when she gained a government pension for her service. Interestingly, she secured the coveted pension in her own name. For Cathy Williams who served as Pvt. William Cathay, this may have been another factor that denied her a pension because officials may have doubted that the two were one and the same.[53]

Unlike the cases of white women who fought in the Civil War as men, a measure of hostility no doubt also played a part in denying the pension that Cathy Williams deserved. Because the Anglo and Hispanic cultures were patriarchal, Cathy Williams was probably viewed as a threat and an alarming presence to those white males who reviewed her case.

After all, here was an independent, free-thinking, outspoken, and strong black woman who was so unlike their own wives, sisters, and daughters, living the life that she had chosen on her own terms, with considerable self-sufficiency and pride in her past accomplishments. These were stereotype-shattering realities that the average white man may have found difficult to either understand or accept at the time.

For most of her adult life, Cathy Williams had accomplished a great deal on her own and without male support or assistance. Hence, besides racial and gender prejudice, a measure of hostility almost certainly developed against her from the beginning, combining with racism to doom her bid to gain an invalid pension.

As so often in the past when a cruel fate seemed to inflict a reversal from which it appeared she would never recover, the denial of a pension did not destroy Cathy Williams. Now that she was all but an invalid and on crutches, she had to somehow once again make her way in life, but under more trying and difficult circumstances than ever before.

With the pension denial, Cathy Williams was delivered the final injustice from an ungrateful nation that she had faithfully served in two wars. Such was not the case in more enlightened and less prejudiced societies. In some European cultures, women warriors who disguised themselves as men were more often rewarded for their military services than in the United States.

One such woman was Marie Schellinck who fought with Napoléon's Grande Armée. She not only received a pension but was also officially recognized, receiving the Legion of Honor and a personal visit from Napoléon himself. What is significant about this case was the different treatment accorded to women who served their respective countries because of more open and tolerant societal values especially in Europe.

Even women soldiers in America's first war, against the British, received more recognition and support than Cathy Williams nearly one hundred years later. Mary Ludwig Hays McCauley fought in the American Revolution, winning a nice lump sum settlement, a lifetime pension, and financial assistance from an organization of military wives from West Point. Unlike the sad fate of Cathy Williams, McCauley was recognized "as an individual who had performed her own meritorious services during the war."

Most significant was the case of the only known black woman, at least identified so by one historian, to have served in the American Revolution, Deborah Sampson-Gannet, who was tall and masculine, like Cathy. After her service in the 4th Massachusetts Regiment during which time she suffered a saber wound—that she treated herself—Deborah was immortalized as an American hero for distinguished service.

After it was determined that her service name and real name identified the same person, John Hancock signed a petition in 1792 that officially recognized Deborah's military service. This assistance resulted in "paying compensation for service performed in the late Army of the United States[, which] exhibited an extraordinary instance of female heroism by discharging the duties of a faithful and gallant soldier, and at the same time preserving the virtue and chastity of her sex unsuspected and unblemished."

But while Deborah served in the struggle that won the American nation's independence, Cathy Williams was fated to have participated in no such idealistic crusade. Instead, she had been engaged in an ugly, thankless war against Native Americans on the remote Western frontier. Unfortunately, this was yet another factor why Cathy Williams would never receive the recognition and appreciation that was bestowed upon Deborah and others.Cathy Williams had performed the same kind of faithful military service for nearly two years as a Buffalo Soldier. Unlike Cathy Williams, however, Deborah received fair treatment both before and after her true identity was ascertained. In addition, Deborah gained an honorable discharge after her sex was discovered by a surgeon in a Philadelphia hospital. Her discharge from service made no mention of her sex to "stain" a distinguished service record.

Clearly, Deborah's sex—a relatively minor detail in this case—was placed secondary in importance to the fact that she fought in a heroic struggle to gain her country's independence. Unfortunately, such was not the case with Cathy Williams. She was immediately discharged from service once her sex was ascertained and expelled from Fort Bayard, with her former comrades angry at her. Such similar hostility undoubtedly played a part in the denial of her invalid pension decades later.[54]

But unfortunately for Cathy Williams and as much as anything else, what had certainly ensured a disqualification for an invalid pension was that she was black in a racist America. Therefore, and unlike the precedents established throughout the annals of military history in countries on both sides of the Atlantic, Cathy was denied her invalid pension as much because of her color as anything else.

In this sense, the pension denial was a disgrace and an injustice, if not a tragedy. At the time Cathy Williams was denied her pension, even the wives and survivors of deceased U.S. soldiers received pensions and full payments for their fathers' and husbands' military service. Such financial reward, however, was never rendered to this Civil War veteran and female Buffalo Soldier. Although she had served her country first from 1861 to 1865 in the Civil War and then from 1866 to 1868 as an enlisted private of the 38th Infantry, her country had betrayed her during her greatest hour of need.

Tragically, in the historiography of African Americans in the American military, such betrayals by white America were not uncommon. Many African Americans who fought with General Washington during the American Revolution were returned to slavery. With justifiable bitterness over the tragic fates of the black patriots who helped to win their nation's liberty, William Eustis, an army surgeon and later Massachusetts governor, described that when the "war [was] over, and peace restored, these [black] men returned to their respective states; and who could have said of them, on their return to civil life, after having shed their blood in common with whites in the defense of the liberties of the country: 'You are not to participate in the rights secured by the struggle, or in the liberty for which you have been fighting'."

In addition, such was also the dismal fate of the soldiers of the San Domingo Battalions of Free Men of Color, who fought with General Jackson at Chalmette, Louisiana, in January 1815. The majority of these Louisiana men, mostly refugee mulattoes from San Domingo, or St. Dominque, who fled the slave revolts that consumed what is today Haiti were denied the freedom, land, and pensions that were promised them for service against the British invader during the War of 1812.

Indeed, "they were forced to be content with honeyed words and stately phrases, lavished upon them before [the battle of New Orleans], but which became empty phrases after the victory." Worst of all after their distinguished service, these African Americans of New Orleans and "their descendants were [eventually] not only asked to leave the city forever, but [also] ordered from the state [of Louisiana], as well."

Despite her failing health and with prospects looking bleak, Cathy Williams somehow managed to survive mostly on her own after the severe blow of her pension denial. A couple of years later in July 1894 and after a trip by rail by way of Raton, Buffalo Soldiers of the 24th Infantry from Fort Bayard, Private Cathay's last outpost, marched through the dusty streets of Trinidad. There is little doubt that such a sight brought a sense of pride to Cathy Williams if she still lived to view the disciplined Buffalo Soldiers once again. To her, it probably seemed not that long ago when she herself marched in the ranks with these black troops of her old regiment, and proudly wore the uniform of blue.

These soldiers had arrived in Trinidad to protect railroad property, officials, the tracks, and the Raton tunnel, in conjunction with Federal marshals, when workers went on strike. This strike resulted partly from an economic depression, which caused dramatic reductions of wages and job losses.

By this period, the Indian hostilities had all but ceased across the frontier. Even the Apache were subdued by this time. Now the new role of the Buffalo Soldiers was that of guardians in the escalating labor unrest in the West. Cathy Williams was undoubtedly glad not to serve in such a role against common working people simply attempting to survive as best they could amid an abusive system of exploitation.

The Buffalo Soldiers encamped in the Trinidad and the Raton areas. Here, they served as a permanent military presence and symbol of national authority to intimidate the strikers and deter violence. Not until September 1894 would the Buffalo Soldiers return to Fort Bayard, after the strike and threats of violence dissipated thanks largely to their presence. These black soldiers had once again helped to ensure the peace in the West.[55]

Sadly, no one knows when the end finally came for the first female Buffalo Soldier, Cathy Williams. The last recorded date of Cathy Williams's life that can be verified was in April 1892. At that time she was still living in Trinidad, crippled but surviving as best she could on her own at age forty-eight.

The period of her life in Trinidad after the denial of Cathy's pension was probably brief. Unable to work, in poor health, nearly destitute, and stricken with diabetes, the tragic end almost certainly came for Cathy before the turn of the century. Indeed, the 1900 census for Trinidad and the Trinidad city directories for 1901 to 1904 indicate no Cathy Williams as a resident, and in her crippled and impoverished condition, it was quite unlikely that she would have relocated to another part of the West or returned to Missouri.

Hopefully, though without family or children, Cathy Williams would have been fortunate enough to have had some close friends to care for her in her final days. The small African American and Hispanic community on the north side of Trinidad might have taken care of her in the matriarchal tradition of black society.

Without a disability pension, Cathy probably never lived to see the onset of the twentieth century. In the end, despite her eventful life, it was diabetes that probably caused Cathy Williams's death. Most likely, her death came not many years after she was denied a pension because she appeared to be too healthy to an unsympathetic Trinidad physician. She could not overcome government bureaucracy, white prejudice, and indifference.

No record can be found in the small town of Trinidad of the final burial place of Cathy Williams. With no family or money, she was probably buried in a poorly marked grave in the black cemetery on the north side of town. Due to the ravages of the elements, her modest wooden grave marker (if any existed at all) remained in place for only a short time.

Without family to attend her grave, the last resting place of this former slave woman was probably forgotten and eventually lost to indifference and modern development. Almost certainly, the spring rains, harsh Colorado winters, and heavy snowfalls have obscured all traces of her grave. Today, the final resting place of Cathy Williams, the first female Buffalo Soldier, lies in a place known only to God.

But in many ways, the surrounding mountains and the pristine beauty of the high plains of southeast Colorado, around her long-time hometown of Trinidad, stand majestically as a silent memorial to overlook the unknown final resting place of Cathy Williams, or Pvt. William Cathay. Here, in the untamed Western lands so far away from her native Missouri, Cathy found a permanent home and a self-sufficient life for herself, after a long journey from slavery to become an independent, proud, and free woman. All in all, Cathy Williams had lived life on her own terms to the very end.

After accomplishing so much against the odds and coming so far in a life of struggle and hardship, she must have died with a hard-earned sense of contentment and peace of mind. Cathy Williams had come a long way from her former life as a helpless Missouri slave girl.

The remarkable success story of Cathy Williams's life was essentially one of the power of the will to endure, overcome, and survive, to triumph over almost insurmountable obstacles, despite little chance or hope for success. In the process, Cathy was able to accomplish what few other women, black or white, could even imagine at the time.[56]

More important and certainly unknown to her at the time, Cathy was in fact a pioneer for the legion of American women who now serve with pride and distinction in all branches of today's U.S. military. She accomplished this feat at a time when it was considered illegal, inconceivable, and perhaps even immoral for her to serve in defense of her country.

In time, however, the American nation and U.S. military have come to recognize the value of women in their service. But this change came far too late for Cathy Williams. At long last, the many unsung contributions and sacrifices of the Buffalo Soldiers are now being recognized and placed in a proper historical perspective for the first time.

Today, the faithful and honorable service of black women in the U.S. military is recognized as essential to the supremacy of the most powerful armed forces in the world. Tens of thousands of African American men and women now serve in the American armed forces. Long ago, an obscure young ex-slave named Cathy Williams indirectly helped to pave the way by her service on behalf of her country.

A fitting epitaph to honor the memory of Cathy Williams, which partly describes her sacrifices and accomplishments in both the Civil War and as a Buffalo Soldier, comes from one of Napoléon's soldiers, who described a brutal reality that could not be denied in regard to her nearly six years of service in behalf of her country: "In the career of glory one gains many things; the gout and medals, a pension[, which Cathy was unfairly denied,] and rheumatism[, which Cathy was not denied]. And also frozen feet[, which Cathy suffered], an arm or leg the less, a bullet lodged between two bones[,] which the surgeon cannot extract. All of those bivouacs in the rain and snow, all the privations, all those fatigues experienced in your youth, you pay for when you grow old. Because one has suffered in years gone by, it is necessary to suffer more, which does not seem exactly fair." Cathy Williams paid a high price for serving her country.

The many struggles, trials, and sacrifices of Cathy Williams tell the story of the intangibles that no one could either deny or take away from her in the end, ensuring her a successful life. Her intact pride and dignity revealed a heroic triumph of the spirit.[57]

Another appropriate eulogy to the life of Cathy Williams, or Pvt. William Cathay, comes from the words of a Union soldier of the Civil War, who paid tribute to Annie Etheridge—the best known woman soldier of the Civil War—who also served with distinction, honor, and courage: "[S]elf-sacrificing Annie, you, I hope, will get your reward in heaven when your campaigns and battles in this life are ended."[58]

In the end, perhaps Cathy Williams finally found in heaven what she had been seeking for most of her life on earth: ever-lasting peace of mind, a sense of contentment, well-deserved recognition, and an appropriate reward for what she had accomplished in a remarkable lifetime of struggle.[59]

APPENDIX

"CATHY WILLIAMS' STORY"
as published in the January 2, 1876 *St. Louis Daily Times*

"My father was a free man, but my mother a slave, belonging to William Johnson, a wealthy farmer who lived at the time I was born near Independence, Jackson county, Missouri. While I was a small girl my master and family moved to Jefferson City. My master died there and when the war broke out and the United States soldiers came to Jefferson City they took me and other colored folks with them to Little Rock. Col. Benton of the 13th army corps was the officer that carried us off. I did not want to go. He wanted me to cook for the officers, but I had always been a house girl and did not know how to cook. I learned to cook after going to Little Rock and was with the army at the battle of Pea Ridge. Afterwards the command moved over various portions of Arkansas and Louisiana. I saw the soldiers burn lots of cotton and was at Shreveport when the rebel gunboats were captured and burned on Red river. We afterwards went to New Orleans, then by way of the Gulf to Savannah, Georgia, then to Macon and other places in the South. Finally I was sent to Washington City, and at the time Gen. Sheridan made his raids in the Shenandoah valley I was cook and washwoman for his staff. I was sent from Virginia to some place in Iowa and afterwards to Jefferson Barracks, where I remained some time. You will see by this paper that on the 15th day of November 1866, I enlisted in the United States army at St. Louis, in the Thirty-eighth United States Infantry, company A, Capt. Charles E. Clarke commanding.

I ENLISTED TO SERVE THREE YEARS!"

The Times man examined the paper and found it to be a genuine document, a discharge from the army dated Fort Bayard, New Mexico, October 14, 1868. The discharge was granted on the surgeon's certificate, and stated that the character of the discharged William Cathy [*sic*] was good. Continuing, the woman said: "The regiment I joined wore the Zouave uniform and only two persons, a cousin and a particular friend, members of the regiment, knew that I was a woman. They never 'blowed' on me. They were partly the cause of my joining the army. Another reason was I wanted to make my own living and not be dependent on relations or friends. Soon after I joined the army, I was taken with the small-pox and was sick at a hospital across the river from St. Louis, but as soon as I got well I joined my company in New Mexico. I was

A GOOD SOLDIER.

As that paper says, I was never put in the guard house, no bayonet was ever put to my back. I carried my musket and did guard and other duties while in the army, but finally I got tired and wanted to get off. I played sick, complained of pains in my side, and rheumatism in my knees. The post surgeon found out I was a woman and I got my discharge. The men all wanted to get rid of me after they found out I was a woman. Some of them acted real bad to me. After leaving the army I went to Pueblo, Colorado, where I made money by cooking and washing. I got married while there, but my husband was no account. He stole my watch and chain, a hundred dollars in money and my team of horses and wagon. I had him arrested and put in jail, and then I came here. I like this town. I know all the good people here, and I expect to get rich yet. I have not got my land warrant. I thought I would wait till the railroad came and then take my land near the depot. Grant owns all this land around here, and it won't cost me anything. I shall never live in the states again. You see I've got a good sewing machine and I get washing to do and clothes to make. I want to get along and not be a burden to my friends or relatives."

In detailing the above the woman sometimes failed to recall dates and the names of places, but otherwise her narrative was smooth and well connected. The TIMES representative returned his thanks for the information and retired with the promise to give a truthful account of what he had been told.

NOTES

CHAPTER 1

1. John W. Blassingame, *The Slave Community: Plantation Life in the Antebellum South* (New York: Oxford University Press, 1972), 2–3.
2. Stanley M. Elkins, *Slavery: A Problem in American Institutional and Intellectual Life* (Chicago: The University of Chicago Press, 1974), 89–98; Deborah Gray White, *Ar'n't I a Woman? Female Slaves in the Plantation South* (New York: W. W. Norton and Company, 1985), 22–23; Charles Johnson, Patricia Smith, and the WGBH Series Research Team (hereafter cited as Johnson et al.), *Africans in America: America's Journey through Slavery* (New York: Harcourt Brace & Company, 1998), 1–5.
3. Robert Coughlan, *Tropical Africa* (New York: Times Incorporated, 1966), 29–31.
4. *St. Louis Daily Times*, January 2, 1876.
5. *Daily Times*, January 2, 1876; Pvt. William Cathay Service Records, RG 94, National Archives, Washington, D.C. (hereafter cited as NA).
6. *Daily Times*, January 2, 1876.
7. Ibid.
8. Pvt. William Cathay Enlistment Papers, vol. 62, NA; Cynthia Savage Speech given to the West Texas Historical Society, April 11, 1997, Cathy Williams File, Arthur Johnson Memorial Library, Raton, New Mexico (hereafter cited as Savage Speech, AJML); William Loren Katz, *The Black West: A Documentary and Pictorial History of the African American Role in the Westward Expansion of the United States* (New York: Simon and Schuster, 1996), 297; Morris F. Taylor, *Trinidad: Colorado Territory* (Trinidad: Trinidad State Junior College, n.d.), 182; Johnson et al., *Africans in America*, x–xi, 341; *Daily Times*, January 2, 1876.
9. *Daily Times*, January 2, 1876.
10. Richard C. Wade, *Slavery in the Cities* (New York: Oxford University Press, 1964), 3–27, 241–81; Savage Speech, AJML; John Lofton, *Denmark Vesey's Revolt: The Slave Plot That Lit A Fuse to Fort Sumter* (Kent, OH: Kent State University Press, 1983), v–xix, 10–15, 123, 131–239; David Nicholls, *From Dessalines to Duvalier: Race, Color and National Independence in Haiti* (New Brunswick, NJ: Rutgers University Press, 1996), 27–32; Alfred

N. Hunt, *Haiti's Influence on Antebellum America: Slumbering Volcano in the Caribbean* (Baton Rouge: Louisiana State University Press, 1988), 84–122; Herbert Aptheker, *American Negro Slave Revolts* (New York: International Publishers, 1974), 98; Johnson et al., 286–90; *Daily Times*, January 2, 1876.

11. Duane G. Myers, *The Heritage of Missouri* (St. Louis: River City Publishers, 1982), 315–16; *Daily Times*, January 2, 1876.

12. Myers, *The Heritage of Missouri*, 315–16; Johnson et al., 341; *Daily Times*, January 2, 1876.

13. R. Douglas Hurt, *Agriculture and Slavery in Missouri's Little Dixie* (Columbia: University of Missouri Press, 1992), ix–xiv, 51–79, 215; Howard Wight Marshall, *Folk Architecture in Little Dixie: A Regional Culture in Missouri* (Columbia: University of Missouri Press, 1981), vii–9; Phillip Thomas Tucker, *History of the First Missouri Confederate Brigade: From Pea Ridge to Vicksburg* (Shippensburg, PA: White Mane Publishing Company, 1993), xx–xxiii; Milton D. Raffferty, *Historical Atlas of Missouri* (Norman: University of Oklahoma Press, 1982), 9–10, 14–15; *Daily Times*, January 2, 1876.

14. Phillip Thomas Tucker, "Above and Beyond . . . African-American Missourians of Colonel Alexander Doniphan's Expedition," *Password* 35, no. 3 (fall 1990): 133–37; *Bolivar (Missouri) Weekly Courier*, May 8, 1858; Bernard DeVoto, *The Year of Decision: 1846* (Boston: Houghton Mifflin Company, 1943), 388–420; Anders Stephanson, *Manifest Destiny: American Expansion and the Empire of Right* (New York: Hill and Wang, 1995), 38–42.

15. Tucker, "Above and Beyond," 133–37; *Weekly Courier*, May 8, 1858; Frank S. Edwards, *A Campaign in New Mexico* (Philadelphia: n.p., 1847), 126–27; David Grant Noble, ed., *Santa Fe: History of an Ancient City* (Santa Fe, NM: School of American Research Press, 1989), 97–113.

16. *Daily Times*, January 2, 1876.

17. DeVoto, *The Year of Decision: 1846*, 419–20.

18. Ibid.; Frank S. Edwards, *A Campaign in New Mexico with Colonel Doniphan* (Albuquerque, NM: University of New Mexico Press, 1996), xxvi; *Daily Times*, January 2, 1876.

19. *Daily Times*, January 2, 1876; Cathy Williams File, AJML; Pvt. William Cathay Service Records, RG 94, NA.

20. *Daily Times*, January 2, 1876; Cathy Williams File, AJML; Pvt. William Cathay Service Records, RG 94, NA.

21. *Daily Times*, January 2, 1876; Cathy Williams File, AJML; Pvt. William Cathay Service Records, RG 94, NA.

22. *Daily Times*, January 2, 1876; Cathy Williams File, AJML; Pvt. William Cathay Service Records, RG 94, NA.

23. Stephen Sayles, "Thomas Hart Benton and the Santa Fe Trail," *Missouri Historical Review* 69, no. 1 (October 1974), 1–22; Taylor, *Trinidad*, 182; Paul Horgan, *Josiah Gregg and His Vision of the Early West* (New York: Farrar, Straus and Giroux, 1972), 3–4, 10, 27, 45–46; *Daily Times*, January 2, 1876.

24. *Daily Times*, January 2, 1876.

25. Douglas T. Miller, *Frederick Douglas and the Fight for Freedom* (New York: Facts on File, 1993), 1–4; *Daily Times*, January 2, 1876.

26. Linda Brent, *Incidents in the Life of a Slave Girl* (New York: Harvest / HBJ, 1973), ix–5; Johnson et al., *Africans in America*, 335–36.

27. White, *Ar'n't I a Woman?*, 119–20.

28. Ibid., 119–22; Johnson et al., *Africans in America*, 2–3; *Daily Times*, January 2, 1876.

29. *Daily Times*, January 2, 1876.
30. Ibid.
31. Ibid.
32. Ibid.; Guy M. Stone, comp., *Marriage Records of Cole County, Missouri, 1821–1900*, Book A (Jefferson City, MO: n.p., 1964), 27; Census Records for the State of Missouri, Cole County, 1850, NA; Rafferty, *Historical Atlas of Missouri*, 32–33; Taylor, *Trinidad*, 182.
33. *Daily Times*, January 2, 1876.
34. Ibid.
35. Johnson, et al., *Africans in America*, 48–49, 135–36.
36. Melton A. McLaurin, *Celia: A Slave* (Athens: University of Georgia Press, 1991), 1–32.
37. *Daily Times*, January 2, 1876.
38. Ibid.
39. Charles Peabody Diary, May 21, 1846–September 11, 1846, Missouri Historical Society, St. Louis, Missouri; Hurt, *Agriculture and Slavery in Missouri's Little Dixie*, 216; White, *Ar'n't I a Woman?*, 143; Katz, *The Black West*, 297; Pvt. William Cathey Enlistment Papers, vol. 62, NA; Taylor, *Trinidad*, 182; Robert E. Acock letter to Maj. Benjamin Franklin Robinson, January 9, 1858, Robert E. Acock Papers, 1854–1866, Collection No. 2166, Western Historical Manuscript Collection, State Historical Society of Missouri, Columbia, Missouri; McLaurin, *Celia: A Slave*, 14–32; Johnson et al., *Africans in America*, 42–49, 274–75; Euola W. Cox and Barbara J. Richardson, *Noteworthy Black Women of New Mexico, Past and Present*, (n.p.: n.p., n.d.), 1; Shannon Lanier and Jane Feldman, *Jefferson's Children: The Story of One American Family* (New York: Random House, 2000), 33–39; Robert F. Dalzell, Jr., and Lee Baldwin Dalzell, *George Washington's Mount Vernon: At Home in Revolutionary America* (New York: Oxford University Press, 1998), 140; Pvt. William Cathay Service Records, RG 94, NA; DeAnne Blanton, "Cathy Williams: Black Woman Soldier, 1866–1868," *Minerva* 10, nos. 3–4, *(fall/winter 1992)*: 1.
40. Joel Williamson, *New People: Miscegenation and Mulattoes in the United States* (New York: The Free Press, 1980), 24–26, 57–59, 65; Myers, *The Heritage of Missouri*, 315–22; Hurt, *Agriculture and Slavery in Missouri's Little Dixie*, x, xi, 221–22; McLaurin, *Celia: A Slave*, 14–32; Catherine Clinton and Michele Gillespie, eds., *The Devil's Lane: Sex and Race in the Early South* (New York: Oxford University Press, 1997), 232–43; Annette Gordon-Reed, *Thomas Jefferson and Sally Hemings: An American Controversy* (Charlottesville: University Press of Virginia, 1997), 169, 175–80; Barbara Murray and Brian Duffy, "Jefferson's Secret Life," *U.S. News and World Report*, November 9, 1998, 58–63; Lanier and Feldman, *Jefferson's Children*, 27–39.
41. White, *Ar'n't I A Woman?*, 14–15; Brent, *Incidents in the Life of a Slave Girl*, v–vi, 6, 51–52; Johnson et al., *Africans in America*, 37–49; *Daily Times*, January 2, 1876.
42. George P. Rawick, *From Sundown to Sunup: The Making of the Black Community* (Westport, CT: Greenwood Publishing Company), 69.
43. White, *Ar'n't I a Woman?*, 83, 156; *Daily Times*, January 2, 1876.
44. Willard Sterne Randall, *George Washington* (New York: Henry Holt and Company, 1997), 208.
45. Miller, *Frederick Douglass*, 3–8.
46. John W. Blassingame, *The Slave Community: Plantation Life in the Antebellum South* (Oxford: Oxford University Press, 1972), 41–42; Rawick, *From Sundown to Sunup*, xix, xx, 77–93; Johnson et al., *Africans in America*, 89, 164–65; *Daily Times*, January 2, 1876.
47. *Daily Times*, January 2, 1876.
48. Julius Lester, *To Be a Slave* (New York: Dell Publishing Company, 1971), 64–65; Rawick, *From Sundown to Sunup*, 72; Johnson et al., *Africans in America*, 358–59; *Daily Times*, January 2, 1876.

49. Rawick, *From Sundown to Sunup*, 77–93; Jean Fahey Eberle, *The Incredible Owen Girls* (St. Louis: Boar's Head Press, 1977), 5–6; White, *Ar'n't I a Woman*, 163; Johnson et al., *Africans in America*, 89.

50. White, *Ar'n't I a Woman?*, 123, 140–41, 163; Johnson et al., *Africans in America*, 89.

51. Rawick, *From Sundown to Sunup*, 51; Johnson et al., 90–92.

52. Lester, *To Be A Slave*, 101–116; Blassingame, *The Slave Community*, 42; Johnson et al., *Africans in America*, 89–91.

53. Winthrop D. Jordan, *The White Man's Burden: Historical Origins of Racism in the United States* (Oxford: Oxford University Press, 1974), 98; Blassingame, *The Slave Community*, 41, 59–61; Johnson et al., *Africans in America*, 91, 286–89, 308–12.

54. Lester, *To Be A Slave*, 106; Blassingame, *The Slave Community*, 49–74; Johnson et al., *Africans in America*, 91.

55. Quintard Taylor, *In Search of the Racial Frontier: African Americans in the American West, 1528–1990* (New York: W. W. Norton and Company, 1998), 112–13; Johnson et al., *Africans in America*, 275–76.

56. Brent, *Incidents in the Life of a Slave Girl*, 17; Blassingame, *The Slave Community*, 27–28; Johnson et al., *Africans in America*, 89.

57. Brent, *Incidents in the Life of a Slave Girl*, 6–7; *Daily Times*, January 2, 1876.

58. White, *Ar'n't I a Woman?*, 22, 157–60, 163; *Daily Times*, January 2, 1876.

CHAPTER 2

1. *Daily Times*, January 2, 1876.

2. James Neal Primm and Steven Rowan, eds., *Germans for a Free Misssouri: Translations from the St. Louis Radical Press, 1857–1862* (Columbia: University of Missouri, 1983), 244.

3. Mahline, "Reminiscences of General Sterling Price," *Ware's Valley Monthly: A Journal of Western Thought and Life* 1, no. 1 (May 1875), 489.

4. Primm and Rowan, *Germans for a Free Misssouri*, 242–44; *Daily Times*, January 2, 1876.

5. Undated edition of the *St. Louis Democrat*, Missouri Commandery M.O.L.L.U.S., pictorial archives, Missouri Historical Society, St. Louis, Missouri; Thomas Fleming, *Liberty: The American Revolution* (New York: Viking, 1997), 192–93; Christopher Phillips, *Damned Yankee: The Life of General Nathaniel Lyon* (Columbia: University of Missouri Press, 1990), 30, 77, 129–204; Pvt. William Cathay Service Records, RG 94, NA.

6. *Daily Times*, January 2, 1876.

7. Rafferty, *Historical Atlas of Missouri*, 33–34; James Neal Primm, *Lion of the Valley: St. Louis, Missouri* (Boulder: Pruett Publishing Company, 1981), 172–74; *Daily Times*, January 2, 1876.

8. Bruce Catton, *Terrible Swift Sword* (New York: Doubleday and Company, 1971), 16; *Battlefields of the South: From Bull Run to Fredericksburg by An English Combatant* (New York: John Bradburn, 1864), 61; Edward A. Pollard, *The First Year of the War* (n.p.: Philip & Son, 1863), 136.

9. *Daily Times*, January 2, 1876.

10. Ibid.

11. Mark Mayo Boatner III, *The Civil War Dictionary* (New York: David McKay Company, 1959), 60; Register of United States Army Officers, 1776–1903 (Washington, D.C.: War Department, 1904), 213; *The Soldier of Indiana in the War for the Union* (Indianapolis: Merrill and Company, 1968), 28; Savage Speech, AJML; Compiled Military Service Records of Union Soldiers Who Served from the State of Indiana, NA; Sketch of the His-

tory of the Eighth Indiana Regiment, Indiana State Archives, Indianapolis, Indiana (hereafter cited as ISA); *Daily Times*, January 2, 1876; Pvt. William Cathay Service Records, RG 94, NA.

12. Brent, *Incidents in the Life of a Slave Girl*, 163–64, 167; Savage Speech, AJML; Thomas Melick, December 29, 1861, letter, Civil War Files of J. W. Bartmess, Indiana Historical Society, Indianapolis, Indiana (hereafter cited as IHS); Sketch of the History of the Eighth Indiana Regiment, ISA.

13. *Daily Times*, January 2, 1876.

14. Elizabeth D. Leonard, *All the Daring of the Soldier: Women of the Civil War Armies* (New York: W. W. Norton & Company, 1999), 152–53.

15. *Daily Times*, January 2, 1876.

16. Ibid.

17. Ibid.

18. Vicki Wendel, "Washer Women," *Civil War Times Illustrated* 38, no. 4 (August 1999) 31–35.

19. Ibid., 31–33; *Daily Times*, January 2, 1876.

20. *Daily Times*, January 2, 1876.

21. Ibid.

22. Ibid.

23. Myers, *The Heritage of Missouri*, 328; Savage Speech, AJML; Taylor, *In Search of the Racial Frontier*, 94–95; *Daily Times*, January 2, 1876.

24. *Daily Times*, January 2, 1876.

25. Ibid.

26. Ibid.

27. Elkins, *Slavery*, 81–91; Savage Speech, AJML; *Daily Times*, January 2, 1876.

28. Wendel, "Washer Women," 31–35.

29. *Daily Times*, January 2, 1876.

30. Glenn W. Sunderland, *Five Days to Glory* (New Jersey: A. S. Barnes and Company, 1970), 23; William L. Shea and Earl J. Hess, *Pea Ridge: Civil War Campaign in the West* (Chapel Hill: University of North Carolina Press, 1992), 332–33; Michael A. Mullins, *The Fremont Rifles: A History of the 37th Illinois Veteran Volunteer Infantry* (Wilmington, NC: Broadfoot Publishing Company, 1990), 41; Boatner, *The Civil War Dictionary*, 226; Lizzie S. Pollock, October 11 and 17, 1861, letters, Civil War Files of Lizzie S. Pollock, IHS; Compiled Indiana Service Records, NA; Sketch of the History of the Eighth Indiana Regiment, ISA; *Daily Times*, January 2, 1876.

31. Albert Castel, *General Sterling Price and the Civil War in the West* (Baton Rouge: Louisiana State University Press, 1968), 65; Mullins, *The Fremont Rifles*, 41.

32. Castel, *General Sterling Price*, 65.

33. *Daily Times*, January 2, 1876.

34. Castel, *General Sterling Price*, 66–71; Shea and Hess, *Pea Ridge*, 20–22, 55–58; Taylor, *Trinidad*, 182; Sketch of the History of the Eighth Indiana Regiment, ISA.

35. Castel, *General Sterling Price*, 71–74.

36. Tucker, *The South's Finest*, 24–27; Castel, *General Sterling Price*, 74–76.

37. Tucker, *The South's Finest*, 24–27; Shea and Hess, *Pea Ridge*, 119.

38. Tucker, *The South's Finest*, 27–30; Shea and Hess, *Pea Ridge*, 201–3, 220–21.

39. Shea and Hess, *Pea Ridge*, 223–71, 332; Castel, *Sterling Price*, 75–78.

40. *Daily Times*, January 2, 1876.

41. Leonard, *All the Daring of the Soldier*, 154.

42. Ibid.

43. Shea and Hess, *Pea Ridge*, 288–89, 332.

44. Michael Fellman, *Inside War: The Guerrilla Conflict in Missouri during the American Civil War* (Oxford: Oxford University Press, 1989), 33–34, 95, 137; David E. Jones, *Women Warriors: A History* (Washington, D.C.: Brassey's, 1997), 239–40; Leonard, *All the Daring of the Soldier*, 86–87.

45. Shea and Hess, *Pea Ridge*, 289–90; *Daily Times*, January 2, 1876.

46. Shea and Hess, *Pea Ridge*, 290–92; Savage Speech, AJML; Sketch of the History of the Eighth Indiana Regiment, ISA; *Daily Times*, January 2, 1876.

47. Shea and Hess, *Pea Ridge*, 291–92; Boatner, *The Civil War Dictionary*, 215; Sketch of the History of the Eighth Indiana Regiment, ISA; *Daily Times*, January 2, 1876.

48. Shea and Hess, *Pea Ridge*, 292–99; Sketch of the History of the Eighth Indiana Regiment, ISA; *Daily Times*, January 2, 1876.

49. Shea and Hess, *Pea Ridge*, 300–301; *Daily Times*, January 2, 1876.

50. Shea and Hess, *Pea Ridge*, 300–301.

51. Shea and Hess, *Pea Ridge*, 301–2; Michael B. Dougan, *Confederate Arkansas: The People and Policies of a Frontier State in Wartime* (Tuscaloosa: University of Alabama Press, 1991), 115–17.

52. *Daily Times*, January 2, 1876.

53. Shea and Hess, *Pea Ridge*, 302–4; Robert L. Kerby, *Kirby Smith's Confederacy: The Trans-Mississippi South, 1863–1865* (Tuscaloosa: The University of Alabama Press, 1972), 33.

54. Shea and Hess, *Pea Ridge*, 301, 303–4, 306; Savage Speech, AJML.

55. Joseph T. Glatthaar, *Forged in Battle: The Civil War Alliance of Black Soldiers and White Officers* (New York: Meridian Books, 1991), 91–92; Ephraim McDowell Anderson, *Memoirs: Historical and Personal, Including the Campaigns of the First Missouri Confederate Brigade* (St. Louis: Times Printing Company, 1868), 285; Tucker, *The South's Finest*, 116.

56. Shea and Hess, *Pea Ridge*, 305; Castel, *Sterling Price*, 154–58; Sketch of the History of the Eighth Indiana Regiment, ISA; *Daily Times*, January 2, 1876.

57. Castel, *General Sterling Price*, 154, 157–58.

58. *Daily Times*, January 2, 1876.

59. Ibid.

60. Ibid.

61. Savage Speech, AJML; Taylor, *Trinidad*, 182; *Daily Times*, January 2, 1876.

62. *Daily Times*, January 2, 1876.

63. Sketch of the History of the Eight Indiana Regiment, ISA; Tucker, *The South's Finest*, 121–210; Edwin C. Bearss, *The Campaign for Vicksburg: Grant Strikes a Fatal Blow* (Dayton, OH: Morningside Press, 1986), 2: 404, 648; *The War of the Rebellion: A Compilation of the Official Records of the Union and Confederate Armies* (hereafter cited as *OR*), 24, ser. 1, part 1 (Washington, D.C.: Government Printing Office, 1889), 625–28.

64. Savage Speech, AJML; Mullins, *The Fremont Rifles*, 223–24; Sketch of the History of the Eighth Indiana Regiment, ISA.

65. *Daily Times*, January 2, 1876.

66. Boatner, *The Civil War Dictionary*, 685; Savage Speech, AJML; Sketch of the History of the Eighth Indiana Regiment, ISA.

67. Boatner, *The Civil War Dictionary*, 685–86; Savage Speech, AJML; Sketch of the History of the Eighth Indiana Regiment, ISA.

68. Boatner, *The Civil War Dictionary*, 685–86; *Daily Times*, January 2, 1864.

69. *Daily Times*, January 2, 1864.

70. Ibid.

71. Edwin Adams Davis, *Louisiana: The Pelican State* (Baton Rouge: Louisiana State University Press, 1972), 202–5; Boatner, *The Civil War Dictionary*, 686–89.

72. Sketch of the History of the Eighth Indiana Regiment, ISA; Ludwell H. Johnson, *Red River Campaign: Politics and Cotton in the Civil War* (Kent, OH: Kent State University Press, 1993), 40–41; Savage Speech, AJML.

73. Sketch of the History of the Eighth Indiana Regiment, ISA; Savage Speech, AJML; Johnson, *Red River Campaign*, 34–36; *Daily Times*, January 2, 1876.

74. Sketch of the History of the Eighth Indiana Regiment, ISA; Savage Speech, AJML; Ronnie C. Tyler, *Santiago Vidaurri and the Southern Confederacy* (Austin: Texas State Historical Association, 1973), 97–128; *Daily Times*, January 2, 1876.

CHAPTER 3

1. Sketch of the History of the Eighth Indiana Regiment, ISA.

2. Ibid.

3. Ibid.

4. *Daily Times*, January 2, 1876.

5. Thomas Froncek, ed., *An Illustrated History: The City of Washington* (New York: Wings Books, 1992), 170–71, 222, 225.

6. Sketch of the History of the Eighth Indiana Regiment, ISA.

7. Ibid.; Thomas A. Lewis, *The Guns of Cedar Creek* (New York: Harper and Row Publishers, 1988), 24–25, 55–56, 331; Boatner, *The Civil War Dictionary*, 743–45.

8. Boatner, *The Civil War Dictionary*, 744–45; Lewis, *The Guns of Cedar Creek*, 31, 55–56; Savage Speech, AJML; Taylor, *Trinidad*, 183.

9. *Daily Times*, January 2, 1876.

10. Lewis, *The Guns of Cedar Creek*, 183–87; Savage Speech, AJML; *Daily Times*, January 2, 1876.

11. Lewis, *The Guns of Cedar Creek*, 192–97.

12. *Daily Times*, January 2, 1876.

13. Lewis, *The Guns of Cedar Creek*, 199–211; Savage Speech, AJML.

14. Lewis, *The Guns of Cedar Creek*, 218–96; Roy Morris, Jr., *Sheridan: The Life and Wars of General Phil Sheridan* (New York: Crown Publishers, 1992), 210–21.

15. Savage Speech, AJML; *Daily Times*, January 2, 1876.

16. Leonard, *All the Daring of the Soldier*, 241–42.

17. Ibid., 243–44.

18. *Daily Times*, January 2, 1876; Savage Speech, AJML.

19. *Daily Times*, January 2, 1868; Sketch of the History of the Eighth Indiana Regiment, ISA.

20. Ibid.

21. *Daily Times*, January 2, 1876; Sketch of the History of the Eighth Indiana Regiment, ISA.

22. Sketch of the History of the Eighth Indiana Regiment, ISA; *Daily Times*, January 2, 1876.

CHAPTER 4

1. William H. Leckie, *The Buffalo Soldiers* (Norman: University of Oklahoma Press, 1967), 6, 19; Taylor, *In Search of the Racial Frontier*, 164–65; Phillip Thomas Tucker, *From Auction Block to Glory: The African American Experience* (New York: Friedman Fairfax Publishing Group, 1998), 18–25.

2. *Daily Times*, January 2, 1876.

3.–11. Ibid.

12. Savage Speech, AJML; Pvt. William Cathey Enlistment Papers, vol. 62, NA; Robert M. Utley, *Frontier Regulars: The United States Army and the Indian, 1866–1890* (New York:

Macmillan, 1973), 11–13, 25; Katz, *The Black West*, 199–200, 281; Monroe Lee Billing-
ton, *New Mexico's Buffalo Soldiers, 1866–1900* (Niwot: University Press of Colorado,
1991), 4; Taylor, *In Search of the Racial Frontier*, 164–65; Sketch of the History of the
Eighth Indiana Regiment, ISA; Jones, *Women Warriors*, 231–40; Linda Wolfe Keister, *The
Complete Guide to African-American Baby Names* (New York: Penguin Books, 1998), 36;
Daily Times, January 2, 1876; Leonard, *All the Daring of the Soldier*, 143–225; Private
William Cathay Service Records, RG 94, NA.

13. Leonard, *All the Daring of the Soldier*, 205.
14. Ibid., 211.
15. White, *Ar'n't I a Woman?*, 23–24; Savage Speech, AJML; Pvt. William Cathey Enlistment
Papers, vol. 62, NA.
16. Pvt. William Cathay Service Records, RG 94, NA; *Daily Times*, January 2, 1876.
17. Blanton, "Cathy Williams," 1; Savage Speech, AJML; Pvt. William Cathey Enlistment
Papers, vol. 62, NA; Francis B. Heitman, *Historical Register and Dictionary of the United
States Army* (Washington, D.C.: Government Printing Office, 1903), 134; Frank N.
Schubert, *Black Valor: Buffalo Soldiers and the Medal of Honor, 1870–1898* (Wilmington:
Scholarly Resources, 1997), 180; James G. Hollandsworth, Jr., *The Louisiana Native
Guards: The Black Military Experience during the Civil War* (Baton Rouge: Louisiana State
University Press, 1995), 100–101; Private William Cathay Service Records, RG 94, NA;
Daily Times, January 2, 1876.
18. Blanton, "Cathy Williams," 1; Pvt. William Cathay Service Records, RG 94, NA.
19. Blanton, "Cathy Williams," 1; *Daily Times*, January 2, 1876; Leonard, *All the Daring of
the Soldier*, 205–6.
20. Blanton, "Cathy Williams," 1; White, *Ar'n't I a Woman*, 161–62; Pvt. William Cathey
Enlistment Papers, vol. 62, NA; Savage Speech, AJML; John Hope Franklin, *From Slavery to Freedom: A History of Negro Americans* (New York: Alfred A. Knopf, 1974), 196;
Daily Times, January 2, 1876; Patricia C. McKissack and Frederick McKissack, *Sojourner
Truth: Ain't I a Woman?* (New York: Scholastic, 1992), 1–2, 6–21.
21. Leonard, *All the Daring of the Soldier*, 209.
22. Ibid., 201–2.
23. Blanton, "Cathy Williams," 1; Pvt. William Cathey Enlistment Papers, vol. 62, NA; Savage Speech, AJML; Utley, *Frontier Regulars*, 71–72, 76–78; Jones, *Women Warriors*, 237;
Daily Times, January 2, 1876.
24. Leckie, *The Buffalo Soldiers*, 9; Savage Speech, AJML; Pvt. William Cathey Enlistment Papers, vol. 62, NA; Utley, *Frontier Regulars*, 27–28.
25. Pvt. William Cathey Enlistment Papers, vol. 62, NA; Utley, *Frontier Regulars*, 11–12;
Katz, *The Black West*, 201; Schubert, *Black Valor*, ix.; Gerald T. Altoff, *Amongst My Best
Men: African Americans and the War of 1812* (Put-in-Bay, OH: The Perry Group, 1996),
102–3, 126–28.

CHAPTER 5

1. Leonard, *All the Daring of the Soldier*, 221.
2. Richard Hall, *Patriots in Disguise: Women Warriors of the Civil War* (New York: Marlowe
and Company, 1994), xi; Leonard, *All the Daring of the Soldier*, 15–19, 100–225.
3. Benjamin Quarles, *The Negro in the American Revolution* (Chapel Hill: University of
North Carolina Press, 1972), 23; Phillip Thomas Tucker, *From Auction Block to Glory:
The African American Experience* (New York: Friedman Fairfax Publishing Group, 1998),
18–22; William C. Nell, *Services of Colored Americans in the Wars of 1776 and 1812* (New

York: AMS Press, 1976), 11; *The American Military on the Frontier: Proceedings of the Seventh Military History Symposium,* U.S. Air Force Academy (Washington, D.C.: Office of Air Force History, 1976), 98; Utley, *Frontier Regulars,* 27–28; Schubert, *Black Valor,* ix; Thomas Fleming, *Lexington* (Washington, D.C.: U.S. Department of the Interior, 1978), 1–7; Jones, *Women Warriors,* xi–xiii, 8–9, 81–93; Blond, *La Grande Armée,* 54–55; John R. Elting, *Swords around a Throne: Napoléon's Grande Armée* (New York: Da Capo Press, 1997), 38–39, 274–75; Dumas, Alexandre, *The Three Musketeers* (New York: Bantam Books, 1984), i; Johnson et al., *Africans in America,* 158–64, 167, 177, 181–82; Rene Chartrand and Francis Back, *Napoleon's Overseas Army* (London: Reed International Books, 1994), 5–40; Richard Walling, *Men of Color at the Battle of Monmouth, June 28, 1778* (New Jersey: Longstreet House, 1994), iv–6, 11–30.

4. Thomas Fleming, *Liberty,* 151, 288–89, 302–3; Quarles, *The Negro in the American Revolution,* 52, 72; Tucker, *From Auction Block to Glory,* 18–22; C. Kay Larson, "Bonny Yank and Ginny Reb Revisited," *Minerva* 10, no. 2 (summer 1992): 48; Jones, *Women Warriors,* 220–28; Hall, *Patriots in Disguise,* xi; *Daily Times,* January 2, 1876; Leonard, *All the Daring of the Soldier,* 102–6, 155–56.

5. James Thomas Flexner, *Washington: The Indispensable Man* (Boston: Little, Brown and Company, 1974), 367; Leonard, *All the Daring of the Soldier,* 165.

6. Aptheker, *American Negro Slave Revolts,* 3; Johnson et al., *Africans in America,* 93–112, 253–57, 286–89, 342–43.

7. Tucker, *From Auction Block to Glory,* 30–122; Schubert, *Black Valor,* ix–8.

8. Tucker, *From Auction Block to Glory,* 52–71, 86–87; Larson, "Bonny Yank and Ginny Reb," 48–49; Katz, *The Black West,* 4–5; William Loren Katz, *Black Women of the Old West* (New York: Atheneum Books, 1995), ix, 3–6; William C. Davis, *Three Roads to the Alamo: The Lives and Fortunes of David Crockett, James Bowie, and William Barret Travis* (New York: HarperCollins, 1998), 29; Edwin C. McReynolds, *The Seminoles* (Norman: The University of Oklahoma Press, 1985), 3–87; Kenneth Wiggins Porter, *The Negro on the American Frontier* (New York: Arno Press, 1971), 244–93; Jones, *Women Warriors,* 206–214, 238; K. Jack Bauer, *Zachary Taylor: Soldier, Planter, Statesman of the Old Southwest* (Baton Rouge: Louisiana State University Press, 1985), 109; Hall, *Patriots in Disguise,* 164–66; *Daily Times,* January 2, 1876; Leonard, *All the Daring of the Soldier,* 70, 152–54.

9. Jones, *Women Warriors,* 81–83.

10. Ibid., 83–88.

11. Ibid., 88–91; Alan Schom, *Napoleon Bonaparte* (New York: HarperCollins, 1997), 145–88; Blond, *La Grande Armée,* 20; Michael Barthorp, *The Zulu War: A Pictorial History* (London: Blandford Press, 1985), 1–69.

12. Martin Ros, *Night of Fire: The Black Napoleon and the Battle for Haiti* (New York: Sarpedon, 1994), 6, 38–39; Peter Earle, *The Sack of Panama: Sir Henry Morgan's Adventures on the Spain Main* (New York: The Viking Press, 1982), 66; Jones, *Women Warriors,* 65–67, 76, 99, 103, 229; Johnson et al., *Africans in America,* 249–55; *Daily Times,* January 2, 1876.

13. Benjamin O. Davis, Jr., *American: An Autobiography* (Washington, D.C.: Smithsonian Institution Press, 1991), ix–3, 67.

14. Alan M. Osur, *Blacks in the Army Air Forces during World War II: The Problem of Race Relations* (Washington, D.C.: Office of Air Force History, 1986), 70.

15. Hall, *Patriots in Disguise,* 20–32, 159.

16. Leonard, *All the Daring of the Soldier,* 191–97.

17. Phillip Thomas Tucker, *The Forgotten "Stonewall of the West": Major General John Stevens Bowen* (Macon: Mercer University Press, 1997), 322–23.

18. Ibid., 20–32, 154–62; Leonard, *All the Daring of the Soldier*, 165–275; *Daily Times*, January 2, 1876.
19. *Daily Times*, January 2, 1876.
20. Ibid.

CHAPTER 6

1. Arlen L. Fowler, *The Black Infantry in the West, 1869–1891* (Norman: University of Oklahoma Press, 1996), xii–xiii.
2. Ibid., xiv.
3. Ibid., 3, 12.
4. Blanton, "Cathy Williams," 2–3; General Colin Powell Speech at the dedication of the Buffalo Soldier Monument, Fort Leavenworth, Kansas; Leckie, *The Buffalo Soldiers*, 260; Savage Speech, AJML; Pvt. William Cathey Enlistment Papers, vol. 62, NA; Utley, *Frontier Regulars*, 11–14, 26–27; Katz, *The Black West*, 36–38, 204; Billington, *New Mexico's Buffalo Soldiers*, 4–5; Schubert, *Black Valor*, ix, 4–5; Taylor, *In Search of the Racial Frontier*, 164; Charles E. Francis, *The Men Who Changed a Nation: The Tuskegee Airmen*, (Boston: Branden Publishing Company, 1993), 7–77.
5. Leonard, *All the Daring of the Soldier*, 203; *Daily Times*, January 2, 1876.
6. Leonard, *All the Daring of the Soldier*, 203; *Daily Times*, January 2, 1876.
7. Hall, *Patriots In Disguise*, 28, 156–57.
8. Bell Irvin Wiley, *The Life of Billy Yank: The Common Soldier of the Union* (Baton Rouge: Louisiana State University Press, 1978), 339.
9. Hall, *Patriots in Disguise*, 159–62; *Daily Times*, January 2, 1876.
10. William C. Winter, *The Civil War in St. Louis: A Guided Tour*, (St. Louis: Missouri Historical Society, 1994), 4–7; NiNi Harris, *History of Carondelet* (St. Louis: The Patrice Press, 1991), 3–19; Blanton, "Cathy Williams," 3; Andrew Burstein, *The Inner Jefferson: Portrait of a Grieving Optimist* (Charlottesville: University Press of Virginia, 1995), 168, 278; Savage Speech, AJML; *Daily Times*, January 2, 1876.
11. *Daily Times*, January 2, 1876.
12. Ibid.
13. Fowler, *The Black Infantry in the West*, 3–4.
14. Ibid., 97.
15. Phil Sheridan, *Personal Memoirs* (New York: Press of Jenkins and McCowan, 1888), 2:282; Morris, *Sheridan*, 293–94; Fowler, *The Black Infantry in the West*, 4–5.
16. Blanton, "Cathy Williams," 3; Savage Speech, AJML; White, *Ar'n't I a Woman?*, 83; Utley, *Frontier Regulars*, 75–77; Taylor, *Trinidad*, 183; Heitman, *Historical Register and Dictionary of the United States Army*, 306; Phillips, *Damned Yankee*, 75; Johnson et al., *Africans in America*, 190–92; Alan S. Brown, ed., *A Soldier's Life: The Civil War Experiences of Ben C. Johnson* (Kalamazoo: Western Michigan University Press, 1962), 9, 13, 17, 29, 38, 41–44; *Daily Times*, January 2, 1876.
17. *Daily Times*, January 2, 1876.
18. Ibid.; Leonard, *All the Daring of the Soldier*, 193, 210.
19. Blanton, "Cathy Williams," 3; Savage Speech, AJML; Utley, *Frontier Regulars*, 98; Scott M. Forsythe, "The Buffalo Soldiers as Infantry" (paper presented at the annual meeting of the Western Historical Association, St. Paul, MN, October 1997); *Daily Times*, January 2, 1876.
20. Harry H. McConnell, *Five Years a Cavalryman; Or, Sketches of Regular Army Life on the Texas Frontier, 1866–1871* (Norman: University of Oklahoma Press, 1996), 212–13; Records of U.S. Army Continental Commands, RG 94, NA; William A. Dobak, "Col-

ored Troops and Buffalo Soldiers: Some Legacies of Southern Reconstruction in the West-ern Army," (paper presented at the annual meeting of the Western Historical Association, St. Paul, MN, October 1997), 2–4; Billington, *New Mexico's Buffalo Soldiers*, 4–5.

21. Robert G. Carter, *On the Border with Mackenzie* (New York: 1961), 46–47; *New York Tri-bune*, November 18, 1893; Evan S. Connell, *Son of the Morning Star: Custer and the Little Bighorn* (New York: Harper & Row, 1984), 132–43; Leckie, *The Buffalo Soldiers*, 19–20; Utley, *Frontier Regulars*, ix–x, 1–2, 115–29; Virginia Irving Armstrong, comp., *I Have Spoken: American History through the Voices of the Indians* (New York: Pocket Books, 1972), 100–101; Billington, *New Mexico's Buffalo Soldiers*, 4–6; Katz, *Black Women of the Old West*, 29; Schubert, *Black Valor*, 15–16; Taylor, *In Search of the Racial Frontier*, 81–86, 169–70; Johnson et al., *Africans in America*, 387.

22. Department of Defense, *Black Americans in Defense of Our Nation* (Washington, D.C.: Department of Defense, n.d.), 25–27; *The American Military on the Frontier*, 6, 13, 86, 95; Connell, *Son of the Morning Star*, 151; Leckie, *The Buffalo Soldiers*, 13–15; Geoffrey Perret, *Ulysses S. Grant: Soldier & President* (New York: Random House, 1997), 99–100; Utley, *Frontier Regulars*, 1–2, 27–29; Frederick Remington, *Frederic Remington's Own West* (New York: Promontory Press, 1960), 69; Katz, *The Black West*, 199–202, 204, 225; Schubert, *Black Valor*, ix–16; Taylor, *In Search of the Racial Frontier*, 164.

23. Blanton, "Cathy Williams," 3; Morris, *Sheridan*, 208, 253–54, 299; Marguerite Mering-ton, ed., *The Custer Story: The Life and Intimate Letters of General Custer and His Wife Elizabeth* (New York: The Devin-Adair Company, n.d.), 190, 195, 197; Connell, *Son of the Morning Star*, 124–27, 171; Leckie, *The Buffalo Soldiers*, viii, 8, 13–14; Savage Speech, AJML; Edward G. Longacre, *Custer and His Wolverines: The Michigan Cavalry Brigade, 1861–1865* (Conshohocken, PA: Combined Publishing, 1997), 35, 195–278; Utley, *Frontier Regulars*, 2–3, 83–85; Katz, *The Black West*, 178–79, 210, 223; Boatner, *The Civil War Dictionary*, 363, 390–91; Heitman, *Historical Register and Dictionary of the United States Army*, 134, 306; Wiley Sword, *Shiloh: Bloody April* (New York: William Morrow, 1974), 383–84, 389–91, 453; Taylor, *In Search of the Racial Frontier*, 98, 169; Jones, *Women Warriors*, 210; Elting, *Swords around a Throne*, 44; Noah Andre Trudeau, *Like Men of War: Black Troops in the Civil War, 1862–1865* (New York: Little, Brown and Company, 1998), 3–7; John W. Ravage, *Black Pioneers: Images of the Black Experience on the North American Frontier* (Salt Lake City: The University of Utah Press, 1997), 73, 78–79; John G. Neihardt, *Black Elk Speaks* (Lincoln: University of Nebraska Press, 1961), 104; Eric S. Lander and Joseph J. Ellis, "Founding Father," *Nature* 396 (November 5, 1988): 13–14, 27–28; *Daily Times*, January 2, 1876.

24. *The American Military on the Frontier*, 137–41; Savage Speech, AJML; *Daily Times*, Janu-ary 2, 1876.

25. Horgan, *Josiah Gregg*, 46; *Daily Times*, January 2, 1876.

26. Horgan, *Josiah Gregg*, 158; Tucker, *The South's Finest*, 25–27; Leckie, *The Buffalo Soldiers*, 8; *Daily Times*, January 2, 1876.

27. Phillip Thomas Tucker, "A Forgotten Sacrifice: Richard Gentry, Missouri Volunteers, and the Battle of Okeechobee, *The Florida Historical Quarterly* 70, no. 2 (October 1991): 150–65; Armstrong, *I Have Spoken*, 98–99; Katz, *The Black West*, 4–5, 16–21, 44, 315; Schubert, *Black Valor*, 15–16; Taylor, *In Search of the Racial Frontier*, 164; Phillip Thomas Tucker, "John Horse: Forgotten African-American Leader of the Second Seminole War," *Journal of Negro History*, 72, no. 2 (spring 1992): 74–83; Journal of the Committee on the Florida Campaign: the Senate and the House of Representatives (of Missouri) to investi-gate the battle fought December 1837 in Florida by the Regular Army and the Missouri Volunteers, Missouri Historical Society, St. Louis, Missouri; Richard Drinnon, *Facing*

West: The Metaphysics of Indian-hating and Empire-Building (Minneapolis: University of Minnesota Press, 1980), 105–9, 219–22.

28. *The American Military on the Frontier*, 3, 11–12; Utley, *Frontier Regulars*, x; Taylor, *In Search of the Racial Frontier*, 164; "Daisy Anderson: Civil War Soldier's Widow, Dies at 97," *Washington Post*, September 27, 1998; *Daily Times*, January 2, 1876.

29. *The American Military on the Frontier*, 141–43; Schubert, *Black Valor*, 15–16; Taylor, *In Search of the Racial Frontier*, 164; "Daisy Anderson," *Washington Post*, September 27, 1998.

30. Blanton, "Cathy Williams," 3; Merington, *The Custer Story*, 209–11; Connell, *Son of the Morning Star*, 125; Thomas P. Sweeney, M.D., letter to author, September 16, 1998.

31. Ramon Powers and Gene Younger, "Cholera on the Plains: The Epidemic of 1867," *Kansas Historical Quarterly*, 37, no. 4 (winter 1971): 351–93.

32. Ibid., 358–59, 377; Connell, *Son of the Morning Star*, 171.

33. Powers and Younger, "Cholera on the Plains," 360–93.

34. Ibid., 364–67, 372.

35. Jay Monaghan, *Custer: The Life of General George Armstrong Custer* (Lincoln: University of Nebraska Press, 1959), 293–94.

36. Fowler, *The Black Infantry in the West*, 17.

37. Monaghan, *Custer*, 294–98.

38. Blanton, "Cathy Williams," 3; Glatthaar, *Forged in Battle*, 167–68, 235; William A. Gladstone, *United States Colored Troops, 1863–1867* (Gettysburg: Thomas Publications, 1990), 22, 111; Phillip Thomas Tucker, "The First Missouri Confederate Brigade's Last Stand at Fort Blakeley on Mobile Bay, *Alabama Review* 42, no. 4 (October 1989): 277–78; Trudeau, *Like Men of War*, 405; Fowler, *The Black Infantry in the West*, 77.

39. Leonard, *All the Daring of the Soldier*, 203–4.

40. Ibid., 204.

41. *Daily Times*, January 2, 1876.

42. Leonard, *All the Daring of the Soldier*, 240.

43. Blanton, "Cathy Williams," 3.

44. Ibid.; David Lavender, *The American Heritage History of The Great West* (New York: American Heritage, 1982), 261; David A. Dary, *The Buffalo Book: The Saga of an American Symbol* (New York: Avon Books, 1975), 93–120, 212; Blanton, "Cathy Williams," 6–7; Sheridan, *Personal Memoirs*, 2: 282, 297–98; Merington, *The Custer Story*, 207–10; Morris, *Sheridan*, 300–301; Connell, *Son of the Morning Star*, 126, 135–36, 155–56, 170–74; Leckie, *The Buffalo Soldiers*, 15–16, 21, 23; Utley, *Frontier Regulars*, 23–24, 91–92, 98, 148; Armstrong, *I Have Spoken*, 100–101; W. C. Vanderwerth, comp., *Indian Oratory: Famous Speeches by Noted Indian Chieftains* (New York: Ballantine Books, 1971), 120–22; Forsythe, "The Buffalo Soldiers as Infantry"; Billington, *New Mexico's Buffalo Soldiers*, 4–5; Francis Stanley, *Fort Union (New Mexico)* (n.p.: F. Stanely, 1953), xi, 172, 183–84, 203, 261–64; Chris Emmett, *Fort Union and the Winning of the Southwest* (Norman: University of Oklahoma Press, 1965), 28–37, 325, 336; *Albuquerque Journal*, Albuquerque, New Mexico, June 22, 1997; Taylor, *In Search of the Racial Frontier*, 83, 185; Powers and Younger, "Cholera On the Plains," 351–93; Blond, *La Grande Armée*, 19–20, 62–63; Elting, *Swords around a Throne*, 137; Horgan, *Josiah Gregg*, 47–48; Cynthia Savage, interview with author, September 21, 1998; *Daily Times*, January 2, 1876.

45. Emmett, *Fort Union and the Winning of the Southwest*, 336–37.

46. Ibid.

47. Ibid.; *Albuquerque Journal*, June 22, 1997.

48. Emmett, *Fort Union and the Winning of the Southwest*, 323–34; *Albuquerque Journal*, June 22, 1997.

49. *The American Military on the Frontier*, 96; Blanton, "Cathy Williams," 3.
50. *The American Military on the Frontier*, 142–43; Connell, *Son of the Morning Star*, 151.
51. Fowler, *The Black Infantry in the West*, 79.
52. Blanton, "Cathy Williams," 3; Ray C. Colton, *The Civil War in the Western Territories: Arizona, Colorado, New Mexico, and Utah* (Norman: University of Oklahoma Press, 1989), 139; Sheridan, *Personal Memoirs*, 282–83; Connell, *Son of the Morning Star*, 145–49; Leckie, *The Buffalo Soldiers*, 27; Savage Speech, AJML; Utley, *Frontier Regulars*, 84–85; Armstrong, *I Have Spoken*, 96–97; Billington, *New Mexico's Buffalo Soldiers*, 4–7, 29–30, 38, 40; Stanley, *Fort Union*, x; Lee Myers, "Mutiny at Fort Cummings," *New Mexico Historical Review* 46, no. 4 (1971): 348; *Daily Times*, January 2, 1876.
53. Savage Speech, AJML; Utley, *Frontier Regulars*, 83–87; Billington, *New Mexico's Buffalo Soldiers*, 26, 28–30; *Daily Times*, January 2, 1876.
54. Billington, *New Mexico's Buffalo Soldiers*, 28.
55. Connell, *Son of the Morning Star*, 126; Leckie, *The Buffalo Soldiers*, 25–26; Schubert, *Black Valor*, 65.
56. Schubert, *Black Valor*, 69; Emmett, *Fort Union and the Winning of the Southwest*, 345–47.

CHAPTER 7

1. Remington, *Frederick Remington's Own West*, 69; Utley, *Frontier Regulars*, 19–23; Russell Duncan, ed., *Blue-Eyed Child of Fortune: The Civil War Letters of Colonel Robert Gould Shaw* (New York: Avon Books, 1992), 2, 15–56.
2. Dobak, "Colored Troops and Buffalo Soldiers," 1–8; *Valentine (Nebraska) Republican*, April 12, 1889.
3. Savage Speech, AJML; Dobak, "Colored Troops and Buffalo Soldiers," 1–8; Trials of Black Soldiers, Thirty-eighth United States Infantry, for the "Mutiny" at Fort Cummings, Office of the Judge Advocate General, RG 153, NA; Gladstone, *United States Colored Troops*, 102; Katz, *The Black West*, 204; Billington, *New Mexico's Buffalo Soldiers*, 8, 38–42; Stanley, *Fort Union*, 258–60; Myers, "Mutiny at Fort Cummings," 337–48; Johnson et al., *Africans in America*, 439; *Daily Times*, January 2, 1876.
4. Heitman, *Historical Register and Dictionary of the United States Army*, 306; Gen. Joseph J. Reynolds to Bvt. Gen. E. D. Townsend, January 18, 1870, Charles E. Clarke Military Service Record, NA.
5. Myers, "Mutiny at Fort Cummings," 347–48.

CHAPTER 8

1. Alvin R. Sunseri, *Seeds of Discord: New Mexico in the Aftermath of the American Conquest, 1846–1861* (Chicago: Nelson-Hall, 1979), 57–59; Paul Horgan, *Great River: The Rio Grande in North American History* (Hanover, NH: University Press of New England, 1984), 61, 220; Utley, *Frontier Regulars*, 379; Armstrong, *I Have Spoken*, 111; Schubert, *Black Valor*, 41–59; Donald E. Worcester, *The Apaches: Eagles of the Southwest*, (Norman: University of Oklahoma Press, 1992), xiii–7, 10, 14, 19, 21, 35, 54–55, 80.
2. Vanderwerth, *Indian Oratory*, 125.
3. Worcester, *The Apaches*, 15, 22–23, 41, 52.
4. Ibid., 37–40.
5. Worcester, *The Apaches*, 10–11, 15, 23, 28–29, 81–82, 96–98.
6. Ibid., 61.

7. Forsythe, "The Buffalo Soldiers as Infantry"; Utley, *Frontier Regulars*, 50–53; Billington, *New Mexico's Buffalo Soldiers*, 16; Worcester, *The Apaches*, 4–7, 29; Neihardt, *Black Elk Speaks*, 93.

8. Forsythe, "The Buffalo Soldiers as Infantry"; Utley, *Frontier Regulars*, 50–53.

9. Forsythe, "The Buffalo Soldiers as Infantry"; Worcester, *The Apaches*, 72.

10. Forsythe, "The Buffalo Soldiers as Infantry"; Utley, *Frontier Regulars*, 51–52; Katz, *The Black West*, 286; Billington, *New Mexico's Buffalo Soldiers*, 13; Jones, *Women Warriors*, 208; Compiled Military Service Records of Civil War Soldiers Who Served from the State of Ohio, NA; *Daily Times*, January 2, 1876.

11. Forsythe, "The Buffalo Soldiers as Infantry"; Utley, *Frontier Regulars*, 71–74, 274–75.

12. Forsythe, "The Buffalo Soldiers as Infantry"; Utley, *Frontier Regulars*, 78; Billington, *New Mexico's Buffalo Soldiers*, 13.

13. Forsythe, "The Buffalo Soldiers as Infantry"; Morris, *Sheridan*, 302–3.

14. Forsythe, "The Buffalo Soldiers as Infantry"; Billington, *New Mexico's Buffalo Soldiers*, 13–14; Worcester, *The Apaches*, 36; *Daily Times*, January 2, 1876.

CHAPTER 9

1. Forsythe, "The Buffalo Soldiers as Infantry"; Morris, *Sheridan*, 301; Connell, *Son of the Morning Star*, 150–51; Leckie, *The Buffalo Soldiers*, 10–11, 13–14, 44; Utley, *Frontier Regulars*, 88–89; Billington, *New Mexico's Buffalo Soldiers*, 12, 29, 31–32; Taylor, *In Search of the Racial Frontier*, 83; *Daily Times*, January 2, 1876; Leonard, *All the Daring of the Soldier*, 212.

2. Sheridan, *Personal Memoirs*, 284; Morris, *Sheridan*, 298–99; Utley, *Frontier Regulars*, 135–36; Armstrong, *I Have Spoken*, 98–100.

3. Utley, *Frontier Regulars*, 147–50; Morris, *Sheridan*, 300, 302–3; Savage Speech, AJML; Billington, *New Mexico's Buffalo Soldiers*, 36, 41, 168–69; *Daily Times*, January 2, 1876.

4. Blanton, "Cathy Williams," 3–4; Utley, *Frontier Regulars*, 84; Billington, *New Mexico's Buffalo Soldiers*, 7–8, 16, 21–23; *Silver City (New Mexico) Daily Press*, February 17, 1965; Fowler, *The Black Infantry in the West*, 82; *Daily Times*, January 2, 1876.

5. Morris, *Sheridan*, 307–8; Connell, *Son of the Morning Star*, 127–32, 179–80; Taylor, *In Search of the Racial Frontier*, 164.

6. Utley, *Frontier Regulars*, 142, 149–50; Boatner, *The Civil War Dictionary*, 390–91.

7. Blanton, "Cathy Williams," 4; Pvt. William Cathey Enlistment Papers, vol. 62, NA; Savage Speech, AJML; Utley, *Frontier Regulars*, 89–90, 143; Taylor, *Trinidad*, 183; *Daily Times*, January 2, 1876.

8. *Daily Times*, January 2, 1876.

9. Savage Speech, AJML; Blanton, "Cathy Williams," 4; Pvt. William Cathey Enlistment Papers, vol. 62, NA; Stanley M. Elkins, *Slavery: A Problem in American Institutional and Intellectual Life* (Chicago: The University of Chicago Press, 1974), 81–89; Herbert Aptheker, *American Negro Slave Revolts* (New York: International Publishers, 1974), 1–5, 11–17, 368–74; Eugene D. Genovese, *From Rebellion to Revolution: Afro-American Slave Revolts in the Making of the Modern World* (Baton Rouge: Louisiana State University Press, 1979), xiii–50; *Daily Times*, January 2, 1876.

10. *Daily Times*, January 2, 1876.

11. Savage Speech, AJML; *Daily Times*, January 2, 1876.

12. *Daily Times*, January 2, 1876.

13. Ibid.

14. Jeffrey, *Frontier Women*, 45, 198–99; Savage Speech, AJML; *Daily Times*, January 2, 1876.

15. Leckie, *The Buffalo Soldiers*, 258–60; Savage Speech, AJML; *Daily Times*, January 2, 1876.

CHAPTER 10

1. Phillip T. Drotning, *Black Heroes in Our Nation's History* (New York: Washington Square Press, 1969), 109–10; Leckie, *The Buffalo Soldiers*, 172; Charles E. Clarke Military Service Record, NA; *Daily Times*, January 2, 1876.

2. Blanton, "Cathy Williams," 6; Leckie, *The Buffalo Soldiers*, 176, 206–7; *Daily Times*, January 2, 1876.

3. Brent, *Incidents in the Life of a Slave Girl*, 172; Katz, *Black Women of The Old West*, 31; Taylor, *In Search of the Racial Frontier*, 17; *Daily Times*, January 2, 1876.

4. *Daily Times*, January 2, 1876; Brent, *Incidents in the Life of a Slave Girl*, 208.

5. W. Sherman Savage, "The Role of Negro Soldiers in Protecting the Indian Territory from Intruders," *Journal of Negro History* 1, vol. 36 (January 1951): 28; Taylor, *In Search of the Racial Frontier*, 18, 81–82, 134–35, 142.

6. Blanton, "Cathy Williams," 6; Savage Speech, AJML; Taylor, *In Search of the Racial Frontier*, 17–23; *Daily Times*, January 2, 1876.

7. Blanton, "Cathy Williams," 5; Savage Speech, AJML; Katz, *Black Women of the Old West*, 31; *Daily Times*, January 2, 1876.

8. Blanton, "Cathy Williams," 5; Savage Speech, AJML; Katz, *The Black West*, 77–79, 155–56, 285, 303; Taylor, *Trinidad* 183; Katz, *Black Women of the Old West*, 32, 40l; Cythnia Savage, interview with author, November 20, 1998; *Daily Times*, January 2, 1876.

9. Savage Speech, AJML; *Daily Times*, January 2, 1876.

10. *Daily Times*, January 2, 1876.

11. Ibid.

12. Wyatt Blassingame, *Bent's Fort: Crossroads of the Great West* (Champaign, IL: Garrard Publishing Company, 1967), 7–85; *Daily Times*, January 2, 1876.

13. *Daily Times*, January 2, 1876.

14. Wyatt, *Bent's Fort*, 65–66; *Daily Times*, January 2, 1876.

15. Savage Speech, AJML; Katz, *The Black West*, 145–46, 190–94; Christoper Phillips, *Damned Yankee: The Life of General Nathaniel Lyon* (Columbia: University of Missouri Press, 1990), 255–56; Taylor, *In Search of the Racial Frontier*, 149, 153–54; Savage interview, November 20, 1998.

16. History Files, Baca House, Santa Fe Trail Museum, Trinidad, Colorado; History Files, Trinidad History Museum, Trinidad, Colorado; "Railroads and Railroad Towns in New Mexico," *New Mexico Magazine*, 3; *Daily Times*, January 2, 1876.

17. Ravage, *Black Pioneers*, 60–61; *Daily Times*, January 2, 1876.

18. Ravage, *Black Pioneers*, 60–61; Savage Speech, AJML; Utley, *Frontier Regulars*, 2; John A. Garraty, *The American Nation: A History of the United States Since 1865* (New York: Harper and Row, 1971), 22–23; Taylor, *In Search of the Racial Frontier*, 18, 104, 123–25, 129; Ravage, *Black Pioneers*, 60–61; Savage interview, November 20, 1998; Limerick, *The Legacy of Conquest*, 27.

19. History Files, Santa Fe Trail Museum; History Files, Trinidad History Museum; Katz, *The Black West*, 147–49, 294, 298; Billington, *New Mexico's Buffalo Soldiers*, 131; Taylor, *In Search of the Racial Frontier*, 17–18; Ravage, *Black Pioneers*, 60–61, 67; Savage interview, November 20, 1998.

20. Savage Speech, AJML.

21.–26. *Daily Times*, January 2, 1876.

27. History Files, Trinidad History Museum; History Files, Santa Fe Trail Museum; Savage Speech, AJML; Taylor, *Trinidad*, 182–83; Taylor, *In Search of the Racial Frontier*, 17–23; Cox and Richardson, *Noteworthy Black Women of New Mexico*, 8; Savage interview, No-

vember 20, 1998; *Daily Times*, January 2, 1876; "Railroad and Railroad Towns in New Mexico," 3.

28. Limerick, *The Legacy of Conquest*, 48; *Daily Times*, January 2, 1876.

29. Savage Speech, AJML; Katz, *The Black West*, 285, 287; Billington, *New Mexico's Buffalo Soldiers*, 158–59; Katz, *Black Women of the Old West*, 39; Schubert, *Black Valor*, 4–5, 10–11; Taylor, *In Search of the Frontier West*, 38, 85; *The Buffalo Soldier Monument Dedication, 126th Anniversary Reunion of the 9th and 10th (Horse) Cavalry Association, July 22–26, 1992, Fort Leavenworth, Kansas* (Topeka: Mainline Printing, 1992), 32; Las Animas County, Colorado, Census Records, Las Animas County Clerk and Recorder Office, Trinidad, Colorado; Cox and Richardson, *Noteworthy Black Women of New Mexico*, 2; Fowler, *The Black Infantry in the West*, 92–93, 105; *Daily Times*, January 2, 1876.

30. Cox and Richardson, *Noteworthy Black Women of New Mexico*, 10.

31. Katz, *The Black West*, 285; Hine and Thompson, *The History of Black Women in America*, 176; Cox and Richardson, *Noteworthy Black Women of New Mexico*; *Daily Times*, January 2, 1876.

32. "Railroads and Railroad Towns in New Mexico," 16–17.

33. Taylor, *In Search of the Racial Frontier*, 27–32, 35, 74–75, 149; Cox and Richardson, *Noteworthy Black Women of New Mexico*, 2, 6; Darlis A. Miller, "Cross-Cultural Marriages in the Southwest: The New Mexico Experience, 1846–1900," *New Mexico Historical Review* 57, no. 4 (October 1982): 335–37, 340; *Daily Times*, January 2, 1876.

34. Limerick, *The Legacy of Conquest*, 237; Miller, "Cross-Cultural Marriages," 335–53.

35. Taylor, *In Search of the Racial Frontier*, 157.

36. "Railroads and Railroad Towns in New Mexico," 16.

37. Jay T. Conway, *A Brief Community History of Raton, New Mexico, 1880–1930* (Raton: Colfax County Pioneers Association, 1930), 1–11, 18, 23; Savage Speech, AJML; Katz, *The Black West*, 48–59, 167–98, 264, 315, 318; Katz, *Black Women of the Old West*, 33–37; Taylor, *In Search of the Racial Frontier*, 17–18, 27–32, 67, 74, 112–13, 104, 120, 135; Castel, *Sterling Price*, 4–5; Savage interview, September 21, 1998; Miller, "Cross-Cultural Marriages," 335–39, 348; Savage interview, November 20, 1998.

38. Conway, *A Brief Community History of Raton*, 7–16, 19.

39. Savage Speech, AJML; Blanton, "Cathy Williams," 6; Robert G. Ferris, *Explorers and Settlers: Historic Places Commemorating the Early Exploration and Settlement of the United States* (Washington, D.C.: U.S. Government Printing, 1968), 70–71; Conway, *A Brief Community History of Raton*, 8; Katz, *Black Women of the Old West*, 58.

40. Blanton, "Cathy Williams," 5–6; Savage Speech, AJML; Hine and Thompson, *The History of Black Women in America*, 176; Katz, *Black Women of the Old West*, x, 31, 55–56; Thomas P. Sweeney, letter to author, September 16, 1998; Ravage, *Black Pioneers*, 63; Cox and Richardson, *Noteworthy Black Women of New Mexico*, 8; Savage interview, November 20, 1998; James A. Bear, Jr., *Jefferson at Monticello: Recollections of a Monticello Slave and of a Monticello Overseer* (Charlottesville: University Press of Virginia, 1967), 40, 84, 128; *Daily Times*, January 2, 1876.

41. Blanton, "Cathy Williams," 5–6; Savage Speech, AJML.

42. Blanton, "Cathy Williams," 5–6; Savage Speech, AJML.

43. Blanton, "Cathy Williams," 5–6; Savage Speech, AJML.

44. Blanton, "Cathy Williams," 5–6; Savage Speech, AJML; *Daily Times*, January 2, 1876.

45. Blanton, "Cathy Williams," 6–11; *Daily Times*, January 2, 1876.

46. Miller, "Cross-Cultural Marriages in the Southwest," 345.

47. Blanton, "Cathy Williams," 6, 8.

48. Ibid., 4, 8–9.

49. Ibid., 8–9; *Daily Times*, January 2, 1876.

50. Hall, *Patriots in Disguise*, 20–21.

51. Ibid.

52. Ibid., 23–24.

53. Leonard, *All the Daring of the Soldier*, 113.

54. Ibid., 113–120.

55. Jones, *Women Warriors*, 74–75, 193, 221–22, 226–28; *Daily Times*, January 2, 1876; Leonard, *All the Daring of the Soldier*, 104–5, 167–69.

56. Billington, *New Mexico's Buffalo Soldiers*, 143–45; Taylor, *In Search of the Racial Frontier*, 186; Drotning, *Black Heroes in Our Nation's History*, 29; Marcus Christian, *Negro Soldiers in the Battle of New Orleans* (Washington, D.C.: Eastern National, 1997), 41–42.

57. Savage Speech, AJML; Savage interview, September 21 and November 20, 1998; Blanton, "Cathy Williams," 11; 1990 Trinidad, Colorado, Census, Las Animas County, Colorado; Trinidad City Directories, 1901–1904, Colorado Historical Society, The Colorado History Museum, Denver, Colorado.

58. Elting, *Swords around a Throne*, 157; *Daily Times*, January 2, 1876.

59. Leonard, *All the Daring of the Soldier*, 99, 106, 110–11.

BIBLIOGRAPHY

PRIMARY SOURCES

Acock, Robert E. Letter to Maj. Benjamin Franklin Robinson. January 9, 1858. Robert E. Acock Papers, 1854–1866. Collection No. 2166, Western Historical Manuscript Collection, State Historical Society of Missouri, Columbia, Missouri.

Buffalo Soldier Monument Dedication, 126th Anniversary Reunion of the 9th and 10th (Horse) Cavalry Association, July 22–26, 1992. Fort Leavenworth, Kansas (Topeka: Mainline Printing, 1992).

Cathay, William, Pvt. Service Records. RG 94. National Archives and Records Administration, Washington, D.C.

Cathey, William, Pvt. Enlistment Papers. Thirty-Eighth U.S. Infantry, vol. 62, National Archives, Washington, D.C.

Census Records for the State of Missouri, Cole County, 1850. National Archives, Washington, D.C.

Census Records. Las Animas County, Colorado. Las Animas County Clerk and Recorder Office, Trinidad, Colorado.

Compiled Military Service Records of Civil War Soldiers Who Served from the State of Ohio. National Archives, Washington, D.C.

Compiled Military Service Records of Union Soldiers Who Served from the State of Indiana. National Archives, Washington, D.C.

Dobak, William A. "Colored Troops and Buffalo Soldiers: Some Legacies of Southern Reconstruction in the Western Army." Paper presented at the annual meeting of the Western Historical Association, St. Paul, Minnesota, October 1997.

Forsythe, Scott M. "The Buffalo Soldiers as Infantry." Paper presented at the annual meeting of the Western Historical Association, St. Paul, Minnesota, October 1997.

History Files. Baca House, Santa Fe Trail Museum, Trinidad, Colorado.

History Files. Trinidad History Museum, Trinidad, Colorado.

Journal of the Committee on the Florida Campaign: the Senate and the House of Representatives (of Missouri) to investigate the battle fought December 1837 in Florida by the Regular Army and the Missouri Volunteers, Missouri Historical Society, St. Louis, Missouri.

Melick, Thomas. Letter. December 29, 1861. Civil War Files of J. W. Bartmess. Indiana Historical Society, Indianapolis, Indiana.

Peabody, Charles. Diary. May 21, 1846–September 11, 1846. Missouri Historical Society, St. Louis, Missouri.

Pollock, Lizzie S. Letters. October 11 and 17, 1861. Civil War Files of Lizzie S. Pollock, Indiana Historical Society.

Powell, Colin. Speech given at the dedication of the Buffalo Soldier Monument, Fort Leavenworth, Kansas.

Records of U.S. Army Continental Commands, RG 94, National Archives, Washington, D.C.

Regular Army Muster Rolls, Company A, 38th United States Infantry, National Archives, Washington, D.C.

Reynolds, Gen. Joseph J. Letter to Bvt. Gen. E. D. Townsend. January 18, 1870. Charles E. Clarke Military Service Record. National Archives, Washington, D.C.

Savage, Cynthia. Speech to the West Texas Historical Society, April 11, 1997. Cathy Williams File. Arthur Johnson Memorial Library, Raton, New Mexico.

Sketch of the History of the Eighth Indiana Regiment, Indiana State Archives, Indianapolis, Indiana.

Trials of Black Soldiers. Thirty-Eighth United States Infantry for RG 153, National Archives, Washington, D.C.

Trinidad City Directories, 1901–1904. Colorado Historical Society. The Colorado History Museum, Denver, Colorado.

SECONDARY SOURCES
Books

Altoff, Gerald T. *Amongst My Best Men: African Americans and the War of 1812.* Put-in-Bay, OH: The Perry Group, 1996.

American Military on the Frontier, Proceedings of the Seventh Military History Symposium, United States Air Force Academy. Washington, D.C.: Office of Air Force History, 1976.

Anderson, Ephraim M. *Memoirs: Historical and Personal, Including the Campaigns of the First Missouri Confederate Brigade.* St. Louis: Times Printing Company, 1868.

Aptheker, Herbert. *American Negro Slave Revolts.* New York: International Publishers, 1974.

Armstrong, Virginia Irving, comp. *I Have Spoken: American History through the Voices of the Indians.* New York: Pocket Books, 1972.

Barthorp, Michael. *The Zulu War: A Pictorial History.* Poole: Blandford Press, 1985.

Battlefields of the South: From Bull Run to Fredericksburg by an English Combatant. New York: John Bradburn, 1864.

Bauer, K. Jack. *Zachary Taylor: Soldier, Planter, Statesman of the Old Southwest.* Baton Rouge: Louisiana State University Press, 1985.

Bear, James A., Jr. *Jefferson at Monticello: Recollections of a Monticello Slave and of a Monticello Overseer.* Charlottesville: University Press of Virginia, 1967.

Bearss, Edwin C. *The Campaign for Vicksburg: Grant Strikes a Fatal Blow,* 3 vols. Dayton: Morningside Press, 1986.

Billington, Monroe Lee. *New Mexico's Buffalo Soldiers, 1866–1900.* Niwot: University Press of Colorado, 1991.

Blassingame, John W. *The Slave Community: Plantation Life in the Antebellum South.* New York: Oxford University Press, 1972.

Blassingame, Wyatt, *Bent's Forts: Crossroads of the Great West.* Champaign, IL: Garrard Publishing Company, 1967.

Blond, Georges. *La Grande Armée.* London: Arms & Armour Press, 1997.

Boatner, Mark Mayo III. *The Civil War Dictionary.* New York: David McKay Company, Inc., 1959.

Brent, Linda. *Incidents in the Life of a Slave Girl.* New York: Harvest/HBJ, 1973.

Brown, Alan S., ed. *A Soldier's Life: The Civil War Experiences of Ben C. Johnson.* Kalamazoo: Western Michigan University Press, 1962.

Burstein, Andrew. *The Inner Jefferson: Portrait of a Grieving Optimist.* Charlottesville: University Press of Virginia, 1995.

Carter, Robert G. *On the Border with Mackenzie.* New York: 1961.

Castel, Albert. *General Sterling Price and the Civil War in the West.* Baton Rouge: Louisiana State University Press, 1968.

Catton, Bruce. *Terrible Swift Sword.* New York: Doubleday and Company, 1971.

Chartrand, Rene, and Francis Back. *Napoleon's Overseas Army.* London: Reed International Books, 1994.

Christian, Marcus. *Negro Soldiers in the Battle of New Orleans.* Washington, D.C.: Eastern National, 1997.

Clinton, Catherine, and Michele Gillespie, eds. *The Devil's Lane: Sex and Race in the Early South.* New York: Oxford University Press, 1997.

Colton, Ray C. *The Civil War in the Western Territories: Arizona, Colorado, New Mexico, and Utah.* Norman: University of Oklahoma Press, 1989.

Connell, Evan S. *Son of the Morning Star: Custer and the Little Bighorn.* New York: Harper & Row Publishers, 1984.

Conway, Jay T. *A Brief Community History of Raton, New Mexico, 1880–1930.* Raton: Colfax County Pioneers Association, 1930.

Coughlan, Robert. *Tropical Africa.* New York: Times Incorporated, 1966.

Cox, Euola W., and Barbara J. Richardson. *Noteworthy Black Women of New Mexico: Past and Present.* N.p.: n.p., n.d.

Dalzell, Robert F., Jr., and Lee Baldwin Dalzell. *George Washington's Mount Vernon: At Home in Revolutionary America.* New York: Oxford University Press, 1998.

Dary, David A. *The Buffalo Book: The Saga of an American Symbol.* New York: Avon Books, 1975.

Davis, Benjamin O., Jr. *American: An Autobiography.* Washington: Smithsonian Institution Press, 1991.

Davis, Edwin Adams. *Louisiana: The Pelican State.* Baton Rouge: Louisiana State University Press, 1972.

Davis, William C. *Three Roads to the Alamo: The Lives and Fortunes of David Crockett, James Bowie, and William Barret Travis.* New York: Harper Collins Publishers, 1998.

Department of Defense. *Black Americans in Defense of Our Nation.* Washington, D.C.: Department of Defense, n.d.

Devoto, Bernard. *The Year of Decision: 1846.* Boston: Houghton Mifflin Company, 1943.

Dougan, Michael B. *Confederate Arkansas: The People and Policies of a Frontier State in Wartime.* Tuscaloosa: University of Alabama Press, 1991.

Drinnon, Richard. *Facing West: The Metaphysics of Indian-Hating and Empire-Building.* Minneapolis: University of Minnesota Press, 1980.

Drotning, Phillip T. *Black Heroes in Our Nation's History*. New York: Washington Square Press, 1969.

Dumas, Alexandre. *The Three Musketeers*. New York: Bantam Books, 1984.

Duncan, Russell, ed. *Blue-Eyed Child of Fortune: The Civil War Letters of Colonel Robert Gould Shaw*. New York: Avon Books, 1992.

Earle, Peter. *The Sack of Panama: Sir Henry Morgan's Adventures on the Spanish Main*. New York: The Viking Press, 1982.

Eberle, Jean Fahey. *The Incredible Owen Girls*. St. Louis: Boar's Head Press, 1977.

Edwards, Frank S. *A Campaign in New Mexico with Colonel Doniphan*. Philadelphia: Carey and Hart, 1847.

Elkins, Stanley M. *Slavery: A Problem in American Institutional and Intellectual Life*. Chicago: The University of Chicago Press, 1974.

Elting, John R. *Swords around a Throne: Napoléon's Grande Armée*. New York: Da Capo Press, 1997.

Emmett, Chris. *Fort Union and the Winning of the Southwest*. Norman: University of Oklahoma Press, 1965.

Ferris, Robert G. *Explorers and Settlers: Historic Places Commemorating the Early Exploration and Settlement of the United States*. Washington, D.C.: U.S. Government Printing, 1968.

Fellman, Michael. *Inside War: The Guerrilla Conflict in Missouri during the American Civil War*. Oxford: Oxford University Press, 1989.

Fleming, Thomas. *Lexington*. Washington, D.C.: United States Department of the Interior, 1978.

———. *Liberty: The American Revolution*. New York: Viking, 1997.

Flexner, James Thomas. *Washington: The Indispensable Man*. Boston: Little, Brown and Company, 1974.

Fowler, Arlen L. *The Black Infantry in the West, 1869–1891*. Norman: University of Oklahoma Press, 1996.

Francis, Charles E. *The Men Who Changed a Nation: The Tuskegee Airmen*. Boston: Branden Publishing Company, 1993.

Franklin, John Hope. *From Slavery to Freedom: A History of Negro Americans*. New York: Alfred A. Knopf, 1974.

Froncek, Thomas, ed. *An Illustrated History: The City of Washington*. New York: Wings Books, 1992.

Garraty, John A. *The American Nation: A History of the United States Since 1865*. New York: Harper and Row Publishers, 1971.

Genovese, Eugene D. *From Rebellion to Revolution: Afro-American Slave Revolts in the Making of the Modern World*. Baton Rouge: Louisiana State University Press, 1979.

Gladstone, William A. *United States Colored Troops, 1863–1867.* Gettysburg: Thomas Publications, 1990.

Glatthaar, Joseph T. *Forged in Battle: The Civil War Alliance of Black Soldiers and White Officers.* New York: Meridian Books, 1991.

Gordon-Reed, Annette. *Thomas Jefferson and Sally Hemings: An American Controversy.* Charlottesville: University Press of Virginia, 1997.

Hall, Richard. *Patriots in Disguise: Women Warriors of the Civil War.* New York: Marlowe and Company, 1994.

Harris, NiNi. *History of Carondelet.* St. Louis: The Patrice Press, 1991.

Heitman, Francis B. *Historical Register and Dictionary of the United States Army.* Washington, D.C.: Government Printing Office, 1903.

Hine, Darlene C., and Kathleen Thompson. *A Shining Thread of Hope: The History of Black Women in America.* New York: Broadway Books, 1998.

Hollandsworth, James G., Jr. *The Louisiana Native Guards: The Black Military Experience during the Civil War.* Baton Rouge: Louisiana State University Press, 1995.

Horgan, Paul. *Great River: The Rio Grande in North American History.* Hanover: University Press of New England, 1984.

———. *Josiah Gregg and His Vision of the Early West.* New York: Farrar, Straus Giroux, 1972.

Hunt, Alfred N. *Haiti's Influence on Antebellum America: Slumbering Volcano in the Caribbean.* Baton Rouge: Louisiana State University Press, 1988.

Hurt, R. Douglas. *Agriculture and Slavery in Missouri's Little Dixie.* Columbia: University of Missouri Press, 1992.

Jeffrey, Julie Roy. *Frontier Women: The Trans-Mississippi West, 1840–1880.* New York: Hill and Wang, 1979.

Johnson, Charles, Patricia Smith, and the WGBH Series Research Team. *Africans in America: America's Journey through Slavery.* New York: Harcourt Brace & Company, 1998.

Johnson, Ludwell H. *Red River Campaign: Politics and Cotton in the Civil War.* Kent: Kent State University Press, 1993.

Jones, David E. *Women Warriors: A History.* Washington, D.C.: Brassey's Books, 1997.

Jordan, Winthrop D. *The White Man's Burden: Historical Origins of Racism in the United States.* Oxford: Oxford University Press, 1974.

Katz, William Loren. *The Black West: A Documentary and Pictorial History of the African American Role in the Westward Expansion of the United States.* New York: Simon and Schuster, 1996.

———. *Black Women of the Old West.* New York: Atheneum Books, 1995.

Keister, Linda Wolfe. *The Complete Guide to African-American Baby Names.* New York: Penguin Books, 1998.

Kerby, Robert L. *Kirby Smith's Confederacy: The Trans-Mississippi South, 1863–1865*. Tuscaloosa: The University of Alabama Press, 1972.

Lanier, Shannon, and Jane Feldman. *Jefferson's Children: The Story of One American Family*. New York: Random House, 2000.

Lavender, David. *The American Heritage History of the Great West*. New York: American Heritage Publishing Company, 1982.

Leckie, William H. *The Buffalo Soldiers*. Norman: University of Oklahoma Press, 1967.

Leonard, Elizabeth D. *All the Daring of the Soldier: Women of the Civil War Armies*. New York: W. W. Norton & Company, 1999.

Lester, Julius. *To Be a Slave*. New York: Dell Publishing Company, 1971.

Lewis, Thomas A. *The Guns of Cedar Creek*. New York: Harper and Row Publishers, 1988.

Limerick, Patricia Nelson. *The Legacy of Conquest: The Unbroken Past of the American West*. New York: W. W. Norton, 1987.

Lofton, John. *Denmark Vesey's Revolt: The Slave Plot That Lit a Fuse to Fort Sumter*. Kent: The Kent State University Press, 1983.

Longacre, Edward G. *Custer and His Wolverines: The Michigan Cavalry Brigade, 1861–1865*. Conshohocken, PA: Combined Publishing, 1997.

Marshall, Howard Wright. *Folk Architecture in Little Dixie*. Columbia: University of Missouri Press, 1981.

McConnell, Harry H. *Five Years a Cavalryman; Or, Sketches of Regular Army Life on the Texas Frontier, 1866–1871*. Norman: University of Oklahoma Press, 1996.

McKissack, Patricia C., and Frederick McKissack. *Sojourner Truth: Ain't I a Woman?* New York: Scholastic Inc., 1992.

McLaurin, Melton A. *Celia: A Slave*. Athens: University of Georgia Press, 1991.

McReynolds, Edwin C. *The Seminoles*. Norman: The University of Oklahoma Press, 1985.

Merington, Marguerite, ed. *The Custer Story: The Life and Intimate Letters of General Custer and His Wife Elizabeth*. New York: The Devin-Adair Company, n.d.

Meyer, Duane G. *The Heritage of Missouri*. St. Louis: River City Publishers, 1982.

Miller, Douglas T. *Frederick Douglas and the Fight for Freedom*. New York: Facts on File Publications, 1993.

Mintz, Sidney W., ed. *Slavery, Colonialism, and Racism*. New York: W. W. Norton and Company, 1974.

Monaghan, Jay. *Custer: The Life of General George Armstrong Custer*. Lincoln: University of Nebraska Press, 1959.

Morris, Roy, Jr. *Sheridan: The Life and Wars of General Phil Sheridan*. New York: Crown Publishers, Inc., 1992.

Mullins, Michael A. *The Fremont Rifles: A History of the 37th Illinois Veteran Volunteer Infantry*. Wilmington: Broadfoot Publishing Company, 1990.

Neihardt, John G. *Black Elk Speaks*. Lincoln: University of Nebraska Press, 1961.

Nell, William C. *Services of Colored Americans in the Wars of 1776 and 1812*. New York: AMS Press, 1976.

Nicholls, David. *From Dessalines to Duvalier: Race, Color, and National Independence in Haiti*. New Brunswick: Rutgers University Press, 1996.

Noble, David Grant, ed. *Santa Fe: History of an Ancient City*. Santa Fe: School of American Research Press, 1989.

Osur, Alan M. *Blacks in the Army Air Forces During World War II: The Problem of Race Relations*. Washington, D.C.: Office of Air Force History, 1986.

Perret, Geoffrey. *Ulysses S. Grant: Soldier and President*. New York: Random House, 1997.

Phillips, Christopher. *Damned Yankee: The Life of General Nathaniel Lyon*. Columbia: University of Missouri Press, 1990.

Pollard, Edward A. *The First Year of the War*. 2 vols. Philip and Son, 1863.

Porter, Kenneth Wiggins. *The Negro on the American Frontier*. New York: Arno Press, 1971.

Primm, James Neal. *Lion of the Valley: St. Louis, Missouri*. Boulder: Pruett Publishing Company, 1981.

Primm, James Neal, and Steven Rowan, eds. *Germans for a Free Missouri: Translations from the St. Louis Radical Press, 1857–1862*. Columbia: University of Missouri, 1983.

Quarles, Benjamin. *The Negro in the American Revolution*. Chapel Hill: University of North Carolina Press, 1972.

Rafferty, Milton D. *Historical Atlas of Missouri*. Norman: University of Oklahoma Press, 1982.

Randall, Willard Sterne. *George Washington*. New York: Henry Holt and Company, 1997.

Ravage, John W. *Black Pioneers: Images of the Black Experience on the North American Frontier*. Salt Lake City: The University of Utah Press, 1997.

Rawick, George P. *From Sundown to Sunup: The Making of the Black Community*. Westport: Greenwood Publishing Company, 1972.

Register of United States Army Officers, 1776–1903. Washington D.C.: War Department, 1904.

Remington, Frederick. *Frederick Remington's Own West*. New York: Promontory Press, 1960.

Ros, Martin. *Night of Fire: The Black Napoleon and the Battle for Haiti*. New York: Sarpedon, 1994.

Schom, Alan. *Napoleon Bonaparte*. New York: Harper Collins Publishers, 1997.

Schubert, Frank N. *Black Valor: Buffalo Soldiers and the Medal of Honor, 1870–1898*. Wilmington: Scholarly Resources, Inc., 1997.

Shea, William L., and Earl J. Hess. *Pea Ridge: Civil War Campaign in the West*. Chapel Hill: University of North Carolina Press, 1992.

Sheck, Ree, ed. *Railroads and Railroad Towns in New Mexico*. N.p.: New Mexico Magazine, 1989.

Sheridan, Phil. *Personal Memoirs*. 2 vols. New York: Press of Jenkins and Mc-Cowan, 1888.

The Soldier of Indiana in the War for the Union, The. Indianapolis: Merrill and Company, 1968.

Stanley, Francis. *Fort Union (New Mexico)*. N.p.: F. Stanley, 1953.

Stephanson, Anders. *Manifest Destiny: American Expansion and the Empire of Right*. New York: Hill and Wang, 1995.

Stone, Guy M, comp. *Marriage Records of Cole County, Missouri, 1821–1900*. Book A. Jefferson City: Private Printing, 1964.

Sunderland, Glenn W. *Five Days to Glory*. New Jersey: A. S. Barnes and Company, 1970.

Sunseri, Alvin R. *Seeds of Discord: New Mexico in the Aftermath of the American Conquest, 1846–1861*. Chicago: Nelson-Hall, Inc., Publishers, 1979.

Sword, Wiley. *Shiloh: Bloody April*. New York: William Morrow and Company, 1974.

Taylor, Morris F. *Trinidad: Colorado Territory*. Trinidad: Trinidad State Junior College, n.d.

Taylor, Quintard. *In Search of the Racial Frontier: African Americans in the American West, 1528–1990*. New York: W. W. Norton and Company, 1998.

Trudeau, Noah Andre. *Like Men of War: Black Troops in the Civil War, 1862–1865*. New York: Little, Brown and Company, 1998.

Tucker, Phillip Thomas. *The Forgotten "Stonewall of the West," Major General John Stevens Bowen*. Macon: Mercer University Press, 1997.

———. *From Auction Block to Glory: The African American Experience*. New York: Friedman Fairfax Publishing Group, 1998.

————. *The South's Finest: History of the First Missouri Confederate Brigade.* Shippensburg, PA: White Mane Publishing Company, 1993.

Tyler, Ronnie C. *Santiago Vidaurri and the Southern Confederacy.* Austin: Texas State Historical Association, 1973.

Utley, Robert M. *Frontier Regulars: The United States Army and the Indian, 1866–1890.* New York: Macmillan Publishing Company, Inc., 1973.

Vanderwerth, W. C., comp. *Indian Oratory: Famous Speeches by Noted Indian Chieftains.* New York: Ballantine Books, 1971.

Wade, Richard C. *Slavery in the Cities.* New York: Oxford University Press, 1964.

Walling, Richard. *Men of Color at the Battle of Monmouth, June 28, 1778.* New Jersey: Longstreet House, 1994.

The War of the Rebellion: A Compilation of the Official Records of the Union and Confederate Armies. 128 vols. Washington, D.C.: Government Printing Office, 1889.

White, Deborah Gray. *Ar'n't I A Woman? Female Slaves in the Plantation South.* New York: W. W. Norton and Company, 1985.

Wiley, Bell Irvin. *The Life of Billy Yank: The Common Soldier of the Union.* Baton Rouge: Louisiana State University Press, 1978.

Williamson, Joel. *New People: Miscegenation and Mulattoes in the United States.* New York: The Free Press, 1980.

Winter, William C. *The Civil War in St. Louis: A Guided Tour.* St. Louis: Missouri Historical Society, 1994.

Worcester, Donald E. *The Apaches: Eagles of the Southwest.* Norman: University of Oklahoma Press, 1992.

MAGAZINES

Blanton, DeAnne. "Cathy Williams: Black Woman Soldier, 1866–1868." *Minerva* 10, nos. 3–4 (1992).

Lander, Eric S., and Joseph J. Ellis. "Founding Father." *Nature* 396 (1988).

Larson, C. Kay. "Bonny Yank and Ginny Reb Revisited." *Minerva* 10, no. 2 (1992).

Mahline. "Reminiscences of General Sterling Price." *Ware's Valley Monthly: A Journal of Western Thought and Life* 1, no. 1 (1875).

Miller, Darlis A. "Cross-Cultural Marriages in the Southwest: The New Mexico Experience, 1846–1900." *New Mexico Historical Review* 57, no. 4 (1982).

Murray, Barbara, and Brian Duffy. "Jefferson's Secret Life." *U.S. News and World Report*, November 9, 1998.

Myers, Lee. "Mutiny at Fort Cummings." *New Mexico Historical Review* 46, no. 4 (1971).

Powers, Ramon, and Gene Younger. "Cholera on the Plains: The Epidemic of 1867." *Kansas Historical Quarterly* 37, no. 4 (1971).

Savage, W. Sherman. "The Role of Negro Soldiers in Protecting the Indian Territory from Intruders." *Journal of Negro History* 36, no. 1 (1951).

Sayles, Stephen. "Thomas Hart Benton and the Santa Fe Trail," *Missouri Historical Review* 69, no. 1 (1974).

Tucker, Phillip Thomas. "Above and Beyond . . . African-American Missourians of Colonel Alexander Doniphan's Expedition." *Password* 35, no. 3 (1990).

———. "The First Missouri Confederate Brigade's Last Stand at Fort Blakeley on Mobile Bay." *Alabama Review* 42, no. 4 (1989).

———. "A Forgotten Sacrifice: Richard Gentry, Missouri Volunteers, and the Battle of Okeechobee." *The Florida Historical Quarterly* 70, no. 2 (1991).

———. "John Horse: Forgotten African-American Leader of the Second Seminole War." *Journal of Negro History* 72, no. 2 (1992).

Wendel, Vicki. "Washer Women." *Civil War Times Illustrated* 38, no. 4 (1999).

NEWSPAPERS

Albuquerque (New Mexico) Journal
Bolivar (Missouri) Weekly Courier
New York Tribune
St. Louis Daily Times
Silver City (New Mexico) Daily Press
St. Louis Democrat
Valentine (Nebraska) Republican
Washington Post

INTERVIEWS

Savage, Cynthia. Interview with author. Midland, Texas, September 21, 1998, and November 20, 1998.

LETTERS TO AUTHOR

Sweeney, Thomas P. Letter to author, September 16, 1998.

INDEX